Young People and Offending

Young People and Offending

Education, youth justice and social inclusion

Martin Stephenson

WILLAN
PUBLISHING

Published by

Willan Publishing
Culmcott House
Mill Street, Uffculme
Cullompton, Devon
EX15 3AT, UK
Tel: +44(0)1884 840337
Fax: +44(0)1884 840251
e-mail: info@willanpublishing.co.uk
website: www.willanpublishing.co.uk

Published simultaneously in the USA and Canada by

Willan Publishing
c/o ISBS, 920 NE 58th Ave, Suite 300,
Portland, Oregon 97213-3786, USA
Tel: +001(0)503 287 3093
Fax: +001(0)503 280 8832
e-mail: info@isbs.com
website: www.isbs.com

First published 2007

Hardback
ISBN-13: 978 1-84392-155-4
ISBN-10: 1-84392-155-3

Paperback
ISBN-13: 978 1-84392-154-7
ISBN-10: 1-84392-154-5

British Library Cataloguing-in-Publication Data

A catalogue record for this book is available from the British Library

Typeset by GCS, Leighton Buzzard, Bedfordshire
Project managed by Deer Park Productions, Tavistock, Devon
Printed and bound by T.J. International Ltd, Padstow, Cornwall

Contents

Section III

Acknowledgements

This book has sprung from involvement in a large number of projects and accrued a corresponding number of debts, too many to acknowledge fully here. The professional and personal support from Frank Joyce of ECOTEC Research and Consulting Ltd., and John Malkin from Nottingham Trent University has been invaluable.

The Esmee Fairbairn Foundation, through its Rethinking Crime and Punishment initiative, funded the research project Unlocking Learning, from which much of Chapter 8 is derived.

The knowledge gained from undertaking several YJB-sponsored evaluation projects has been vital, and the enthusiastic support of Maggie Blyth was much appreciated, as was the help of Robert Newman. Roger Smith was generous with his time in helping shape this book.

I am very grateful for stimulating discussions over the years with John Graham, Geoff Hayward and Carl Parsons, and their work has been very influential on me, although they bear no responsibility for the views expressed here.

Maree Adams helpfully prepared the graphs in Chapters 3 and 4.

Thanks also to Samantha McLean for tireless work on the preparation of the manuscript, and to Brian Willan for his stamina and understanding in the publication of this book.

Martin Stephenson
October 2006

List of figures

Glossary

ADHD	Attention Deficit Hyperactivity Disorder
ASSET	the Youth Justice Board's assessment tool
DTO	Detention and Training Order
E2E	entry to employment
EBD	emotional and behavioural difficulties
EOTAS	education otherwise than at school
FE	further education
ISSP	intensive supervision and surveillance programme
LASCH	local authority secure children's home
LSC	Learning and Skills Council
LSU	learning support unit
MLD	moderate learning difficulty
NEET	not in education employment or training
Ofsted	Office for Standards in Education
PE	physical education
PRU	pupil referral unit
SEN	special educational needs

SEU   Social Exclusion Unit

STC   secure training centre

YJB   Youth Justice Board

YOI   young offender institution

Yot   Youth Offending Team

Foreword
by Rod Morgan (Chair, Youth Justice Board)

It may be too much to say that if we reformed our schools, we would have no need of prisons. But if we better engaged our children and young people in education we would almost certainly have less need of prisons. Effective crime prevention has arguably more to do with education than sentencing policy. What is curious is that this connection, which has implicitly been at the heart of juvenile justice policy ever since it developed with the foundation of juvenile reformatories and industrial schools towards the end of the nineteenth century, has been so little explored by contemporary criminologists and educationalists. That children and young people who are disengaged from education are much more likely to be involved in antisocial and criminal behaviour is well established. What, however, is the nature and direction of the causal relationship? Is the starting point the characteristics of the disengaged individuals and groups concerned – such pathologies as ADHD and Asberger's syndrome or the allegedly disaffected underclass. Or is social exclusion imposed upon such groups by an educational culture and institutions forged in the vested interests of the dominant middle classes? Whatever the causal connections, what are the long-term consequences?

There are few persons better equipped than Martin Stephenson to analyse these and other questions, which are among the most important for British social policy. Martin was a founder member of the Youth Justice Board established in 1998. Since leaving the Board in 2002, he has undertaken a series of education-related commissions for the Board and has sifted the murky statistics regarding youth 'detachment', the neutral term which he contends best enables us critically to analyse what is possibly the most extensive and damaging form of contemporary social exclusion. Of the five and a half million 10–17-year-olds in England and Wales, an estimated one-third to one-half a million are, for one reason or another, not engaged in education or training, thereby missing out on what is generally regarded as essential preparation for entry into an increasingly sophisticated and demanding adult labour market. Most absenteeism is authorised and short-term, but the long-term non-participants include the 'permanently' and 'informally' excluded, those who have fallen between the cracks and who, astonishingly, are not on any school roll, and the long-term non-attenders, most of whom become the NEET (not in education, employment or training) 16- and 17-year-olds. Young offenders, whether in custody or subject to community orders, are drawn overwhelmingly from this population: aged 15–17, their street experience is often more akin to that of 25–30-year-olds, combined with the literacy and numeracy attainment of 10- or 11-year olds.

What is absolutely clear is that once young offenders have become detached from education and training, it is extraordinarily difficult for them to get back into it. The 'system' does not readily cater for them. As Martin Stephenson emphasises, responsibility for them is passed like a baton between the various authorities, and frequently dropped. It is to be hoped that this study contributes to the formation of a more effective relay team. Better still, that it promotes a more inclusive education system and, as a corollary, the criminalisation of fewer children and young people.

Rod Morgan
Chair, Youth Justice Board
October 2006

Preface

The interrelationship between education and youth crime has long been recognised in terms of both social policy and public opinion. Concerns about ill-disciplined young people in school and crime on the streets are both highly topical and long-standing. While engagement in education has at different times been proposed either as the treatment for social ills or as a central part of coercive retraining, recent government initiatives have been seen as becoming so preoccupied with crime that social policy has become 'criminalised' (Muncie 2002; Pitts 2004). Yet, neither the widespread conflation in the media of school discipline problems and crime in the community nor that of low achievement at school and a disaffected underclass is as widely reflected in the academic or professional literature. Understandably, both, with some exceptions, tend to run on parallel lines of education and youth justice with relatively little convergence.

In contrast to public perceptions, professionalism tends to divide up these territories so that what goes on in schools is the province of teachers, and crime belongs to social workers and probation officers, police officers and prison staff. Occasionally, these professional defences are breached, as in the case of the education of young people in the care system, where a body of literature has grown over the last 25 years to bring about a wider recognition of systemic failure and eventual social policy reform (see, for example, Stein and Carey 1986; Jackson 1987; Biehal *et al*. 1992). This is not yet the case in youth justice.

Reports by government bodies, such as the Social Exclusion Unit (SEU) (SEU 1998 and 1999) and, more specifically and comprehensively, by the Audit Commission (2004), have highlighted educational issues in relation to offending. The academic literature has not yet mirrored this.

For example, a recent comprehensive survey of antisocial behaviour by young people (Rutter *et al.* 1998), although discussing the possible effects of school organisation on offending, makes no reference to exclusions from school and their apparent effect on offending. The educational demographics of young people in the youth justice system are largely unknown (Youth Justice Board (YJB) 2006). Within youth justice, the two very different cultures of custody and community confront each other, and the relevant literature tends to fall either side of this divide. While there has been a focus in recent years on topics such as exclusion from school and the apparent association with offending, there is no single broad text exploring educational issues in youth justice.

The objectives of this book, then, are to examine the links between the youth justice and education systems, estimate the educational demographics of the young people in the youth justice system and critically survey the research evidence for the role of education in offending, and assess current social policy development. The social exclusion/social inclusion discourse is given considerable emphasis both in being used as the theoretical framework for much of the analysis and in assessing the effectiveness of government social policy.

With such a wide topic, the inevitable constraints mean that some important areas, such as the educational and youth justice experiences of young people from particular ethnic minority backgrounds, as well as gender issues, are not dealt with in detail.

There are three broad sections. Section I deals with the theoretical background, summarises the evolution of the education system in relation to youth justice, and examines the value of social exclusion as an explanatory framework particularly for the development of social policy over the last 15 years. Section II assesses the evidence on educational risk factors for offending, such as the effects of low attainment or becoming detached from mainstream school, and looks in detail at the impact of custodial education. The final section assesses public opinion and the views of specific stakeholders, such as magistrates, on education and youth justice; surveys the evidence on what works; and explores the effectiveness of government social policy both in terms of the targets it has set and in relation to the relevant risk factors.

Section I

Chapter I

Background: theories and evidence

The socialisation functions of schools have been discussed since their inception. Debates from at least the nineteenth century have contested the capacity of schooling as a prophylactic to prevent outbreaks of disorder among the young. It is now commonplace that young people spend up to one-quarter of their waking hours in formal education, so at the very least a school or college has considerable potential as an agent of social control. The school, then, takes its place alongside the family and the community in both polemical and research literature as a potentially powerful influence on the development of young people, including their involvement in offending.

There are, however, very different theoretical views attributed to the influence of schooling on the commencement in, persistence of and desistance from offending by children and young people. This is partly a reflection of the weakness of the empirical evidence and the significant gaps in the knowledge base. Surveying the different theories provides the context for discussion in later chapters on the potential of the school to influence delinquency and the relationship of educational characteristics such as low attainment or detachment from school with offending.

Definitions

From a criminological perspective, delinquency is often defined more narrowly in terms of a young person breaking the law. In an effort to include those individuals who are below the age of criminal responsibility and related behaviours that are (currently) outside the criminal code, some commentators have used the term 'antisocial behaviour' (Rutter *et al.* 1998).

In order to incorporate those behaviours usually deemed a problem within a school, Gottfredson (2001) used a broad definition of delinquency, including

> such behaviors as cussing at a teacher, biting a classmate, shirking homework, being late to class, writing on school walls, cheating on tests, bullying classmates, lying, fighting, stealing, joyriding, drinking alcohol, having sex, selling drugs, assaulting or robbing others, setting fire to property, raping and murdering (Gottfredson 2001:4).

The inclusion of defiant, disobedient or even lazy actions alongside grave crimes arguably slips too comfortably into the current general expansion of youth justice which is seen as colonising new areas of behaviour (Muncie and Hughes 2002). In a wider sense, it could be seen as part of the current widespread construction of youth as a problem. Equally, it will be argued that the histories of the education and youth justice systems are inextricably intertwined and have been shaped by the same forces that too clear a distinction in behaviours may obscure.

It is not always possible to tell from studies whether broad or narrow definitions are being used, but 'delinquency' is used here in relation to offending while 'antisocial behaviour' is applied to a wider range of behaviours. Specific definition of those behaviours that particular staff in various educational institutions find very difficult or unacceptable is almost impossible without introducing dubious and arbitrary categories. As Topping (1983), in dismissing the term 'maladjustment', emphasised, 'if it is pointless to spend pages on categorising the indefinable, there is even less point in debating questions of incidence and causation' (Topping 1983: 11).

The term 'antisocial behaviour' is often used in studies on youth offending, but as it has become increasingly politicised, its currency has been debased. The Crime and Disorder Act 1998 defined 'antisocial behaviour' as acting in a 'manner that caused or was likely to cause harassment, alarm or distress to one or more persons not of the same household'. The elasticity of this definition is of considerable political value. Contrasting the use in American studies of less emotive terms such as 'incivilities' or ones applying to communities rather than individuals such as 'disorder' Burney (2005: 2) argues that the recent use of the term 'antisocial behaviour' has 'politicised an almost limitless range of behaviour drawn into the net of new controls. It signals exclusion and rejection, trumpeted as a means of rescuing social order and strengthening communities.' The shifting balance between the 'incivilities' of young people and crime causes real problems when trying to establish, for example, whether it is behaviour in schools or expectations and levels of tolerance that have changed. Similarly, a recent work argues for more consideration of the long-standing notion of deviance 'because "anti-social behaviour" is such a highly problematic, value-laden, subjective and politically-loaded construct' (Squires and Stephen 2005:185).

While these problems must be borne in mind, many relevant studies do refer to antisocial behaviour in relation to educational attainment and detachment (Rutter *et al.* 1998). Clearly, what happens before the age at which children can be prosecuted needs examining too. Consequently, this text does use the term in certain places.

The ready acceptance of definitions could potentially limit analysis. The unquestioning adoption of terms such as 'disruptive', 'truancy', or 'emotional and behavioural difficulties' could result in misleading conclusions. The assumption that, for example, 'truancy' is a unitary concept assists the identification of correlates. If it turns out this is a catch-all term bundling only superficially similar behaviours together that have a multiplicity of causes, then significant distortions are introduced into studies. This distortion is possibly exaggerated by the arbitrary definitions of local administrators charged with collecting data. As Furlong (1985: 73) has warned:

> It can be argued that researchers who treat official statistics and definitions of school deviance as facts and then attempt to explain their causes may therefore simply be revealing the common-sense theories of school deviance employed by those who are agents of social control – teachers, magistrates, educational welfare officers.

Main theories

There are significant differences among criminologists about the nature of the relationship between schools and delinquent behaviour. Given the limitations in the empirical evidence, there is no consensus on the transmission mechanisms and even the direction of the relationship. Understandably competing theories have flourished (see, for example, Rutter *et al.* 1998; Gottfredson 2001; Farrington 2002).

Those conflict theories rooted in the wider economic system analyse schools as either preparing young people for the alienation of employment, with the inevitable rejection by some, or inducing strain on those young people who do not attain appropriate middle-class standards. Similarly, social disorganisation theorists perceive schools as reflecting a wider process of community disintegration which diminishes their capacity for effective socialisation. From these perspectives, if the school system does not promote delinquency, neither does it inhibit it.

Again theories which put great emphasis on the importance of individual characteristics, such as the absence of self-control (which usually includes such features as impulsiveness, risk-taking, weak perception of consequences and antisocial personality), sometimes see few independent effects of the school. Academic failure or detachment from school is portrayed as having little or no causal relationship with offending and as being due to the playing out of a lack of self-control in an educational context.

Theories adopting a more situational perspective, such as routine activity theory, perceive schools as potentially increasing the risk of crime by grouping together the most at-risk members of the population where 'must-have' consumer goods are frequently on display. In the absence of effective supervision by the school, crime will therefore tend to increase.

Those theories which assign the greatest importance to the role of the school do so through its perceived socialisation effects. It acts either as reinforcement to the family in inhibiting delinquent behaviours and promoting pro-social attitudes, or as a counterbalance where families are unable to offer this developmental protection. Attachment to school is seen as second in importance only to positive family bonds in providing a source of social control.

Labelling theory was very influential in the juvenile justice arena in the 1980s and gave academic authority to both policy and practice. In relation to schools, labelling theory has been analysed as a process within several theoretical traditions but has several distinct features - it is less concerned with the perceived causes of particular behaviour but focuses rather on the reactions of teachers to it. Adherents argue that if teachers consistently categorise particular young people as academic failures or disruptive or non-attenders, this will shape the young person's responses and influence other professionals (Furlong 1985; West and Pennell 2003).

More recent theories place emphasis on the effects of age. The emergence of antisocial behaviour could be shaped by influences such as family and school quite differently according to the age of the young person. This has led to propositions of different pathways or stages to delinquency that might be followed in a particular order (Herrenkohl *et al.* in Loeber and Farrington 2001).

Two important developmental theories that identify common educational risk factors for delinquency yet adopt very different stances on causation are the Farrington theory (Farrington 2002) and the social development model (Hawkins *et al.* 2003). The interpretations and implications of these theories could lead to quite different emphases on interventions to prevent offending where education is concerned. Both theories are integrative and draw on classic delinquency theories. The Farrington theory posits school failure and subsequent weak employment careers as being largely the result of developing antisocial tendencies and low intelligence.

According to this theory, schools are the arenas where the effects of low intelligence and high impulsivity are played out:

Children with low intelligence may be more likely to offend because they tend to fail in school and hence cannot achieve their goals legally. Impulsive children, and those with a poor ability to manipulate abstract concepts, may be more likely to offend because they do not give sufficient consideration and weight to the possible consequences of offending. Also, children with low intelligence and high impulsivity are less able to build up internal inhibitions against offending (Farrington 2003: 168).

This cycle of poverty and low intelligence is seen as leading to early school failure, which is exacerbated by absenteeism, resulting in few or no qualifications and culminating in unemployment and not achieving goods, status and excitement legitimately.

The social development model is an integrated developmental theory that seeks to explain behaviour by combining hypotheses of social learning, differential association, and social control theories. The role of educational institutions has much more emphasis in this approach, as they supply the opportunity or lack of it for association with either pro- or antisocial peers, potential reinforcement and punishment of behaviour, and the chance to form social bonds with the school. School provides one of the main settings for the prosocial bonding that leads in this model to a stronger belief in the moral order, which is seen as directly influencing behaviour (Hawkins *et al.* 2003).

This model draws insights from several theoretical perspectives. It takes social learning and social control theory to propose that when the processes of socialisation integrate opportunities for interactions with others with the necessary involvement, participatory skills and reinforcement from others, a social bond develops. This social bond could be either pro- or antisocial depending on the nature of the socialising unit. This social bond attaches the individual powerfully to the group or institution. Once created, this bond can independently influence behaviour.

The creation of social bonds is set within a context whereby both structural influences and individual characteristics make available differing opportunities both pro- and antisocial for young people. Schools afford critically important opportunities for social bonding. This model also stresses developmental aspects by locating these socialisation processes within child developmental phases. Behaviour is learned in different ways as the balance between family, community, and schools alters.

Educational theories

In education, much theoretical discussion in this context has been led by psychologists, often focusing on adjustment, although a clear definition proves as elusive as it has for emotional and behavioural difficulties. The dangers of this approach are emphasised by Topping (1983: 12):

> 'Maladjustment' was always a rag-bag term, and discrimination between the 'maladjusted' and 'not-maladjusted' always highly arbitrary. It makes no more sense to suppose that children can be neatly divided into the disruptive and non-disruptive, with appropriate educational placement following automatically from the application of the (very sticky) label.

These education psychology approaches tend to fall into two main categories – psychodynamic and behavioural learning theories. Psychodynamic theories tend to emphasise the quality of parenting experiences in infancy. Weak attachment or emotional deprivation in the early years is seen as inhibiting children from learning how to respond appropriately within the school and other environments, possibly demonstrating hostile and angry reactions to teachers.

Learning theorists, in contrast, argue that inappropriate and appropriate behaviour first in the family and later in school is learned by a process of imitation or reinforcement rather than resulting from individual pathology. Schools in this instance have a potentially significant role through both the behaviour of peers and the authority role of teachers.

Educational sociological theories relating to deviance (usually defined as absenteeism and disruptive behaviour) often place the creation or maintenance of an antischool subculture centre stage. This can range from 'status-deprived' young people, particularly those who have not been successful academically who can gain status from an antisocial culture, through to conscious class resistance in a Marxist analysis (Furlong 1985).

In the context of the alleged high incidence of learning disabilities (although the validity of some special needs constructs is controversial) among young people who offend, three hypotheses have been advanced (Coffey and Gemignani 1994). The susceptibility theory holds that children and young people with learning disabilities will have a predilection towards poor behaviour in school, while the school failure theory claims that their poor academic performance leads to not only behavioural problems but also weakening attachment to school and involvement in delinquent peer groups. In contrast, the differential treatment hypothesis suggests that children and young people with learning disabilities are not necessarily engaging in more difficult or delinquent behaviour but that their behaviour is dealt with more harshly within school and particularly in the youth justice system because they are far less adept in dealing with professionals and avoiding confrontations with the law.

Nature of the evidence

Longitudinal studies are particularly important in trying to identify key associations, the causal order, and the direction of relationships. One of the main difficulties in disentangling risk factors is not only that they are interrelated but also that they tend to coincide. Where education and offending are concerned, much of the effect may be indirect, and there is a range of intervening variables such as disruptive behaviour or absenteeism.

The main studies fall into two broad categories – cross-sectional tests of various theories of antisocial behaviour and offending and longitudinal studies charting criminal careers. Cross-sectional surveys have generated large amounts of evidence and have highlighted correlations. However, these assessments are at a single point in time, constraining the ability to draw inferences about causation. If we cannot establish the temporal order, the causal order remains largely speculative. Collecting data on the explanatory variable and the outcome variable simultaneously establishes just one association. For example, if non-attendance is taken as a potential explanatory variable for offending and a single correlation is generated by the data, then several causal relationships are logically possible. While it may be that non-attendance leads to increases in offending, equally it could also be true that offending leads to non-attendance, or there may be a reciprocal relationship between them. Yet, again, it could be a spurious relationship derived from an underlying common cause such as low attainment.

Cohort studies take time into account and, due to their usually large sample size, provide a great deal of detailed information on the commencement, duration and severity of criminal careers. They can have two significant drawbacks. They have often been drawn from official record-keeping systems of schools or police, for example, and there can be gaps regarding potential explanatory variables such as family or peer relationships. More importantly, some mainstream recording systems fail to include young people who may be involved in the most delinquent behaviours, as they have become detached from school, training or employment and may be existing in the grey economy. Equally, cohort surveys that rely on questionnaire return or household interviews may well omit some young people who are at most risk.

Consequently, individual-based panel studies evolved as the main method to assess the validity of different theories. The studies all share certain core design features but vary significantly in their examination of offending careers. In order to establish the causal order, studies usually select young people before or around the age of commencement of delinquent careers. As the primary purpose is explanatory, they not only establish offending career patterns but also investigate the precursors of antisocial behaviour and offending. In addition, some studies attempt to assess the consequences of offending behaviour over the life course.

There are a number of limitations to panel designs some of which particularly affect educational issues. Focusing on individual-level analysis restricts assessment of the impact of influence of groups and their interactions within a school. They also tend not to take account of contextual changes, such as the reorganisation of a school, or wider shifts in professional opinion or practice, such as the increase in exclusions which may be unrelated to changes in individual behaviour.

Sample selection and retention effects may act differentially against those most at risk educationally in that those with poor literacy and numeracy skills, those with low educational self-esteem, and those subject to non-attendance or exclusion may not participate initially or be more likely to drop out later. Retention rates have been found to have a differential effect (Thornberry *et al.* 2003). Similarly, those surveys which interview less than 75 per cent of the target sample may come to findings that are serious underestimates of the actual level of offending (Farrington 2003).

Several of the major longitudinal panel studies rely on self-administered questionnaires in schools. In the initial Houston school survey, for example, 82 per cent of questionnaires were returned, but this had dropped to 41 per cent at the third sweep (Kaplan 2003).

Typically, initial take-up appears to be around 85 per cent (Huizinga *et al.* 2003; Loeber *et al.* 2003). It must be questioned whether those young people who are not on any school roll or are in often part-time segregated educational provision are fully represented.

These problems probably have an even greater impact on cohort studies and other surveys. The Youth Cohort Study and the 1970 British Cohort Study are both influential sources of information for social policy development and have very large samples. They have major shortcomings in examining educational links with offending, such as non-participation and low attainment. Not only are they both postal and thus highly likely to have a differential effect on non-participants or those with literacy problems, but the Youth Cohort Study does not include young people who are excluded from school or attending special schools (Social Exclusion Unit (SEU) 1999). The recent Crime and Justice Surveys in 2003 and 2004 were based on private households and therefore missed out young people in custody, residential care homes, residential special schools, hostels, and bed and breakfast, as well as homeless and traveller children. The majority of these young people are likely to be at high risk of both educational failure and involvement in offending.

Similarly, the Youth Justice Board (YJB) has commissioned a series of nationally representative surveys of the views of young people on offending and various risk behaviours (e.g. YJB 2000b). This is conducted with a representative sample of young people in mainstream schools. In order to compensate for those young people unlikely to be in a mainstream secondary school on a given day, this was balanced by an 'excluded' survey. Although given wide currency, this sample is at best indicative and does not even consist of representative ages (young people above compulsory school age who therefore cannot be formally excluded are in the sample), and not all the same questions are asked.

While representing a significant advance on other cross-sectional studies, panel studies lack the rigour of true experimental designs, and there may be problems with their internal validity such as testing effects through repeated interviews.

There can be major theoretical differences between panel studies, which are partly reflected in the methodologies and more substantially in interpretations of the findings. Some studies are closely associated with a particular theoretical model (Farrington 2003), while others are more eclectic (Hawkins *et al.* 2003). There is generally far more consensus on the risk factors and their antecedents than on the conceptual framework. This has important implications for social policy and devising and implementing effective interventions.

One of the potentially major weaknesses in longitudinal studies is the much greater emphasis on individual characteristics and the relative neglect of social, political, cultural and environmental factors. The focus tends to be on the young person rather than on the teachers and the school.

In the context of social exclusion, the use of panel studies could have a tendency to focus on the careers of individuals. Again, this can deflect attention from the exclusionary pressures within social structures (Byrne 2005). Charting life courses is essential for improving understanding of causation but could be limiting if these life courses are viewed in isolation from the whole social order. Significant changes in the educational system, such as the abolition of corporal punishment and the subsequent increase in exclusions, could easily be missed by particular cohorts.

Shifts in political and public opinion also tend to be ignored, although these may be implicated in, for example, the dramatic rise in custodial sentences in the 1990s, which was apparently unrelated to trends in crime. The very significant rise in school exclusions in the 1990s is also given little or no prominence in some reviews (Rutter *et al.* 1998; Farrington 2002). Movements in public and professional opinion could change the boundaries for socialising or socially excluding particular groups of young people, such as young black men, who figure disproportionately in both exclusions and custodial sentences. Existing longitudinal surveys of offending in the UK were undertaken when the social context was significantly different. Their samples tend not to reflect the increased ethnic diversity of the population and changes in the labour market, or to develop knowledge about risk factors for young women and protective factors generally (Farrington 2002).

In any event, in studies that do focus on schools, even when weakening social bonds are discussed, the fact that many, possibly the majority of young people, in the youth justice system are not receiving a full-time education at a mainstream school is not considered. If educational institutions do have significant socialising (both pro- and anti-) potential, what are the effects of segregated education such as pupil referral units (PRUs), special schools and home tuition? What is the effect on young people who spend many months or even several years completely outside education or training?

Paradoxically, while there are very high-profile individual cases and an increase in the general media focus on troublesome youth, once such youth are detached from mainstream education, they become largely invisible. When they are dispersed among a range of usually small providers, often with lengthy gaps without any educational provision, recording systems become attenuated, and the most basic details on attendance, learning needs and progression become very difficult to ascertain. Indeed, this cannot be achieved with confidence even for those young people detained in young offender institutions (YOIs) (ECOTEC 2001; YJB 2003c, 2004b).

Increasingly, given the changes in the youth labour market and the pressure of global competition in skills, social policy focuses on the teenage years. This is illustrated by initiatives such as the Connexions service (ages 13–19), Yots (up to 18) and the Tomlinson review on education (14–19). Accordingly, it makes sense to look at the evidence for the effects of all educational institutions up to the age of 18 rather than just schools and compulsory education to 16.

Similarly, the educational context for many young people at risk cannot be viewed in isolation from the other professional interventions to which they can be subject such as entering the care system, particularly residential care. Not only do care and segregated educational institutions have potentially significant socialising roles but also their interactions could amplify certain behaviours of both the young people and the associated professionals.

Risk and resilience factors

Despite the very different theoretical backgrounds, most studies adopt a risk and resiliency approach in trying to disentangle the causes of delinquency. While risk factors increase the likelihood of the commencement, frequency and duration of offending, protective factors reduce the probability of such outcomes despite these risks. Not only do risk factors tend to be interrelated and occur at the same time but they may also be symptoms rather than potential causes. For instance, in this context, absenteeism may be highly associated with poor academic attainment, and both may be correlated with delinquency. There are several possible directions of influence. Not being in school could be either a cause or an effect of low attainment. Similarly, both risk factors could be the cause or effect of delinquency. Alternatively, an independent variable, such as low intelligence or high impulsivity, may be creating these intervening variables.

The balance of longitudinal research is far more towards risk factors rather than protective factors that might inhibit the onset or duration of delinquency. The literature, both longitudinal and cross-sectional, with varying degrees of emphasis, identifies educational risk factors in relation to low attainment, weak bonds to school, and certain aspects of school organisation. While these are the educational risk factors with empirical support for both general offending and its onset among children and young people, the strength of the evidence varies. Poor academic performance is relatively straightforward to define and is well attested as a predictor of behavioural problems in school and delinquency (Maguin and Loeber 1996 and see Chapter 5).

In contrast, the effect of weak bonding to school has problems of definition and more equivocal evidence underpinning it. The literature here covers child (and parent), educational aspirations and motivation towards education. From an educational perspective, the area is gaining more coherence with the development of the definition and analysis of engagement (see Chapter 4).

Studies of those characteristics of school organisation and process that may constitute risk factors for delinquency are relatively rare. Most of those studies that provide insight into the influence of schools on the development of antisocial behaviour relate to secondary schools. Even if school level effects are detected, there is a wide range of potential variables. Relevant school features might include school size, sector and location; teaching and non-teaching staff; resources; and pupil intake. Given the focus on the potential social control role of the school, assessment of the quality of relationships between teaching and other staff and the young people is important but very difficult to achieve. While there is evidence that several of the characteristics of schools may be associated with the development of antisocial behaviour in school and possibly delinquency out of school, precise identification is difficult. One of the most important studies in this area (Rutter *et al.* 1979) was criticised for its attribution of causes to the catch-all 'school ethos' whenever any statistical significance in relationships occurred (Graham 1988).

With regard to those educational issues that may be implicated in the development of a delinquent career, there is significant common ground over the risk factors and to some extent over protective factors. Summarising the findings of seven major panel studies that included many thousands of young people (mainly from the USA, but also Canada and the UK), Thornberry and Krohn (2003) concluded that:

> Children spend a substantial portion of their lives in school. What they learn and the completion of a high school education can have an important effect on their life chances. … Low school performance and commitment to school are consistent predictors of delinquency and other problematic behaviours.

This emphasis on attachment to school and interaction with peers will be discussed in detail, particularly in the context of young people who have become detached from mainstream school. While the social development model provides a more useful platform for consideration of a range of educational issues, a different framework is needed to examine the potential processes within education that may contribute to the development of offending. Equally, the wider social and political environment needs to be examined to judge what impact shifts in, for example, the tolerance level of behaviour in schools has on offending.

Adopting a framework of social exclusion helps to take account of some of these broader influences. Not only does the social exclusion discourse focus on those processes of detachment and multiple disadvantage that are highly relevant but it is also the motif of New Labour's policy reforms.

Conclusions

Whatever theoretical position is taken, there are real difficulties with the current evidence, such as the direction of the relationship between cause and effect with particular risk factors. Does low attainment make young persons more likely to absent themselves or are those who absent themselves more likely to be low attainers? Does being excluded from school lead people into offending, or are actual or potential offenders more likely to be excluded?

It is also unclear as to exactly how exposure to a particular risk factor is translated into committing crime. Does being out of school for long periods of time, for example, often lead to increased opportunities for offending by getting drawn into an older and more delinquent peer group, or, alternatively, through their increased exposure to substance misuse?

In exploring the relationship between education and offending in subsequent chapters, the limited extent of current knowledge will become increasingly apparent. This does not mean, of course, that fresh insights cannot be gained or that recent research has not improved the evidence base. It will be argued, though, that this ignorance is symptomatic of both competing professional interests and of a wider cultural indifference to the education of many young people. There has been a tendency to focus social policy development, supported by the assumptions inherent in some research, on the deficiencies of young people at the expense of critical study of the broader structural influences and particularly the vested interests of institutions and professionals.

Summary

❏ There are significant differences among criminologists about the nature of the relationship between schools and delinquent behaviour. While most agree that low attainment and detachment from school are indicators of risk, there is considerable disagreement about whether or not this is due to a causal relationship either direct or indirect in nature.

❏ There is a major divide between those theories that emphasise the importance of individual features, such as poor self-control and low intelligence, that could lead to school failure and those that see school as having the potential for positive or negative socialisation effects.

❏ Compared with North America, there are relatively few UK longitudinal or panel studies that enable an assessment of school influences on delinquency.

❏ Within many studies, there are potential selection and retention effects that may affect young people in the youth justice system disproportionately due to lower levels of literacy and numeracy, much greater detachment from mainstream schools, and transient housing, all of which could limit participation in questionnaire responses.

❏ Most relevant studies examining potential school effects do not take account of the fact that a majority of young people in youth justice are either not participating at all or are in some form of segregated education.

Chapter 2

The evolution of education and youth justice

If the misery of the poor be caused not by the laws of nature but by our institutions, great is our sin.

Charles Darwin

Of no institution is it truer than of education that to understand its history is to understand its contemporary character

Eric Midwinter (1970: 3)

This chapter examines some of the recurrent themes that surround education and youth justice in a historical context. It is not intended to be a definitive history of the development of education or youth justice but rather to identify some of the early debates that have continued to resonate until the present day. While it is important to avoid anachronisms, there is no denying the fact that current concerns about exclusion and ill discipline, non-attendance, and crime echo those of the nineteenth century. Equally, the campaigns to end the imprisonment of children and young people and the call by the recently appointed Children's Commissioner for England to recreate the spirit of the nineteenth-century child-rescue movement also underline how long-standing have been public concerns over the schooling and reform of delinquent youth (Aynsley-Green 2003).

The early Victorian construction of childhood and its relationship to the various reform movements shaped developments in social care, youth justice and education. The interrelationship between these reforms and their expression in the separation and rescue of children from families, the founding of reformatory schooling, the introduction of mass compulsory education and the development of special education will also be explored. The emphasis on the 'pivotal moments' of the nineteenth century is not to ignore the antecedents of youth justice and education (Shore 2003: 111). The growth of the different agencies that had a vested interest in the categorisation and subsequent segregation of young people who either offended or were troublesome in other ways for mass education is discussed too.

Since the late nineteenth century, education has been seen to have a powerful and unique role as a universal service that offers the opportunity for children and young people to equip themselves with the skills and knowledge to gain employment. But, for many people, it has always had other equally if not more important functions in terms of socialising young people and inculcating the prevailing moral and behavioural standards. Issues of control and behaviour within the school and the wider community have always been inherent within the education system since the advent of universal education in the nineteenth century. 'How a society selects, classifies, distributes, transmits and evaluates the educational knowledge it considers to be public reflects both the distribution of power and the principles of social control' (Bernstein 1975: 25).

More benign, functionalist views of education portray it locked in a symbiotic embrace with the economy and preparing young people for their social destination: 'Education is the influence exercised by the adult generations upon those that are not yet ready for social life. Its object is to arouse and to develop in the child a certain number of physical, intellectual and moral states which are demanded of him by both the political society as a whole and the special milieu for which he is specifically destined' (Durkheim 1956: 71).

A strong functionalist theme still runs through social policy in education from literacy and numeracy strategies at primary school through to the expansion of higher education as a means of competing in the global market. This ignores the potential for education in creating and sustaining social divisions or the fact that the Fordist structure and organisation of schools may be maladapted to the demands of a post-Fordist, post-industrial economy. Parsons (1999) identified six main functions of education, all operating within the fundamental tension between social discipline and individual development: custodial; civilising; creating a national identity; skilling; credentialling; and selecting, organising and transmitting public knowledge. Each of these functions, he argued, is best seen as a continuum representing movement towards or away from exclusion.

A brief survey of the evolution of educational and youth justice policy and the rise in segregated provision alongside mainstream state education provides some useful insights into the current policy context, institutional structures and associated professions that characterise twenty-first-century educational and youth justice systems. This includes charting the many educational categories that were developed for young people who were to be educated outside mainstream school. Much less may have changed about our basic approach to education in the last 150 years than we might like to think.

In studying the institutional and cultural relationships between crime and youth justice, it is useful to examine the origins of segregated education and its relationship to the introduction of mass education in the nineteenth century. It could be argued that the shape of education, social welfare, health and criminal justice services mirrors the prevailing organisational structures and processes of the predominant form of production in a society (Midwinter 1970; Stephenson 1996). Even today the Victorian origins of modern schools can be detected: 'Schools are still modelled on a curious mix of the factory, the asylum and the prison' (Hargreaves 1997: 162).

Construction of childhood

Childhood, rather than being simply a distinct biological phase, is often treated as a variable concept that has been socially constructed and reconstructed. Definitions of childhood appear both to reflect and to influence the societies from which they emerge (Frost and Stein 1989; Hendrick 2002; May 2002).

The period from 1780 to the mid-nineteenth century has been identified as shaping the construction and institutionalisation of a universal notion of childhood across all social classes (Hendrick 2002). The profound effects of industrialisation through urbanisation with its concentration of visible poverty and the rise of class politics were accompanied by the development of the social sciences and saw a different identity of childhood emerge. The discovery of juvenile delinquency was an intrinsic element of this reconstruction, as was the process of compulsory schooling (Platt 1969; Magarey 2002).

The wage-earning child of the late eighteenth century, who in many ways, certainly in the eyes of the law, was treated as an adult, was gradually replaced by one who needed protection and nurturing through education. Within this reconceptualisation, children were to be returned to a state of innocence and dependency and treated differently from adults (May 2002). Three powerful themes emerged that dominated the nineteenth-century reconstruction of childhood: reform of the dangerous classes, rescue of the perishing classes and compulsory schooling for the masses.

By mid-century, the 'Artful Chartist Dodger' was looming large for

Middle England, combining threats of both criminality and political insurrection. Juvenile crime was often portrayed as a precursor to social revolution (Pearson 1983).

Reformers such as Mary Carpenter, Lord Ashley and Micaiah Hill perceived the juvenile delinquent to have been corrupted into precocious adult vices. Matthew Davenport Hill thought the juvenile delinquent 'a little stunted man' who 'knows much and a great deal too much of what is called life' and Micaiah Hill even asked, 'Can these be *children*?', seeing them 'as diminutive men' (Pearson 1983: 167). In criminal justice terms, it was argued that children and young people should be treated differently from adults, particularly where imprisonment was concerned. At the same time as the criminal law and the powers of the newly formed police force were extended to cover acts principally regarded as nuisances and which fell disproportionately on children (Magarey 2002), state recognition of reformatory and industrial schools in 1854 introduced a radical change in penal policy (May 2002).

The Youthful Offenders Act 1854, supplemented by further acts in 1857, 1861 and 1866, was the first recognition in legislative terms of the distinct category of juvenile delinquency. It was also important in that childhood, as defined by *doli incapax* (incapable of crime), was extended from seven years old to 16 years old. The Industrial and Reformatory School Acts introduced the principle of separate custodial provision for young people, which was built around compulsory education.

Moral reclamation

In order to combat the twin threats of political unrest and crime by children and young people, many reformers, philanthropists and politicians saw education as the means of providing moral training. The preoccupation with religious moral training in particular was prominent throughout the educational developments for most of the nineteenth century. From the missionary zeal of the Sunday School Movement from the late eighteenth century through the foundation of Ragged Schools in the first half of the nineteenth century and into both the monitorial and pupil teacher systems there ran a rich vein of religious doctrine that emphasised obedience as crucial in moulding the child.

The concern with both moral reclamation and preventing social disorder was often overt. Kay Shuttleworth, the influential educationalist, emphasised the national need for 'school-houses with well-trained masters, competent and zealous to rear the population in obedience to the laws, in submission to their superiors and to fit them to strengthen the institutions of their country by their domestic virtues, their sobriety, their industry and forethought' (quoted in Furlong 1985: 5).

The links between crime and ignorance were often made, but illiteracy was not necessarily the major concern. Mary Carpenter, who was pre-eminent in calling for the use of education rather than imprisonment for children and young people, saw religious-based moral training as a higher priority than literacy (May 2002). The 1867 inspection report on reformatory and industrial schools underlined this with the assertion that 'the business of a Reformatory is to correct rather than to instruct' (Carlebach 1970: 71). The inculcation of religious precepts and the instilling of these essential industrial characteristics of 'habits of order, punctuality, industry and self-respect' were applied to 'the young ... the depositories of all hopes and expectations', as Thomas Beggs wrote (quoted in Pearson 1983: 182).

Despite the many eloquent testimonies to the grinding poverty of the urban working classes, it was the want of morality rather than money that was highlighted as the cause of crime. Mary Carpenter and many other philanthropists believed that 'It is from the mis-management or low moral condition of the parents, rather than from poverty, that juvenile crime flows' (quoted in Pearson 1983: 175).

Both contemporary and current commentators have queried just how benign the rescue and reform movement really was and how far working-class parental rights were removed and replaced by a state-administered regime derived from the bourgeois ideal of the family (Platt 1969; Pearson 1983; Clarke 2002). Philanthropy was no friend of popular movements such as Chartism, and the Chartists, in turn, were very wary of the educational reform movement. The *Northern Star* proclaimed in 1848 that 'Educationalists [are] the pretended friends, but the real enemies of the people' (Pearson 1983: 181).

Similar analyses have been offered of the equivalent child-saving movement in the USA in the late nineteenth century. Contrary to the notion of socially disinterested, enlightened reformers who developed humanitarian judicial and penal institutions for children and young people and defended the poor, it has been argued that: 'the child-saving movement was a coercive and conservatizing influence' (Platt 2002: 180). Child savers helped define delinquency as a problem for social and not political policy. Treatment, therapy through moral guidance, rather than the redistribution of power and resources, was seen as the solution.

An alternative view of the child savers would see them not so much as libertarians or disinterested humanists but as having fairly paternalistic and romantic notions that nevertheless were backed up by new coercive powers. The interventions provided led to young people being sentenced to lengthier periods in reformatories and industrial schools, segregated in special schools, or made to live in residential homes. In each of these areas there was an emphasis on long hours of labouring at monotonous tasks and, generally, the inculcation of Christian and middle-class values.

Four agencies

The social exclusionary pressures on young people at the start of the twenty-first century can be better understood if placed in the context of the emergence of the four groupings of social welfare, criminal justice, education and health services that coalesced around central government departments and were mirrored at local government level. The struggle for power and status within and between these departments, the tensions between central government planning and local implementation, and the growth of a powerful charitable sector were important features historically and still remain today.

Social welfare – the development of residential care

Despite the perceived malleability of children, it was widely believed by the charitable organisations which sprang up that a new environment was needed, which initially was seen to be that of residential care. Increasingly, the model of the factory was adopted here too. With economies of scale, large residential establishments were created where regimented practices echoed the production-line processes of Victorian factories and mills. Many of these homes offered training and became certified as industrial schools.

Although the popular image then and now was of the collection of waifs from conditions of shocking poverty where they were in effect parentless on the streets, the majority of entrants came from several sources of referral. These might be poor law guardians, individual supporters or branches around the country, or the parents themselves, and they might have been referred as a result of decisions taken in court.

In fact, it is impossible to disentangle the complex skeins of referrals in terms of the origins and the characteristics of children and the financial issues involved. Many of the organisations were able to pick and choose, requests for admission running well ahead of acceptance. One of the criteria used was the distinction between the children of 'deserving' and 'undeserving' parents. Illegitimacy, for example, was grounds for refusal by several organisations (Parker 1990).

Criminal justice

Alongside the rapid growth of the homes came the development of reformatory and industrial schools. They were the start of the lineage of approved schools, community homes with education and, more recently, secure training centres. This line represents the detention of children below the level of the penal service. Although connected closely with offending behaviour, this soon extended to a whole range of antisocial behaviour. The history of these institutions charts the early grouping together of the criminal justice agencies and their separation of children from families and mainstream education. The forces that shaped these agencies had considerable similarities to those that led to the creation and sustaining of the homes. Culturally, it was also underpinned by the child-rescue movement, but the issue of criminality meant that there was a powerful punitive undercurrent. This has maintained the sector that detains children compulsorily largely but not exclusively on criminal behaviour grounds, down to the present time. This intermingling of compulsory detention on both criminal and welfare grounds continues today in some local authority secure children's homes, which contain a mixture of young people detained either on the grounds of their offending or for their welfare.

The great push for establishing these institutions came from the 1850s, and the motivations behind them were encapsulated in the title of a contemporary work: *Reformatory Schools for the Children of the Perishing and Dangerous Classes and for Juvenile Offenders*. A select committee report in 1853 supported state aid for reformatories on the grounds that many children who committed offences required 'systematic education, care, and industrial occupation [rather] than mere punishment' (Grigg 2002: 293). The disease metaphor was a powerful influence in establishing these institutions. Sydney Turner, the inspector of reformatory schools in 1859, confidently proclaimed their function as a 'hospital to cure real disease' (Carlebach 1970: 169).

An important distinction was made in that reformatory schools were for convicted children under 16 who could be sentenced to a reformatory school for a period of two to five years. Industrial schools were for children aged between 7–14 for any length of time up to their fifteenth birthday. Initially, this was for children charged with vagrancy but was widened in 1866 to include 'any child under the age of fourteen found begging or receiving alms ... wandering, and not having a home or settled place or abode, or any visible means of subsistence, or [who] frequents the company of reputed thieves' (May 2002: 110). The 1866 Act introduced not only a new category of children, those 'in need of care and protection' but also the fundamental principle that the

23

state could become the parent where the birth parents had failed in their duties. It also muddied the waters by making industrial schools a sentencing option for younger children who committed criminal offences. So blurred became the referral criteria that by 1896 the only real difference in the view of a departmental committee was age, and they concluded that industrial schools acted as junior schools and reformatories as secondaries (Grigg 2002: 300).

The growth in the numbers of children detained in these schools was substantial, rising to 25,000 by the end of the century. Responsibility for directing the disparate groups of children towards the industrial schools was given to the new school boards created to oversee compulsory elementary education. The schools also provided an outlet for those children who did not comply with attendance orders. In 1881, failure to attend school was second only to drunkenness in the number of cases dealt with at petty sessions in England and Wales, 100,000 cases a year being brought before the courts (Grigg 2002). It was ironic that the introduction of education for all should accelerate the move to separation from families and communities for those in greatest need.

While the neat division of reformatory training for delinquent children and industrial training for at-risk children was much more confused, in practice the important principles established by this legislation and the creation of these institutions helped to pave the way for mass compulsory education later in the century (May 2002). Such was the ascendancy of the industrial and reformatory school movement that it has been asserted that 'during the later nineteenth century, developments in juvenile justice were largely concerned with the Reformatory School system' (Shore 2002: 167).

Mass education

Universal schooling completed the process of the reconstruction of childhood. 'By virtue of its legal authority, and on a daily basis through teachers and school attendance officers, it was able to impose its vision upon pupils ... and upon their parents' (Hendrick 2002: 31). From its earliest days, mass education was inextricably bound up with the prevention of crime, as Lord John Russell asserted in 1839, 'by combining moral teaching with general instruction the young may be saved from the temptations to crime' (Midwinter 1970: 34).

Despite the powerful religious dynamic, the factory both in architecture and regimented organisation supplied the mould. Morality and manufacture fused together in creating the method of teaching known as the monitorial system – 'a vast moral steam-engine', as Coleridge described it (Midwinter 1970: 29).

The role of the teacher and the extension of supervision initially through the monitorial system of education were honed to a much greater emphasis on the inculcation of the appropriate moral principles

> where the teachers become the precept and model for the pupil. ... Hence the poor would gain the basis for an improved domestic economy, the 'perishing class' would be insulated from the contagion of the criminal class, and this latter would come to realise the folly of its erstwhile amoral pursuits and have some device to turn away from these pursuits to seek a living and different manner (Copeland 1999).

Current educational debates have eerie echoes of the controversies of the last years of the nineteenth century. In order to progress from one class to another, a child had to achieve a standard (tests set by HMI determined whether a child had reached the standard). Many unsuccessful older children as a result remained with children as young as five. Class sizes often rose in Standard I to 70 and more with self-fulfilling results.

Evidence to the Sharpe Committee in 1898 reported that teachers were 'conscious to get rid of those children to improve their own work and cause them less trouble'. Their pressures would be all too familiar 100 years later in that the committee also had heard that they were 'all bound up in the idea of the standards and ... codes and they have the inspector after them' (Cole 1996: 7). A further pressure was that until 1890 teachers' pay was related to performance in that it was linked to pupils passing the standards tests, and the unsuccessful pupils could lower salaries.

While the industrial and reformatory school movement was in the ascendant and dominated developments in juvenile justice in the second half of the century, the rise of mass education started to make itself felt by the turn of the century in several ways. The growing authority of the educational system meant a jostling for power with the Home Office over control of the reformatory and industrial schools (Shore 2002). More influential, though, was the development of the discourse of mental deficiency, which replaced notions of moral deficiency as concepts of special educational needs, and the influence of psychologists was felt.

Special education

The history of special educational needs parallels the segregation of children by social welfare and criminal justice groupings. It has proved more enduring, as it has been rooted in ostensibly scientific classification and selection rather than in simple moral and economic arguments. Defining difference permits specialism of provision and justifies removal. Prejudices, stereotyping and a belief in the heritability of a simplistic notion of intelligence are powerful undercurrents that have swirled below the surface of apparently scientific debates of educationalists.

The medical profession had a considerable influence over the development of attitudes towards, and provision for, children. Despite the authority accorded to the profession, its supposed scientific basis was often negligible. Even at the end of the nineteenth century, doctors as the accepted experts in child development still firmly believed in phrenology. The gradient of foreheads, and the size and shape of ears and chins, were all expertly diagnosed to enable the classification of children according to their intellectual capabilities and deviant tendencies.

Increasingly, the medical profession became preoccupied with definition and ranking of different kinds of defect. The introduction of mass education after the Elementary Education Act 1870 saw the development of the idea of special rather than ordinary education for different groups of children. The notion of feeble-mindedness was used to classify one group alongside those with more distinct disabilities such as blindness. By the early twentieth century, the new scientific profession of psychology had acquired a key role in defining and selecting which children should go into special education.

School medical officers gained an increasingly important role as the arbiters of feeble-mindedness and later mental deficiency. However, this concept of feeble-mindedness when applied was nebulous, its incidence varying according to each school medical officer. In 1910, for instance, the chief medical officer queried the disparities in judgements by comparing Warrington, where, out of almost 1,000 children examined, none was diagnosed as feeble-minded, with Northampton, where almost one in five children were deemed feeble-minded (Cole 1996).

The notion also developed that many defects were hereditary and were closely associated with crime, unemployment and promiscuity. This debate has recurred regularly and is currently reflected in the work of Charles Murray and others (McDonald 1997). Famous contemporary scientists, such as Lombroso, advocated screening children for various stigmata before they started school.

Anthropological examination, by pointing out the criminal type, the precocious development of the body, the lack of symmetry, the smallness of the head, and the exaggerated size of the face explains the scholastic and disciplinary shortcomings of children thus marked and permits them to be separated in time from their better-endowed companions and directed towards careers more suited to their temperament (Lombroso 1911, quoted in Gould 1996: 166).

The late nineteenth and early twentieth centuries saw new definitions appear and significant legislative change and a dramatic expansion in separate provision on educational grounds. This was consolidated by the rise of standardised IQ testing and the construction of another category of children requiring special schooling – the maladjusted. Their discovery appears to be linked to the establishment of child guidance clinics and the increasing prestige of psychologists.

In the lineage of terms to describe those young people whose behaviour some teachers and/or some schools deem too inappropriate for their classrooms, the 'maladjusted' held sway only to be displaced in time by 'emotional and behavioural difficulties' (EBD). But, as a comprehensive recent review on behalf of Ofsted observed, 'Defining challenging behaviour, EBD, Attention Deficit Hyperactivity Disorder (ADHD), disaffection, disruption or other terms preferred by different professional groups, has always been an unsatisfactory exercise' (Visser 2003: 10). In the fruitless search for a clearly defined homogeneous group, many definitions and labels have been essayed, but, as Kauffman (2001) admitted in an American context, 'One reason it is so difficult to arrive at a reliable definition is that an emotional or behavioural disorder is not a thing that exists outside a social context but a label assigned according to cultural rules. ... Typically, it is that which is perceived to threaten the stability, security, or values of that society' (Kauffman 2001; cited in Visser 2003: 12).

The 1981 Act, following the Warnock Report, attempted to replace an educational caste system with the concept of a 'continuum of need'. This attempted to sidestep the problems of definition and categorisation and the proliferation of classification. Critics, however, argue that this has largely been a rhetorical shift and that the 'needs' often relate to the needs of mainstream education to remove the child.

Welfare and justice

The new construction of childhood having started to define children as a problem population and one that needed to be treated separately from adults led to further divisions. The dualism between the deprived and the depraved, expressed through assessments of deservingness, was manifested in youth justice through the justice:welfare debate, which has been sustained in various forms for at least 200 years. The shifting boundaries have had significant implications for the education system.

While the classic justice model treating juveniles who offended as adults prevailed, the first decisive welfare distinctions were made through the statutory recognition of reformatory and industrial schools. Crudely, the former were for the depraved and dangerous while the latter were for the deprived and neglected. In practice, the boundaries became increasingly permeable. Welfare legislation increasingly entwined the emerging justice and welfare systems. The Children Act 1908, which was arguably the first comprehensive attempt at childcare legislation, also introduced a source of fundamental tension and confusion, in that juvenile courts were to have jurisdiction over both those who offended and those who were poor and in need. It also established borstals for 16–21-year-olds as an intermediary institution between reformatories and prison. They had similarities with the reformatories, and the function of education had a dual role of training for work but also to 'elevate and instruct' (Stratta 1970: 149). They were later to adopt a particular approach modelled on the public school environment.

Special education also began to focus on the link between crime and poverty but increasingly in terms of inherited deficiency. This shifted the justification for intervention and separation from a moral to a medical basis. The Mental Deficiency Act 1913 introduced the category of 'moral imbecile' and defined these as 'persons who from an early age display some permanent mental defect coupled with strong vicious or criminal propensities, on which punishment had little or no deterrent effect' (Copeland 1999: 181).

The welfare net was cast further over children who might need protection or care by the Children and Young Persons Act 1933. In addition to requiring the juvenile court to take account of the welfare of the child, it accepted the overlapping roles of reformatory and industrial schools by combining them into Approved Schools. The report of the departmental Committee on the treatment of young offenders in 1927, which paved the way for the 1933 Act, asserted: 'The idea of the tariff for the offence as of making the punishment fit the crime dies hard; but it must be uprooted if reformation rather than punishment is to be – as it should be for young offenders – the guiding principle' (Bailey 1987: 57).

Segregated education has always been very attractive to proponents of a welfare approach combining control and retraining. Inevitably, it tends towards detention for relatively lengthy periods of time. Entries into approved schools increased significantly in the aftermath of the 1933 act.

The raft of reforms following the Second World War saw a fusing of welfare and justice approaches with the creation of children's departments by the Children Act 1948 and the Criminal Justice Act 1948, which introduced attendance centres, remand centres for delinquents and detention centres. The high-water mark in a welfare approach whereby delinquency was perceived as largely symptomatic of deprivation was probably the Children and Young Persons Act 1969. Although never fully implemented, it replaced approved schools with community homes with education and the approved school order with the care order. Non-attendance at school had become increasingly seen as a care issue and potential grounds for separation from family. Even in the late 1980s, more than 2000 young people were on care orders for not attending school (Frost and Stein 1989: 102).

Despite the enormous efforts that have been put into developing methods of assessment and placement of children and young people in residential establishments for the past 200 years under the aegis of different government departments, force of circumstance has often been most important.

> Whether the 'problem child' has been 'cared for', 'punished', 'educated' or 'treated' has often been a matter of chance depending upon which individuals in which agency happened to pick up his or her case. A child's placement often depended on where the vacancies were when the child was perceived by particular professionals to have reached crisis point or when funding became available (Visser 2003: 11).

The decommissioning of the residential institutional sector through the 1970s and 1980s was accompanied by a growth in community interventions initially dubbed intermediate treatment. Many of these activities were educational in nature. An assortment of group work, outward-bound activities, literacy and numeracy classes, vocational activities and personal development projects provided loose-knit educational programmes that lacked a formal curriculum. Interestingly, in time, a correctional curriculum using cognitive-behavioural approaches was marketed to practitioners. These activities were usually provided as an adjunct to supervision and later became explicit attachments to supervision orders. The boundaries between formal education and such provision, which was usually centre based, occasionally in surplus school premises, became indistinct. Some young people at risk were drawn into these activities while for some young people on court orders, this was their main source of education.

This blurring meant that some LEAs referred excluded or young people deemed disruptive to intermediate treatment schemes. If that young person subsequently appeared in court, this could adversely affect sentencing. Graham (1988: 18) suggested that 'in effect, an informal tariff may be operating which starts much earlier than the formal juvenile court tariff and acts as a feeder into the formal juvenile justice system'.

Critics of the rise of the welfare model of dealing with young people who offend were concerned that more young people were drawn inadvertently into the remit of the juvenile justice system through being at risk, that the lack of determinacy in sentencing led to longer periods of separation from families and mainstream school, and that there was little evidence that these welfare interventions worked. To make matters worse, it was argued that through a process of labelling this approach could be even increasing the number of young people who continue to offend by drawing them into formal welfare and justice systems rather than allowing them to grow out of this behaviour.

The reconciliation of the tensions between a welfarist approach and a punitive, authoritarian one has often been achieved through an educational treatment discourse. Reformatories and approved schools gained their legitimacy through disciplined labour, and education. The inherent dangers of the welfare approach leading to longer periods of deprivation through educational facilities was exemplified by the Gault case. Gerald Gault, a 15-year-old American, was committed to a state industrial school for six years in 1964 after being found guilty of making obscene telephone calls to his teacher. The same offence committed by an adult carried a maximum punishment of a $60 fine or up to two months' imprisonment (Cromwell and del Carmen 1999).

There were parallels in education where the proliferation of units for young people who did not fit into school during the 1970s was justified as meeting their needs. There were criticisms too of this approach on similar grounds. Topping (1983) argued that two-thirds of young people who display disruptive behaviour stop doing so irrespective of any interventions. This 'spontaneous remission rate' had important implications: 'One is that the widespread belief that the most effective way of preventing serious problems is by early identification and prevention seems to be something of a non-starter'. Another is that notions of treatment, 'especially if directed at within-child "disease" processes, seem to be nonsensical' (Topping 1983: 12).

The community homes with education were run down largely as a result of economics and the challenges of operating large-scale institutions for young people, but were also subject to sustained criticism over the educational outcomes for young people in the care system. Care orders on the grounds of school non-attendance were ended by the Children Act 1989. Large-scale residential care for young people who offend or are at risk of offending has ended, but the institutional response remains in the shape of the significant out-of-school population in pupil referral units (PRUs) and the purported centrality of education in young offenders institutions, local authority secure children's homes (LASCHs) and secure training centres (STCs).

Equally, the justice:welfare debate has moved on but remains relevant to education. The politics of behaviour whereby indiscipline in school and delinquency outside it are blended together may have intensified exclusionary pressures within schools and stimulated the growth of a large out-of-school sector. Non-attendance at school by young people is treated as an offence by their parents, on occasion leading to imprisonment. At any point in time, some 6,000 young people are subject to Detention and Training Orders (DTOs), with a further 3,000 on intensive surveillance and supervision programmes. Critics of this approach see both a 'carceral bonanza' and net widening as Yots (youth offending teams) increase their remit for prevention, including, for example, schemes for police involvement in schools.

Vested interests

Ostensibly, much of the impetus behind the creation of a separate criminal justice system for children and the introduction of universal education was purely humanitarian and benign. However, it is just as possible that the development of both the education and juvenile justice systems represented the interests of prevailing powerful interest groups. Tomlinson (1982) has emphasised the importance of being suspicious when one group claims to be doing good to another group, particularly when there is a power imbalance and legal coercion is involved. From this perspective, certain professional groups came increasingly to have a vested interest in the definition and removal of troublesome children and young people.

At a time when there is both a systematic demonising of young people about their delinquency through the media and by many politicians and calls for a child-rescue movement, it is salutary to reflect on the motives and the outcomes of the work of the nineteenth-century reformers who had such a profound effect on both the educational and youth justice systems. Before the altruism and humanitarianism expressed often through charitable enterprises is accepted at face value, it is important to note that they were operating within a particular social context, and they often reflected wider social and economic political interests. These interests were also political in relation to the maintenance of order and social control, professional in terms of the developing expertise in the segregation and treatment of young people, and commercial, as running many of these institutions involved personal and competitive interests.

From the perspective of special schooling, some commentators have downplayed the social control thesis, preferring to see this as 'subservient to humanitarian motives and inevitably, government financial restraints, whatever the age' (Cole 1989: 170). No doubt, many were, and are, motivated by compassion and other benign motives in intervening to separate children from families and segregate them educationally. However, the assumption that these interventions are intrinsically beneficial and untainted by personal and political vested interests is arguably not only naive but also unsupported by convincing evidence. On the contrary, the institutional responses across social welfare, youth justice, education and health to what are overwhelmingly the children of poor, working-class families, reinforced by whole industries of professionals and experts, could also be exerting social exclusionary pressures.

In the late nineteenth and early twentieth centuries, there was a convergence of vested interests whereby teachers and others in mass education needed special education in order to keep results up. It gave a powerful role to psychologists and others in the medical profession, and the growing special school sector in turn needed defective but educable children (Tomlinson 1982). These push-and-pull pressures with varying relative strengths arguably have continued ever since.

While the vested interests of professionals and agencies have been emphasised in the separation of children from families and segregation of children educationally, the nature and availability of the buildings must not be ignored. The nineteenth century saw a massive investment in building institutions for those who were deemed to be in need of reforming or rescuing (Shore 2003).

The architect is very influential in education and residential services for young people: 'However much the method and content of education may have changed, education is remorselessly geared to its physical fabric. Buildings once erected must be used, and, in turn, they dictate the basis of education' (Midwinter 1970: 54). This dynamic extends more widely. Capital investments by their nature are more durable than services.

The idea that those to be separated should have their own building has proved enduring. Once built, these institutions by their structure encourage their use. In economic theory, Say's law (supply creates its own demand) has long been discredited but holds true for services for socially excluded groups – 'problems always expand to utilise the resources available to solve them' (Topping 1983: 11). Administratively, it has always been easier to select children from mainstream institutions or their families than to gain significant extra resources for the school or family. The growth of these services is still claimed to be evidence of the needs of the young people rather than the needs of teachers in mainstream schools: 'The rapid expansion of numbers in PRUs reflects a clear and continuing need for their place in an array of services' (Daniels *et al.* 2003: 124).

The self-interest of the new institutions and later the associated professionals meant that the avowed purposes of reformatory and industrial schools diverged significantly in reality in two main ways. Despite the aim of turning out reformed young people who could lead productive, crime-free lives, increasingly the emphasis was on work that made profits for the institutions, as Carlebach has documented:

> There was, first of all, a gradual trend from work carried out for training purposes to work which would increase profit. A number of institutions eventually confined themselves to employments which were not only useless in the training sense, but were very harmful to the children in order to achieve maximum profit from their labour. Amongst such employments were brick-making, wood-chopping and paper-salvage for boys, and laundry work for girls (Carlebach 1970: 68-9).

There were powerful incentives for these residential establishments to remain full and to retain children for as long as possible. Per capita grants from the Home Office meant that schools needed to be kept full, and the internal economies of these establishments took up most of the children's time, and such work was classed as 'industrial training'. There was a premium on retaining children until they were older, as the profits on the goods purchased were a significant component of the income of these establishments. In these circumstances, the education and training received was inadequate, as the children 'existed for the benefit of the institution. The institution had not existed for their benefit as a place of attempted rehabilitation' (Hurt 1984: 45).

Thus, paradoxically, while children in mainstream education were receiving increasing legal protection from labouring and were involved in education instead, these establishments were exempt from such regulations, and children who had been detained through their non-attendance at school were now spending most of their time labouring rather than being educated. Of course, the rationale used was that work in itself instilled virtuous habits whether it be picking oakum or hair-teasing. In addition to the fervent belief in the morally restorative powers of monotonous labour was the pervasive view that separation from parents protected this process of inculcation and moral regeneration. Middle-class paternalistic attitudes neglected the emotional ties of family activities and undervalued the family 'atmosphere of emotional warmth, spontaneity and solidarity, which compared favourably with the uniform, depersonalized and rigidly supervised organization characteristic of the Reformatory' (Humphries 1981: 215).

By their very existence and powerful hold on the public imagination, the voluntary societies exerted a strong influence on legislation. They also had several reasons why they needed to expand and were thus committed to increasing the supply of children to their residential establishments. Maintaining economic viability for large residential establishments depended on the recruitment and retention of large numbers of children. A growth in the numbers rescued was a vital part of the marketing of these organisations to maintain charitable donations, particularly given their intense sectarian rivalry.

The operational economics of these establishments sometimes inhibited the inclusion of children into schooling. Such large establishments required a substantial labour force, and the children were both consumers and producers, as they provided much of the workforce while being instilled with the beneficial habits of routine work. On average, the profits of their work contributed about seven per cent of the total income of all industrial schools in addition to a substantial contribution to their internal economy through domestic duties (Parker 1990). Even as late as 1925, Home Office inspectors, when urging voluntary homes to ensure attendance at local schools, were told this was impossible, as 'we should never get the housework done'.

The emphasis, echoed today in the prison service's stricture on 'purposeful activity', was not on the acquisition of specific skills but rather the routines and subordination for work. The overwhelming dominance of the professional perspective in the historical and present accounts of the benefits of interventions may well obscure the unpleasant, subjective reality of the experiences for many young people. Despite the benign motives, the regimes of many reformatory and industrial schools were unremittingly harsh with exhaustingly long days.

Legislation might change the brand name and ostensible purpose, but many institutions survived, and it may be suspected that little perceptible difference was noticed by the children and young people.

Blackbrook House in St Helens was first certified as a reformatory school in 1869 (Lancashire Reformatory School for Girls), and 30 years later it was certified as an industrial school (Industrial School for Roman Catholic Girls), becoming the Sisters of the Sacred Heart, Approved School, from 1933 onwards. Later, it became Blackbrook House Secure Unit.

Not attending school, for example, has been categorised variously as a symptom of psychological disturbance – 'school phobics' – grounds for a care order (until 1989), and a quasi-criminal activity. Similarly offending behaviour by a young person could result in removal to a special school, a community home with education, or a secure training centre. The rescue or retribution surges in political opinion are mirrored at an individual level where non-mainstream provision is used to get rid of difficult young people but also as a sanctuary. As Munn *et al.* (2000) have illustrated: 'The existence of the provision can be used as a warning or threat to pupils – 'You realise that if you don't behave you might be sent to a residential school and you wouldn't like that, would you?' – which then becomes translated into different language when the threat becomes reality – 'You are going to this school because it will really help you' (Munn *et al.* 2000: 126).

Conclusions

The origins of the current educational and youth justice systems are closely entwined. The reconstruction of childhood and the child-rescue movement had a profound effect on the shaping of a separate justice system for children and young people. This new justice system placed schooling centre stage with reformatories for those who had offended and industrial schools for those who were destitute. With the advent of mass education, those schools acted as a safety valve for ordinary schools. In time, they merged, became approved schools and later community homes with education. Their legacy lies in the remaining voluntary sector therapeutic communities, the STCs and PRUs.

The exclusionary pressures on ordinary schools, including those of payment by results, coupled with the growing medical and psychological interest in deficiency, led to the establishment of special education. The diagnosis and classification processes could never become precise because the behaviours to be classified varied between teachers, schools and over time. Consequently, constructs such as moral defective, maladjustment, and emotional and behavioural difficulties have been used to justify either removal from school or, more recently, the attraction of resources in. The proliferation of categories of disability led by the

1980s to more of an emphasis on a continuum of educational needs, shifting the emphasis from medical and psychological to educational. The problem of definitions that are so dependent on context has not gone away.

The vested interests of different groups of professionals in intensifying exclusionary processes is highlighted here as a counterweight to the focus on the deficiencies within the child or its family. Their interests centred on the process of classification. Mainstream teachers saw classification as a means of organising their teaching and class to best effect, their counterparts in special schools or classes relied on classification to supply them with pupils, and those from a medical background controlled the assessment process leading to classification. Other staff in the separate institutions also had a vested interest in keeping the establishment full. Large institutions tended to keep young people for lengthy periods of time, as they relied on them as part of the workforce.

The development of a specific juvenile justice system and the introduction of both penal schooling for the few and education for the masses were closely allied. There were, however, fundamental tensions. Education through moral reclamation at a general level and removal to residential establishment for individuals were designed to maintain social control and curb crime. But if the segregation of groups of youths of itself increased their likelihood of offending (through creating delinquent groups, denying them ordinary family lives, restricting their acquisition of skills and reducing their future employment), then schooling was not just the solution but also part of the problem.

Summary

❑ The child-rescue and reform movement gave rise to a distinct approach to children within the criminal justice system with an emphasis on providing more training and guidance to those who were seen as lacking it. This movement evoked an institutional response, with a wide-ranging building programme of new care and educational institutions being established for those who offended and those believed to be at risk of offending through destitution.

❑ Penal schooling became the dominant feature of juvenile justice in the later nineteenth century and paved the way for the introduction of mass education. Most interventions in youth justice can be seen as 'educational' in that they seek to instruct and facilitate learning.

- ❑ From its inception, mass education contained inherent exclusionary pressures in order to maintain discipline and standards of achievement. This stimulated the growth of special education and sustained the use of reformatory and industrial schools for those who impeded the running of ordinary schools.
- ❑ The emerging medical and psychological professions became important stakeholders in the assessment and classification of those who might need to be removed from ordinary schools. Issues of mental and moral deficiency came to the fore.
- ❑ Selection at ordinary schools on behavioural grounds was formalised with the introduction of a maladjusted category that later became emotional and behavioural difficulties, but both concepts defy consistent definition and assessment, and appear to be social constructs.
- ❑ Important vested interests have been established in the categorisation and removal of children who impede the smooth running of ordinary schools through their behaviour and/or their low attainment.

Chapter 3

Social exclusion and youth crime

Exclusion is an idea which poses the right kind of questions.
D. Donnison (1998: 5)

Social exclusion is a term that has gate-crashed the debate about the direction of social policy without paying the entrance fee of a definition.
P. Teague and R. Wilson (1995: 79)

The previous chapter outlined the development of processes of educational segregation and separate provision, often benign in intent, that tended to detach children and young people who were delinquent or destitute from their families, communities and ordinary schools. Social exclusion may provide a useful unifying concept to examine the way in which the youth justice and education systems currently interact.

Social exclusion has been one of the dominant political discourses since the late 1990s. It has provided the principal social policy framework for the analysis of individuals and group disadvantage, encompassing and superseding other approaches that historically have defined objectives in terms of combating poverty or inequalities. Can this discourse provide a conceptual bridge between education and youth justice studies?

Social exclusion and youth justice

It must be noted straightaway that the language of social exclusion is conspicuous by its absence in YJB reports. The lack of a vocabulary seems indicative of the failure of the discourse of social exclusion to penetrate policy formulation in youth justice. In fact, it has been commented that 'the system appears to have little in the way of a fundamental philosophy but rather is marked by a series of overlapping – sometimes complementary, sometimes conflicting – discourses' (Muncie and Hughes 2002: 7).

There are several possible explanations. The new approach since the election of the New Labour government in 1997 was emphasised by having little truck with the 'failed' past. The focus was on reorganising the system and its infrastructure and ensuring more effective management. Notions of minimal intervention, labelling by the criminal justice system, or net widening were simply seen as irrelevant or as features of the ancien régime.

The espousal of an actuarial approach to risk combined with cognitive-behavioural interventions naturally focuses attention on the actions of the individual rather than their social context. Commentators have portrayed the crime discourse as being more powerful than that of social exclusion, leading to the criminalisation of social policy (Pitts 2005). An alternative perspective is that the YJB's remit was to be 'tough on crime' while other agencies were charged with being 'tough on the causes of crime'. The closest that the youth justice system comes to entering into the social exclusion discourse is implicitly through the construction of Yots and their steering groups which were designed to engage the mainstream and specialist services to ensure the access of young people who offend to, for example, mainstream education and primary and specialist health care.

Educational definitions of exclusion

The engagement of education in this discourse is distorted by the fact that both 'exclusion' and 'inclusion' have particular educational definitions. Exclusion is largely taken to mean formal disciplinary exclusion from school and focuses on the behaviour of individuals rather than an examination of wider processes that restrict access, participation and progression in mainstream education. Similarly, inclusion is discussed very much in terms of the integration of children and young people with special educational needs rather than an approach to all young people.

Significantly, the SEU's first report covered these topics and encapsulated government thinking in 1998 in placing exclusions and non-attendance at the centre of its exposition of social exclusion for young people:

The problem – Truancy and exclusions have reached a crisis point. The thousands of children who are not in school on most schooldays have become a significant cause of crime. Many of today's non-attenders are in danger of becoming tomorrow's criminals and unemployed.

Why it matters – This damages the children themselves and everyone else: the children themselves lose out because they stop learning. This is self-evident for truants, but it is also a problem for excluded pupils. … These lost years matter: both truancy and exclusion are associated with a significantly higher likelihood of becoming a teenage parent, being unemployed or homeless later in life, or ending up in prison; the wider community suffers because of the high levels of crime into which many truants and excluded pupils get drawn. Time lost from education is a direct 'cause of crime' … The police and the public are paying a huge price (SEU 1998: 1).

Definitions

The term 'social exclusion' has provided, in a relatively short time, some parameters for debate that are now common to politicians, academics, and professional bodies across education, social care and health.

The biggest challenge we face: the growing number of our fellow-citizens who lack the means, material and otherwise, to participate in economic, social, cultural and political life in Britain today … [It] is about more than poverty and unemployment. It is about being cut-off from what the rest of us regard as normal life. It is called social exclusion, what others call the 'under class' Mandelson 1997: 1).

So wide-ranging has the use of this term become that it is a political pastiche. Even the definition used by the SEU arguably lacks focus:

a shorthand label for what can happen when individuals and areas suffer from a combination of linked problems such as unemployment, poor skills, low incomes, poor housing, high crime environments, bad health and family breakdown (Levitas 2005: 148).

More useful perhaps are definitions that emphasise the detachment *processes*, such as:

multi-dimensional disadvantage which severs individuals and groups from the major social processes and opportunities in society, such as housing, citizenship, employment and adequate living standards. It may be manifested in various forms, at various times and within various sections of the population (Barry 1998).

Three versions of the social exclusion discourse have been identified (Levitas 2005). These are characterised as RED – the redistributionist discourse of traditional social democratic approaches to social policy; MUD – the moral underclass/dependency discourse that is particularly associated with the American New Right commentators, such as Charles Murray, but has permeated the approach of UK political parties; and SID – the social integration discourse that places particular emphasis on integration through the labour market. The relative newness of the term and its political origin leave social exclusion open to very different conceptualisations with markedly different social policy implications.

The issue of agency is pivotal – is social exclusion a product of self-determination or socially imposed? The former conceptions have been characterised as 'weak' and the latter as 'strong' versions (Byrne 2005). Clearly, in the context of education and offending, the weak thesis would emphasise the self-exclusion by individuals through antisocial behaviour, albeit socially engendered as members of an underclass. Stronger propositions would examine the role of the educational, social care and youth justice structures in detaching and isolating young people. Emphasising deficiencies in motivation and capability at the expense of opportunities can completely reverse the relationship between structure and agency. Structural unemployment for adults is a problem 'of' the economy and society, but tracing its origins back to alienated youth becomes a problem 'for' society (Young 2002).

Conceptual limitations

The prevalence of the weak thesis, particularly politically, is made clear by the linguistics of the discourse. Social exclusion is often used as an adjective rather than a verb – it describes the outcome and condition rather than what is done to people (Fairclough 2000).

While the discourse offers some new conceptual and practical insights, it has limitations. One criticism has been that it shifts the policy focus on to the role of the socially excluded individual in order to broaden the electoral appeal of New Labour. Social exclusion offers a theoretical framework within which the policies that characterise New Labour – drawing from both the traditional Left and Right – can be given concrete expression. The aim has been to try to create a unifying political appeal and offer a new synthesis of Left and Right for the development and delivery of social policy. Many commentators, particularly in the criminal justice field, have expressed considerable scepticism about the cosmetic nature of this new synthesis, perceiving it as a continuation of policies that in fact blame the individuals who have multiple disadvantages, rather than the underlying systemic problems that are themselves fundamental barriers to access and participation for some groups within society (Goldson 2000).

If the policy emphasis is on individual responsibility, the risk is that those who are socially excluded are seen as being detached from the moral order. Responsibility is thus shifted to the excluded persons, requiring that they conform to the prevailing cultural norms.

Young (2002) presents social exclusion as an inevitable and growing feature of late modernity manifested through exclusion from the labour market, civil society and the state. Here the main driver is globalisation, as market forces increase criminogenic factors such as pressures on families and residual communities while simultaneously eroding informal controls. Applied to education, this approach would locate the exclusionary impact of market forces and parental choice within schools, one of its symptoms being the scale of detachment of young people from education. The enormous rise in formal exclusions from primary and secondary schools, the pressure on staying-on rates, the virtual collapse of the youth labour market and accelerated transitions could all be viewed as manifestations of a more exclusionary social order that increases the likelihood of offending. And if not more exclusionary, then it is certainly more polarised.

Other criminologists have highlighted the inherent tensions within the social exclusion discourse in that, arguably, the 'criminal law is, by virtue of its historical origins, substantive offences, and current outcomes, directed at social *exclusion*' (Sheehy 2004: 74). Once excluded via the criminal law, an exclusion that tends to deepen social and economic deprivation, people who offend also have the right to sympathy removed. This is paralleled in young people excluded from school for antisocial behaviour or so-called truants who have a quasi-criminal image.

Two related difficulties arise in using social exclusion as an analytical tool in this context. Despite the original structural emphasis of early conceptualisations, particularly on the effects of labour market changes, there is a tendency for this to be reversed and the focus to be on the individual and so-called self-imposed exclusion. Collectively, such individuals have been claimed to constitute an underclass who are rejected by society.

Both difficulties may have a political origin, as third-way politics is based upon replacing the polarity of agency and structural beliefs with a triangulation famously illustrated by Tony Blair's 'tough on crime, tough on the causes of crime'. More prosaically, the SEU attempts a similar balance: 'social exclusion can happen as a result of problems that face one person in their life. But it can also start from birth. Being born into poverty or to parents with low skills still has a major influence on future life chances' (www.socialexclusion.gov.uk).

The underclass?

The concept of the 'underclass' is not new and simply recasts the fears of the dangerous poor with their unholy trinity of crime, single motherhood and unemployment within a new mould. It has great political utility in that it neatly expresses a range of fears and prejudices it rooted in notions of the undeserving, work-shy poor and, at least in the USA, it comes close to fuelling beliefs in racial inferiority. In the UK, it is often used in respect of antisocial youth.

Social commentators in the nineteenth century with fundamentally differing theories of poverty and social and economic development all identified a distinction between the deserving and undeserving poor. From Malthus to Marx, an impoverished, redundant, morally corrupting, dangerous class roamed the edges of society. Economic exclusion is always portrayed as being accompanied by a set of threatening cultural characteristics of underclass members – they are idle, criminal and promiscuous. It has been a short step for many commentators to attribute the circumstances of the socially excluded to personal choice and responsibility or biological determinism, and to view them as a class entity.

Underclass proponents, such as Charles Murray, believe that deviant youth absorb from their parents a distaste for work and an antipathy to the traditional family, and actively choose involvement in crime and welfare dependency. These attitudes and behaviours are subsequently culturally transmitted to their own children. The development of certain forms of psychological testing, particularly that of ranking according to IQ has had a profound impact not just on our educational system but also in ranking different groups by innate worth (Gould 1996). It is no accident that commentators such as Charles Murray fuse their arguments regarding an underclass with the proponents of IQ as a fixed measure of innate intelligence that explains the different roles in society of, for instance, black people or single mothers. While educational failure is a common feature of many discussions of the underclass, it is often presented as almost predetermined.

43

The notion of an underclass has been hotly contested, and its social and political utility appears to be more significant than the evidence supporting it (MacDonald 1997). Critics have argued that it crudely lumps together problem groups, and where young people are concerned it is inadequate to capture the diversity of their routes into and out of social exclusion (Baldwin *et al.* 1999).

Of course, while the empirical evidence may be weak and the creation of an underclass may not be a corollary of social exclusion, the negative stereotypes of young people relentlessly portrayed by the media may create a public perception of a clearly delineated, homogeneous group of antisocial people. This could become self-fulfilling, as the perception and accompanying punitive populism may well intensify exclusionary pressures on young people both within schools and in the community.

Disaffection

Where young people are concerned, the predominant interpretation is that of the disaffection discourse. This elastic term is stretched to include those who exhibit such disruptive behaviour that results in permanent exclusion from school through to the 'passively disaffected' who attend but do not engage in mainstream education (Parsons 1999). More recently the disaffected were described as young people 'who encounter significant problems in the worlds of education, training and employment, are often in trouble with the criminal justice system, or exhibit other forms of problematic behaviour' (Newburn and Shiner 2005: 1).

In fact, there is no widely accepted definition of disaffection in either the academic literature or official reports. Its use creates the impression of a specific category of young people. The use of the term tends to focus on the young people as agents, and rarely on the structures that are doing the disaffecting. The blanket use of the term also tends to oversimplify the potential complexity of a young person's relationship with learning in general and particular educational institutions. Conceptually, it rests easily alongside theories of the underclass and also with the idea of delinquent subcultures and anomic youth who resist schooling (Williamson and Middlemiss 1999).

The processes of classification are derived from particular discourses and are expressed by academics through the construction of typologies which filter through into practice. At its crudest, this may be the 'bad', 'sad' and the 'mad' hidden behind the window dressing of particular labels – 'oppositional defiance disorder', 'school phobic', and 'dyslexic'. Of course, practitioners and others often use these more palatable words for public and professional consumption but use more obviously pejorative terms in private (Sayer 1993 cited in Thomas and Loxley 2001).

While there may be heuristic reasons behind some of the categories and constructs created, this can have serious implications. The disaffection discourse, for example, provides oxygen for the burgeoning of the politics of behaviour but also absolves schools and practitioners in youth justice from ensuring that all young people gain access to, participate and progress in mainstream education. Difficulties that a young person is experiencing with, say, particular teachers or acquiring skills very readily become diagnosed as symptoms of a broad alienation from learning and education.

Many of these constructs are remarkably resilient; only the branding has changed. They are so enduring because of their usefulness at both a macro- and individual level. It may be that mass education from its inception has always had a symbiotic relationship with a range of providers who have offered special education, therapy and care, control, and training. The balance of political forces has determined which professional/bureaucratic grouping has had dominance at a particular time, but their existence is dependent on a supply of children and young people. Equally, their very existence confirms the view of those in mainstream education that they cannot educate all young people.

The clinical mindset is almost universally appealing and has a long history in education and offending behaviour. The vocabulary of 'dosage', 'treatment', 'disorder' and 'dysfunction' invokes a scientific basis for the removal of young people from mainstream education and provides comfort to practitioners in education, social care, youth justice and health. Attributing events principally to the disposition of a young person rather than to the shortcomings of an institution or agency is much easier. Infringements by young people against the school's rules regulating activity, time, and behaviour in speech and clothing have been reconceptualised as an alleged expression of emotional needs (Thomas and Loxley 2001). Apparently more benign, the 'needs-led' approach central to social work can be very receptive to the diagnoses of special educational needs. It is not common for social workers to uncritically accept terms such as oppositional defence disorder, dyslexia or ADHD – a condition diagnosed by specialists that leads to treatment directs the professional and parental gaze upon the young person.

The evidence is so limited that it is understandable that different discourses proliferate, but what is unhelpful is that the perspectives should often be monocular and focus almost exclusively on individual young people. Far less attention is paid to how agencies and their practitioners often, perhaps unintentionally or covertly, have a significant role in the cultural and social reproduction of social exclusion through segregation. If the direction of causation is an open question when analysing issues such as exclusion and offending, so, too, is the explosive growth in certain kinds of professionals in the last 50 years and the perceived growth in misbehaviour and offending by young people (Graham 1988).

In this context, truancy is portrayed as the archetypal expression of disaffection. Again, for analytical purposes, this term is so limited as to become distorting. The widespread use of a term that originated as a medieval form of abuse and retains a quasi-criminal image in most minds surely obscures a wide range of motivation, behaviour and circumstances. The focus is unwaveringly on the young person.

The term 'young offender' can also be unhelpful, particularly in an educational context where, aside from the influence of stigma on educators and other young people, it runs the risk of creating a potentially spurious category of learner. Given the ubiquity of offending behaviour, the casual use of this term can slip into inadvertent assumptions about learning needs. For example, many young people who enter the care system will also enter the youth justice system, yet, despite shared experiences and behaviours, they will be subject to very different social policy responses.

Consequently, this text adopts a stronger conception of social exclusion which attempts to focus on the process of detachment and on those who do the detaching, and which does not assume the existence of an underclass and sees little value in the use of terminology around 'disaffection', 'truancy' and 'young offenders'.

The current context

Since the 1970s, significant economic changes have had a major impact on the educational careers of young people and probably on the nature and volume of youth crime. This has been accompanied by a fundamental shift in the politics of law and order. The rise of the politics of behaviour has seen a convergence not just of the New Labour and Conservative positions on law and order (Downes and Morgan 2002) but also of social policy on education and youth justice. The language of criminal justice is now increasingly applied to education, a minister of state for education expounding a policy of 'zero tolerance' of disruptive behaviour. This is to include such transgressions as 'backchat' (Smith 2005). How has this come about and what is the empirical basis for this latest breakdown of discipline by young people?

Young people have been represented as a problem, particularly in relation to crime, since at least the nineteenth century and probably long before (Pearson 1983). What is striking is the recurrent discovery of the degeneracy of youth and how much worse their behaviour is than in some golden age in the past – 'youth cultures and youth crime assume the appearance of ever-increasing outrage and perpetual novelty' (Pearson 1994: 1168). This is paralleled by educators in both mainstream and special schools (Visser 2003). Public opinion tends to overestimate consistently the scale and trend in offending, and this applies to crime by young people too (Roberts and Hough 2002; Stephenson 2004). While we bear this in mind, it is equally important to assess the evidence for substantive changes in the behaviour of young people and the context in which this occurs.

What may often be forgotten by the public and particular groups of professionals is that offending by young people is not, and arguably never has been, an unusual event. There are nearly five and a half million 10–17-year-olds in England and Wales, and about a quarter of them will have committed a criminal offence in the last year (Audit Commission 2004). Out of these, about 268,500 were arrested. While about a quarter of all recorded crime is committed by 10–17-year-olds, half of all males under the age of 25 have admitted criminal offences (Newburn and Shiner 2005). Out of these, a small minority of young people who offend commit a disproportionate number of offences.

Labour market influences

Changes in the labour market and the position of youth within it have often had a profound impact on the social exclusion of young people. The nature of the labour market has also shaped the provision for young people who offend. The entry of children and young people to the labour market has been progressively delayed over the last 150 years through both regulation and rising skills thresholds.

The collapse of the youth labour market since the 1970s with the consequent increasing polarisation of access, participation and progression in education and employment for young people can be seen as symptomatic of post-industrial capitalism, as politics converges around a norm of structural social exclusion (Byrne 2005). The relative position of young people has altered both within the cohort and in relation to adults.

This is demonstrated in several ways. Relative incomes of young people have declined dramatically. In 1975, 16-year-olds earned 45 per cent of national average wages and 25-year-olds earned 100 per cent. Despite a downward demographic trend with far fewer new entrants to the labour market, this had declined to 38 per cent and 84 per cent respectively in 1999. Comparisons of outcomes for young people from different longitudinal studies show a marked deterioration for those from poor families (Byrne 2005).

The notion of a school-to-work transition has almost disappeared. In the early 1970s when two-thirds of young people left school at 15, the great majority of those readily found employment. This has now dropped to less than one-fifth (Newburn and Shiner 2005). Even when employment levels have risen the nature of work available has changed. The vocational route with high-quality training has narrowed significantly, and most of the jobs available are casual, low-skilled and insecure. The rise in A-level participation has narrowed the availability for those wishing to continue learning at Level 2 and increased the risk of these young people being lost from the education and training system (Hayward *et al.* 2005).

Comparing the evidence from the National Child Development Study with those in the 1970 British Cohort Study, Bynner (2002) found significant changes over time. There was a continuing and increasing disparity in employment outcomes and transitions to independence between those who gained high-level qualifications and those who did not. The latter often experienced accelerated transitions which tended to be characterised by more episodes of unemployment, early parenthood and low income. Prolonged transitions, including the development of the single lifestyle, was the prerogative of those who were most advantaged educationally.

The gap between the high-qualifications/high-employment status group of young people and those with few if any formal qualifications has grown significantly in the last 30 years. In the post-industrial world with the rise of the knowledge-based service industries, the acquisition of advanced credentials is of much increased significance (Byrne 2005). Not only have staying-on rates in further education increased from 48 per cent in 1989 to 71 per cent in 2000 but also participation in higher education is projected to grow equally rapidly. While just 7 per cent of UK 24-year-olds possessed a degree in 1975, this has risen to over 30 per cent in 2005 with a government target of 50 per cent participation in higher education for those under 30 by 2010.

Standards have also risen. Those achieving the equivalent of five or more high-grade GCSEs increased from 23 per cent in 1975 to 56 per cent in 2005 (West and Pennell 2003; DfES 2005a). The gap between the actual scores of the top and bottom quarters of young people taking GCSEs widened between 1993 and 2000 and widened even more significantly between the top and bottom 10 per cent (West and Pennell 2003).

Increasing income inequality during the 1980s and 1990s is likely to have played a part in the polarisation of educational attainment and participation, as both the relative share of the national income and real incomes fell of the poorest 10 per cent between 1979 and 1990 (Levitas 2005). The association between poverty and lower school attainment is well attested. If we use free school meals as a proxy measure, those schools with 5 per cent or fewer young people known to be eligible achieved 67 per cent achievement of five or more grades A to C in GCSEs. Where eligibility for free school meals was more than 50 per cent, the equivalent achievement figure fell to 21 per cent (West and Pennell 2003).

The relationship between the labour market and participation in education is not always straightforward. For example, participation rates rose in the late 1980s as unemployment was falling. More recently, participation rates have declined, and this may well be due to many young people with low levels of attainment joining the labour market for lower skilled jobs (Hayward et al. 2005).

The attenuated link between compulsory schooling and entry to the labour market is only one, albeit possibly the most influential, of the increasingly delayed and complex transitions facing young people. The decline in the youth labour market has had knock-on effects on the domestic and housing transitions (Coles 2000).

In this much more uncertain environment and facing a wider range of risks, those young people who become detached from mainstream education may well be growing in numbers and have a greater chance of becoming involved in delinquency. In the face of greater choice and uncertainty, effective decision-making and planning skills become much more significant, yet those young people already at risk are unlikely to accumulate this socio-cultural capital through family or mainstream school (Alexander et al. 1993).

In fact, 'transition' may be a misnomer for those young people with multiple adversities who become detached from education and enter the care or custodial systems. So chaotic are their experiences that the key milestones in life, such as formally leaving secondary school or moving into independent living in a structured and supported way, may be almost meaningless from their perspective.

While there is a growing literature on the impact of changes in the labour market and other transitions on young people, it is less extensive on the effect of these changes on public and professional perceptions of young people. Within a much more uncertain environment, the public and professionals may be viewing young people as a more magnified threat. It is reasonable to conjecture that many teachers perceiving a more insecure career path with increased pressure on performance may view certain behaviours or groups of young people as more threatening. The general public may feel pulled by the tension between an increasingly 24-hour-a-day youth-dominated media culture and the extension of youth dependence into a more negative view of behaviour and crime.

The growth of the quasi-market in education could be viewed as part of a process of legitimising competitive post-industrial capitalism (Byrne 2005) or, in New Labour terms, as a crucial part of their electoral strategy to keep the middle classes attached to public services. There is evidence to suggest that the interplay of market forces is intensifying the polarisation of educational outcomes in terms of attainment and post-16 destinations. The educational reforms commencing in the 1980s have profoundly affected school structures through changes to funding, enabling parental choice, and allowing various forms of selection. Although social segregation is apparently related to changing levels of poverty, this segregation may have been intensified by these educational reforms (West and Pennell 2003).

Schools have much greater incentives for both selecting in and selecting out certain young people. It is not a well developed area of educational research, but changes in the socio-economic and educational attainment intake can create negative effects on peer groups – compositional effects. Increased concentrations of underperforming young people appear to have a disproportionate impact on school performance over and above what might be expected. These compositional effects mean that the educational outcomes will tend to be lower for young people in schools where the intake is skewed towards more disadvantaged students than if there was a more balanced intake.

While market-oriented reforms could have some positive effects within particular LEAs, many schools will not be in a position to select in the high-achieving young people. 'Overall, the evidence suggests that selection benefits the advantaged, is likely to increase segregation and has negative consequences on disadvantaged pupils' (West and Pennell 2003: 144).

However, in the context of delinquency, the selecting-out effects across all of mainstream education may be even more significant. Growing numbers of young people were formally excluded from school (which is associated with offending) during most of the 1990s, and the segregated education sector, principally comprising off-site units (PRUs), was given much greater legitimacy (DfE 1994) and appears to have increased considerably in size since the mid-1990s – Daniels et al. (2003) estimated a growth of 64 per cent between 1995 and 1999 alone. Both educational and youth justice research would identify the systematic grouping together of young people who have been identified as behaving disruptively, significantly underachieving and beset by a range of other adversities as a significant risk factor (Tremblay *et al.* 2003).

Social exclusionary impulses may be increasing, rippling outwards from the classroom, whereby more young people are detached from mainstream classes into on-site units or groups, and growing numbers are formally or informally excluded from the school. While the PRU population has grown, so, too, might the population in alternative projects and those without provision. The number of 16–18-year-olds not in education, training or employment has remained stubbornly high, and this is surprising given the strength of the labour market over the last decade. But it is not simply a matter of greater numbers being rejected by mainstream classes and schools. The very existence of segregated provision accelerates this by providing both a justification in helping to define a problem and by apparently offering a solution. Equally, the pervasive inability or unwillingness of local and central government to measure the scale and trends in this population could simply be masking a static problem for which increased if inadequate provision is now being made.

Categorisation

People detached from mainstream life have always been victims of stereotyping, as they are inherently threatening. But popular myths of the menacing, work-shy poor are perhaps less dangerous than the tendency of professionals to split multifaceted continuums into dichotomies – educable and uneducable, normal and feeble-minded. A rather old-fashioned, Fordist view prevails within and between the professions. Specialisation of functions delineates territories where teachers teach and social workers work with families. It is ironic that most professionals profess a belief in 'holistic' working or the needs of the whole child while holding as sacrosanct the divisions between professions.

Within each of the four main institutional groups of education, social care, criminal justice and health, separate cultures have evolved that of necessity define the characteristics of these who do not conform. Diagnosis of these characteristics rapidly acquires its own expertise with quasi-scientific devices that place children in particular categories. While most institutions either overtly or covertly develop practices that locate problems within children and/or their families even where the apparent focus is on 'need', an observer could be forgiven for thinking that there are clearly distinct groups of children around whom specialist staff and facilities are grouped.

In fact, there is little evidence that the groups of children, as defined by social policy makers, around whom central and local government organises itself actually exist as discrete categories.

For example, there is a considerable overlap between those who have been excluded and those not attending school in the youth justice system (Baker *et al.* 2002). The characteristics of these supposedly quite distinct groups of young people – serious/persistent young offenders, young people deemed to have emotional and behavioural difficulties, children being looked after by local authorities, children permanently excluded from school, and homeless young people – are all very similar and rooted in poverty and social exclusion.

It is legitimate to question how far the invention and reinvention of categories of young people are constructs that protect the existence of certain professions. Public sector professions tend to be immortal in contrast to some parts of the private sector where technological change and the unforgiving market have had a huge impact on the shape, status and existence of certain professional roles. Similar shifts are fiercely resisted in the public sector, where the major changes have been limited to the rather snobbishly titled 'paraprofessional' in, for example, health and education. Equally, the invention of new professions is usually blocked. Despite the accumulation of evidence that there are often simply too many professionals involved in the lives of young people with multiple challenges, the initial attempts of the Connexions Strategy to create a new professional were defeated, and the confusion of accountabilities was added to by the allocation of the role to different existing professionals with yet another assessment system.

Moral panics

It has been argued recently that the sociological theory of deviancy amplification through moral panics needs updating to take account of a much more diverse media and more sophisticated interactions between the various audiences (McRobbie and Thornton 2002). It may also be that the convergence on law and order of the main political parties has also tended to elevate concern regarding the antisocial activities of young people into a chronic moral ferment (Downes and Morgan 2002). In an increasingly risk-conscious society, the use of the term antisocial behaviour encompasses offending, indiscipline in schools and incivilities on the streets. It gives a new resonance to age-old concerns about rowdy youth and intensifies calls for exclusionary policies.

Despite evidence that the last 15 years has seen a stable or downward trend in offending by young people (Audit Commission 2004), public opinion is convinced that it has worsened over the period (Hough and Roberts 2004; Stephenson 2004). Fear of the increasing lawlessness of youth appears to be continually rediscovered and is used as a justification for introducing punitive measures (Pearson 1983). One constant in the recurrent episodes of outrage regarding the antisocial and criminal behaviour of young people is a harking back to a golden age of discipline, courtesy and law-abiding behaviour. As Pearson (2002: 48) admonishes: 'The fact that we seem able to persuade ourselves in the 1990s that we are passing through an unprecedented crisis of public morals, while expressing our fears in a language which is indistinguishable from that of generations which are long dead, is an extraordinary historical paradox which reflects an equally extraordinary historical amnesia about even the more recent past.'

Antisocial behaviour has such political utility because it is so elastic. Lacking precision, it cannot be measured over time in the way that crime can. As Burney has pointed out, the simple question, 'are people behaving worse?' cannot be answered satisfactorily, as there are no benchmarks (Burney 2005). Instead, each generation of older members of the community supply a folk memory of respectful youth and dutiful pupils.

Stories about the breakdown of school discipline are one feature of such episodes, but again the evidence for any trend is weak. From an educational perspective, there were episodes of concerns that could be termed moral panics in the 1840s over juvenile delinquency, in 1911 following the school strikes across the country, in the mid-1950s over behaviour in secondary moderns following the 'blackboard jungle novels', and fairly continuously through the last decade at least. Again each episode is characterised by popular images of a lost innocence and obedient pupils, but, as Furlong (1985: 25) has revealed, 'it takes only a little scratching of the surface to show that like today some pupils played truant, some were rude and disruptive and some were aggressive towards their teachers; indiscipline at school is a permanent not a purely contemporary phenomenon.' Similarly, Graham's (1988) review of the evidence could discern no trend of growing indiscipline, and Topping (1983: 11) found the term 'disruptive' to be so 'semantically loose, [and] vernacular' that he would not attempt to define it. What evidence there is tends to consist of more or less rigorous surveys of teaching union members. While leaders of these unions periodically claim that rising exclusions are indicative of deteriorating behaviour, it is noteworthy that they never claim that falling exclusions represent an improvement in behaviour. It is likely that recorded exclusions are no more an accurate indicator of rising levels of disruption than surges in the juvenile custodial population are necessarily a reflection of increasing crime.

In fact, the British Crime Survey responses suggest that violence against teachers has fallen in line with the overall trend in crime by young people. While 1.8 per cent of teachers reported assaults between 1994 and 1998, this had dropped to 1 per cent in 2002 and 2003. A similar fall was recorded in verbal threats against teachers over this period (Abrams 2005). It may be that the perception particularly by teachers but also by the general public is that the levels of disruption in schools have increased significantly in the last 30 years (Graham 1988).

Indices of social exclusion

If, then, youth crime and indiscipline in schools are not rising, exclusions from school and custodial sentences may well be acting as barometers of exclusionary pressures exerted by public, political and professional opinion. If so, similarities in their rate of change over time might be expected. In fact, not only are there pronounced trends in both indices between 1990 and 2005 but they are also highly correlated with each other (r=0.79.) (see Figure 3.1).

Particular short-term fluctuations may be identified such as, for example the fall in permanent exclusions by approximately one-third between 1998 and 2001, which followed the first report of the SEU and the consequent government target for reduction accompanied by a series of measures for schools and LEAs. The subsequent retraction of the target for exclusions saw a renewed rise. Custodial populations are also sensitive to changes in legislation and particular events that arouse public opinion to which sentencers respond. The sharp rise in the juvenile custodial population in 2001 followed closely on the pronouncements of Lord Justice Wolf on mobile phone street robberies. The Audit Commission (2004) suggested that the proportion of those excluded who were in the youth justice system was growing.

While scandals and a public outcry followed by an inquiry often lead to reforms of policy and practice, there are occasions when they can arouse moral panic. The abduction and murder of two-year-old James Bulger in 1993 by two ten-year-old boys dramatically focused public

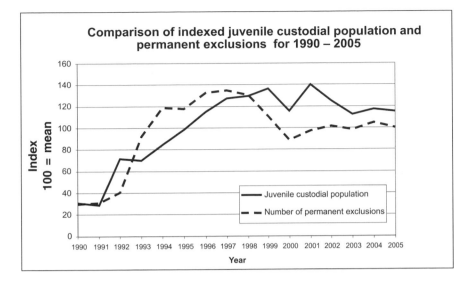

Figure 3.1 Comparison of indexed juvenile custodial population and permanent exclusions for 1990–2005.

Juvenile custodial population figures

- 1990–9 figures were sourced from:
  NACRO (2005) *'A Better Alternative: Reducing Child Imprisonment'*. NACRO: London.
- 2000–5 figures were sourced from:
  Quarterly returns data held by the YJB (unpublished).

Permanent exclusions data

- 1990–4 figures were sourced from:
  Parsons, C. (1996) 'Measuring the real cost of excluding children from school,' paper presented at The National Children's Bureau conference, Exclusion or Inclusion and the School System – Retaining or Rejecting the Disaffected Child, London, 9 July.
- 1995–2004 figures were sourced from the annual Statistical Press Release on exclusions from the Department for Education and Employment (later the DFES) for the years 1995–6 to 2004–5.
- DFEE (1999) *Permanent Exclusions from Schools in England 1997/98 and Exclusion Appeals Lodged by Parents in England 1997/98*. Statistical Press Release SFR 11/1999, 16.

Figure 3.1 Comparison of indexed juvenile custodial population and permanent exclusions for 1990–2005.

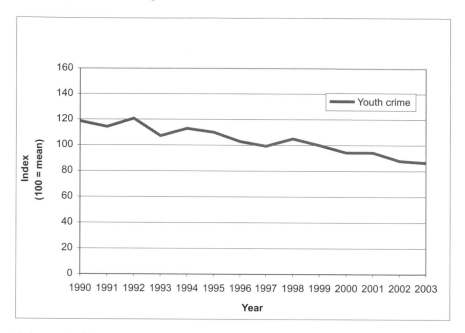

Crime rate data

- 1990–2003 figures were sourced from an annual publication from the Home Office, *Criminal Statistics for England and Wales*. Home Office (1991) *Criminal Statistics for England and Wales 1990*. Norwich: The Stationery Office.

Figure 3.2 Number of young people found guilty or cautioned 1990–2003/04.

attention in what was already an emerging moral panic (Newburn 2002). Later that year, the notorious 'prison works' speech to the Tory Party conference by Michael Howard confirmed a return to the populist punitiveness that was also endorsed and extended by a nascent New Labour (Downes and Morgan 2002). The gradient of the rise in the juvenile custodial population illustrates this profound shift.

It is of course widely believed that both indices simply reflect the increase in disruptive behaviour in school and the crime committed in the community. There are a number of good reasons for not accepting this as a complete explanation. Youth crime over the period appears to have largely followed a downward trend and changes in custodial populations are often unrelated to changes in the scale and nature of offending (Morgan 2002). (see Figure 3.2).

Against the backdrop of increased anxiety about antisocial behaviour, it may be more plausible to view the rapid rise in exclusions in such a short period of time as being due at least in part to the cumulative effect on teaching morale of the reorganisation in the 1980s and the distorting effect of concentrating on an achievement target that many young people currently will have little chance of reaching.

The influence of institutional factors rather than deteriorating behaviour is clearly shared by senior educational managers. A survey of directors of education found that while eight per cent believed that poorer behaviour had led to the rise of exclusions, more than 40 per cent attributed it to increased competition between schools (Sparkes and Glennerster 2002).

Whether the level and trend in exclusions represents a safety valve or is a direct measure of indiscipline or a combination of the two does not preclude a causal relationship with offending and ultimately the juvenile custodial population. Both indices, however, could well be symptomatic of the increasing social exclusionary pressures on certain young people.

Movements in segregated populations

One of the features common to social care, segregated education and youth justice systems is the way in which their populations can change very rapidly. These shifts occur in such short periods of time that it is unlikely to be as a result of changes in behaviour. These population changes often appear to be a consequence of new legislation, although this in itself may be the result of growing public concern. The effects may spill over into different sectors.

It may not be coincidental that major social welfare legislation has often been succeeded by surges in the care, youth justice or special education populations. This can be seen following the mid-nineteenth-century legislation on reformatory and industrial schools, the Children Act 1908, the Children and Young Persons Act 1933, the Criminal Justice Act 1948, the Children Act 1948 and the Children and Young Persons Act 1969. While it could be argued that these were simply reforms to meet growing identified needs among young people or to deal with a problem, the acquisition of new powers of intervention and the establishment of extra provision are always used and draw more young people into their remit irrespective of putative need. So-called welfare approaches are perhaps just as likely as more punitive ones to lead to increases in formal interventions, often with negative consequences.

In special education, for example, following the Education Act 1944 the number of children in schools for the educationally subnormal

(ESN) nearly doubled in the eight years 1947–55 (12,060 to 22,639 and an additional 27,000 waiting for a place). Initially, it appears that mainstream schools were exploiting the rather vague definition of the term – schools for the 'maladjusted' were still relatively few in number. The width of this category and its usefulness to mainstream schools is illustrated by a contemporary Ministry of Education pamphlet: 'it has become less difficult to place the really troublesome educationally sub-normal boy or girl, whose mental disability is compounded by behavioural difficulties and perhaps a record of delinquency' (Ministry of Education 1956 quoted in Tomlinson 1982: 52). The expansion of the numbers of maladjusted pupils did in time rise significantly from 587 in special schools in 1950 to 17,653 by 1976 (Graham 1988).

The scale and nature of the care population has also proved sensitive to legislative change, often initiated by widely publicised scandals of child abuse. The Children Act 1948, for example, which advocated the use of fostering rather than institutional care initiated a rise from 29 per cent of the care population fostered to 37 per cent by 1956 (Frost and Stein 1989). The total care population can move significantly in a short space of time in a way clearly unrelated to the needs of children and young people. There was, for example, a remarkable growth of the numbers of children and young people in the care system in the 1970s, reaching an all-time high of 101,000 in 1977. This increase cannot be attributed to changes in the size of the juvenile population but to a combination of absorbing those on approved school orders, longer stays in the care system and a greater use of care orders (Parker 1990).

The numbers of young people sentenced to custody each year can also change rapidly, apparently irrespective of either demographic or offending trends. The number of custodial sentences for juveniles more than doubled between 1970 and 1978 from 3000 to over 7000 (Newburn 2002). Equally, it could move in the opposite direction just as quickly, the population halving between 1984 and 1988.

Just as juvenile custodial populations crashed in the 1980s, for example, so too, did the number of units for troublesome young people to the extent that the Elton report (1989) foresaw the educational landscape being dominated by schools supported by specialist teams rather than outcrops of units and special projects. This paralleled the situation with custody, where 'in the early 1990s it was not inconceivable to suppose that the wholesale imprisonment of children might be abolished before the end of the century' (Moore 2000, quoted in Goldson 2002: 389).

These abrupt movements in the socially excluded populations of young people are intended to illustrate the point that much more may be going on than simply deteriorating behaviour among young people or weakening of family structures. The short timescales and magnitude of the changes indicate changes in the political climate or local government finance or shifts in the behaviours of organisations and their professionals. Graham (1988: 15) posed the challenging and still relevant question: 'Is it possible that the increasing numbers of pupils referred for special education in general and to disruptive units in particular could be a product of the increasing number of professional experts skilled in the assessment and definition of such children, and the increasing provision of a resource which relieves schools of the burden of coping with their most disruptive pupils?'

The segregation of children on a variety of grounds has often been seen as the outcome of philanthropic motives but from a conflict perspective such actions could be part of the 'ideology of benevolent humanitarianism' that has been repeatedly invoked to justify governmental and professional intervention to remove young people from their families on care grounds, to segregate others on educational grounds, and to sentence others to reformatories, approved schools or latterly secure training centres to curb their delinquency. Most professionals operating in these contexts genuinely believe that they are acting from benign motives and perhaps do not appreciate their economic and professional stake in these systems.

Conclusions

The social exclusion discourse, then, despite its inherent contradictions particularly in its weak versions for implementing social policy, provides an explanatory framework for understanding the dynamics within the changing structures of education and their possible relationships within the youth justice system. In historical terms, it highlights the endemic and systematic attempts to classify and segregate certain young people. In the more recent past, the social exclusion discourse includes the convergence of zero tolerance in the school and the community, where educational credentials are more significant but participation and progression are more polarised, and where segregated education has expanded nearly as rapidly as the 'carceral bonanza' of the custodial population (Bateman and Pitts 2005).

Summary

❑ Social exclusion provides a useful framework for analysing the detachment of young people from mainstream education and their processing within the youth justice system.

❑ Three discourses of social exclusion have been identified: redistributionist (RED), moral underclass (MUD) and social integrationist (SID). Depending on which one is adopted education failure and delinquency can be viewed as the result of either agency or structural causes.

❑ The discourse of social exclusion is largely absent from youth justice, although it is implicitly recognised in the emphasis on the role of mainstream agencies such as education.

❑ It is difficult to justify the existence of an underclass on the evidence available.

❑ Exclusionary pressures on young people have increased in the last 30 years through changes in the labour market, increasing poverty, and truncated transitions intensified by more punitive public and professional opinion.

❑ The two critical indicators of social exclusion, exclusion from school and custodial sentences, appear to have risen substantially during the 1990s, at least partly irrespective of equivalent increases in crime or school indiscipline.

❑ To all intents and purposes, there may be an ill-defined group of young people beset by multiple disadvantages who usually have difficulty in gaining access to, participating in and progressing within mainstream education.

Section II

Chapter 4

Detachment: exclusion, absenteeism, non-participation and unemployment

Till a man learns that the first, second and third duty of a schoolmaster is to get rid of unpromising subjects, a great public school will never be what it might be, and what it ought to be.

Thomas Arnold (Rugby)

'Wag, sir. Wagging from school.'
'You mean pretending to go there and not going?' said Mr Carker.
'Yes sir, that's wagging, sir ... I was chivvied through the streets, sir, when I went there, and pounded when I got there, so I wagged, and hid myself, and that began it.'

Charles Dickens, *Dombey and Son* (1848), ch. 22

Out-of-school or unemployed youth has been a topic of political, public and professional concern since at least the mid-nineteenth century. The association with delinquency has been equally long-standing. Yet, a number of basic questions remain unanswered: How many young people are out of education or training and how many of these are involved in offending? What is the relationship between being detached from mainstream education and beginning or continuing to offend?

These questions have to be answered in the context of a series of complex influences both formal and informal that tend to detach young people from their compulsory schooling and post-16 education and training. There is an increasing use of the law to select out certain young people but also to compel their attendance. Headlines regarding the exclusion of young people are accompanied by those on the imprisonment of parents for failing to secure the attendance of their children at school. Partly as a result of these legal distinctions, different and often spurious categories ('excluded', 'emotional and behavioural difficulties' (EBD), 'truant', and 'not in education, employment or training' (NEET)) have arisen. In youth justice, the issue was highlighted by the Audit Commission in 1996 and has been given considerable prominence by the YJB.

The term 'detachment' is used here for a number of reasons. It emphasises the range of exclusionary pressures within our education systems on young people and draws attention to the importance of attachment of young people to their schooling. It is more neutral than 'disaffected' or 'truant' and recognises the limitations of our knowledge. Such is the variation in responses to similar behaviours of young people by institutions and professionals that many of the current categories could be better viewed as social constructions (Vulliamy and Webb 2001).

Detachment here is taken to occur through exclusion (permanent, fixed-term, and informal including not being on a school roll), absenteeism (authorised and unauthorised) and the statementing process for special educational needs (SEN) (particularly for EBD) and potentially culminates in non-participation post-16 (NEET or status zero).

This is not to claim that these young people represent a discrete group, although many are likely to share disadvantages relating to their physical and mental health, housing and family stability. These factors have a complex interrelationship with access to education and to participation and progression, which in turn will escalate other risk factors.

This approach also tries to capture the complexity of the educational experiences of these young people, which often includes multiple exclusion, persistent absenteeism and finally omission from school rolls altogether. Not only do these young people move between the different categories of exclusion and absenteeism, but also the record keeping and information transfer are often so poor that detailed tracking is impossible (Ofsted 2004).

Placing non-attendance at school within the definition of social exclusion used here, that is, children who do not have access to and/or have difficulty in maintaining themselves within mainstream education, stresses the diversity of reasons for absence from school and the links to a range of exclusionary pressures on young people.

There are three main routes by which young people move and are moved out of mainstream education – formal exclusion, non-attendance and the statementing process. Each of these routes is linked and all share common features. In particular, they often appear to be guided by the notion that the problems are located within the child and ultimately the child will be removed from mainstream education.

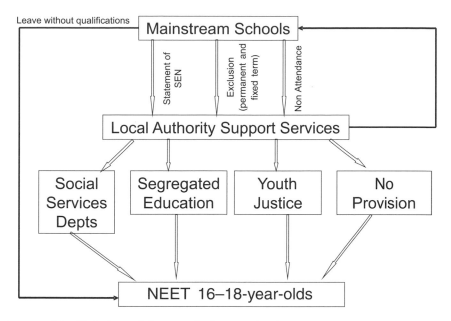

Figure 4.1 Detachment from mainstream schools.

The diagram (Figure 4.1) illustrates the flows of young people out of mainstream secondary schools and the services they may be filtered through. It is somewhat misleading in that it suggests an ordered, systematic approach. The reality often appears to be a relatively chaotic interaction of education, social care, health and criminal justice systems (Blyth and Milner 1996).

Exclusion

Schools have always had a final sanction involving the removal of a pupil. Prior to the Education Act 1986, this was known as suspension (temporary) and expulsion (permanent). There are no continuous national statistics before the 1990s to give an indication of either scale or of any trends. These measures were the highest tariff of disciplinary sanctions available to a head teacher. This tariff also included corporal punishment until 1986. The impression is that suspension and expulsion were rare.

In terms of the current legislation, exclusion is perceived as an event which is the consequence of an extreme breach of an authority relationship. This tends to obscure some of the underlying causes which can lie within the culture of a particular school and can be both complex and cumulative in relation to a specific exclusion. Rather than being a one-off event, exclusion is perhaps better appreciated as often being the culmination of a young person's gradual detachment from school as the relationship deteriorates. The school attendance can also have been characterised by lengthy periods of absence or fixed-term exclusions (Berridge *et al.* 2001).

With regard to trends in permanent exclusions, the evidence suggests that from the mid-1980s the national totals began to increase quite rapidly from a relatively low base, with a dramatic increase in the early 1990s, a fall at the end of the decade, and the resumption of an upward trend by 2001, which has since stabilised (see Figure 3.1, Chapter 3).

In 2004/2005, there were 389,560 fixed-term exclusions in England. The number of pupils affected (once repeat exclusions were accounted for) was 220,840, which is 2.9 per cent of the school population. The average length of a fixed-term exclusion is just under four days but can be up to 45 days (DfES 2006b).

The third type of exclusion is that which could be dubbed 'informal'. This is an illegal practice and is therefore impossible to quantify with any precision. Schools that do not wish to go through the bureaucracy and potential publicity may occasionally indulge in this practice. Ofsted (1996) noted that the practice seems to be growing of 'inviting' parents to find another school, in lieu of exclusion.

For obvious reasons, this is an area where it is extremely difficult to obtain anything other than anecdotal information. One recent study, though, has revealed that in the one LEA prepared or able to disclose the numbers of informal exclusions, significant numbers of days were lost to young people who have experienced this, nearly 1,000 days of potential learning being denied to these 20 young people (ECOTEC 2001). Over a fifth of the sample in another study had been informally excluded (Berridge *et al.* 2001).

Of the minority ethnic groups, black Caribbean children and young people have the largest number of excludees and the highest rate of exclusion. Black Caribbean pupils are over three times as likely as white pupils to be permanently excluded, and those designated 'black other' are excluded at a little under three times the rate of white children. They had experienced a consistent drop in their over-representation until a rise after 2000/1.

Self-fulfilling teacher expectations have been given even greater prominence with regard to particular ethnic minority groups of young people, particularly African-Caribbean males. Historically, they have been over-represented in off-site units and special schools and are significantly more likely to be excluded. Gillborn has emphasised the tensions and conflicts between the expectations of a teaching workforce that is overwhelmingly white (ethnic minority teachers are under-represented in the workforce (West and Pennell 2003)) and African-Caribbean young people, 'who are generally seen as lacking ability and presenting disciplinary problems' (Gillborn 2002: 16).

Ironically, given that exclusions can result in prolonged out-of-school experiences, even in the mid-1990s non-attendance was the reason given for permanent exclusion in one-eighth of the cases analysed in one study (Mitchell 1996). Many of these students cite difficulties with literacy and/or numeracy as a factor for frustration/embarrassment that leads to disruptive behaviour. Research from Daniels *et al.* (2003) shows that 42.1 per cent of their sample was reported as having SEN. Students with SEN relating to EBD are more likely to be excluded – at 36 per 1,000, this is considerably higher than for secondary students in general.

Looked-after children are also widely referred to in the literature as being at increased risk of exclusion. Additional interlinking factors include, for example, their often high mobility, frequent change of carer, lack of constant nominated social worker, and the reasons they are in local authority care (Osler 1997; SEU 2003). Once excluded, young people are particularly vulnerable to their care placement breaking down (Pearce and Hillman 1998), creating problems that fall between social services and education departments (Vernon and Sinclair 1998).

Absenteeism

What, then, are the current scale, nature and trends in non-attendance? Despite the high profile of school attendance under successive governments, it is impossible to answer these basic questions with any kind of precision. The DfES statistics revolve around the number of days lost through authorised and unauthorised non-attendance. They do not enable a detailed analysis of the patterns of non-attendance. This can vary considerably in terms of exposure to risk. For example, an individual who does not attend at all for one month has a similar impact to someone who misses one day a week for a term. The causes of the respective non-attendance and the impact on the individual, particularly in relation to risks of offending, could be very different in both instances. It is very difficult to differentiate between non-attendance at particular lessons while at school, sporadic non-attendance at school, regular but involving no more than one day a week, and those young people who rarely or never attend.

Given the limited state of knowledge about non-attendance, trend analysis can be little more than surmise. However, there must be a strong suspicion that the pressures behind the rise in exclusions would also affect chronic non-attendance.

There are virtually no reliable data on long-term absenteeism, and no official definition of what constitutes it or of when unauthorised absence becomes long-term absence. It has been suggested (Blyth and Milner 1996) that young people who have attended for less than 50 per cent of the previous term could be designated as long-term non-attenders.

Some researchers have divided children who do not attend school into two categories: truants and school refusers, the difference apparently being that truants wilfully miss school without parental consent or knowledge, while school refusers are too afraid to attend school and may stay at home perhaps with parental consent.

The truant is seen as displaying antisocial and conduct disorders while the refuser is suffering from a neurotic condition and may well be labelled as school phobic. This tends to be overlaid with a gender split, with the aggressive boys on the streets and the withdrawn girls at home. In reality, little is known about gender or ethnic patterns of non-attendance. It could be conjectured that there is a greater proportion of females who are not attending school for a variety of reasons than have been formally excluded.

Reid (1999) has proposed three, if not four, categories of truants which he believed were easily identified: the traditional or typical truant, the psychological truant and the institutional truant. He also suggested a fourth category of the generic truant. Rather optimistically, he asserted that 'it is extremely probable that the three categories can be sufficiently refined and amended to highlight possible different treatment approaches by group for the different caring professionals who interact with truants' (Reid 1999: 6).

From the perspective of managers and practitioners, these categories could seem simplistic, obscuring the complex realities, and too static. If young persons decide not to attend school without parental knowledge and initially engage in overt antisocial activities but later, even when the parents are aware of the situation, are too fearful to return to school – are they truants or school refusers?

One study, for example, that examined the effects of non-attendance on later psychiatric disorders (Berg and Nursten 1996: 119) defined non-attendance at two levels:

a) a broad definition skipping school at least twice in one year;
b) a strict definition skipping school at least five times a year in two or more school years.

Even these subdivisions do not enable the identification of the chronic non-attenders as distinct from less frequent non-attenders. The Cambridge study (West and Farrington 1973) in delinquent development, for example, does not stratify non-attendance when examining the association between delinquency and non-attendance. One national survey of non-attendance (O'Keeffe 1994) quantified large-scale non-attendance, with particular emphasis on non-attendance at particular lessons while actually attending school. This methodology had a notable omission in that the data were derived from responses to questionnaires completed by young people who were actually in school on a given day. The chance therefore of gaining information on those who do not attend at all or very rarely was negligible.

This is a highly sensitive issue in that schools may continue to receive money for sometimes quite significant numbers of young people who do not attend at all. A survey of 250 young people in Sunderland established that in the previous two years, almost a quarter had stayed away from school 'a lot of the time' and five per cent claimed to have done so 'all the time' (Wilkinson 1995: 24).

Causes of non-attendance

The balance of research has shifted from a concentration on the familial and personal backgrounds of non-attenders from the 1950s until the 1970s towards analysis of the influence of school organisation (Zhang 2003).

In terms of the impact of personality, there is no substantial agreement in the literature. While some researchers have found an association between non-attendance and unhappiness and unsociability (Carlen *et al.* 1992), others have argued that there is not a significant correlation between non-attendance and concepts of 'maladjustment'.

A much greater degree of consensus is reached over the impact of the family on school non-attendance. A whole range of family difficulties have been identified. These obviously include poverty, unemployment, over-crowding, disrupted home lives and criminal parents. Again, these are the features common to most young people who are socially excluded.

Graham and Bowling (1995) examined the correlates of non-attendance and found that for both males and females delinquent friends, weak parental supervision and weak attachment to family and siblings were strongly associated. Single-parent families, for males, and being members of social classes III M, IV and V, for both sexes, were also correlates of non-attendance. The closeness of the relationship between non-attendance and having delinquent peers, which in turn was found to be closely associated with parental supervision and family structure, led Graham and Bowling to conjecture that family influences were the most important influence on non-attendance. They did also point out that their study had not collected information on the quality of the school environment, which, they felt, had a crucial role in explaining non-attendance. Research in Scotland has indicated that chronic non-attendance could be related to parental attitudes to school and parental levels of education (Scottish Office Education Department 1991).

One interesting variant on the school as 'problem' is the idea of the pupil acting as a rational consumer. Baroness Cox, for instance, argued that non-attendance results from 'rational choice rather than social deviance' (*Times Educational Supplement* (TES) 3 November 1989). Another commentator echoed this viewpoint, in a review of a work on non-attendance, that 'children who choose to miss particular lessons are engaged in the purest form of decision making. Truants are rational consumers. By taking the school menu a la carte, they reveal which subjects or teachers are unsatisfactory and require remedy' (J. Burrell, *The Times*, 7 December 1992). While these analogies of non-attenders acting as rational consumers are a distortion of their vulnerable and powerless position, it does at least switch the pathology from the child to the institution.

Another neglected area is the unintended consequences of non-educational agency interventions. Care placement moves are associated with changes in school placements, and such multiple disruptions may be influential in causing chronic non-attendance (Firth and Horrocks 1996; Brodie 2000). Similarly, the involvement of a young person in the criminal justice system may accelerate that young person out of the education system. The disruption, loss in school time and labelling effect of multiple court appearances could tend to disrupt education, and this could be exacerbated by the involvement of youth justice workers, which can lead to the perception by schools that the appropriate place for the child is with the youth justice team.

Part-time employment may also have a significant impact, perhaps luring young people from low-income families.

A survey in Birmingham of a sample of 1,800 children aged 10–16 years showed that 43 per cent had a job (not including babysitting, and other unregulated employment). Almost three-quarters of those who were working were doing so during school hours (Pond and Searle 1991). Extrapolating these figures nationally results in a figure of from 1.75 to 2 million children aged 10–16 years working. Other research has concluded that participation in part-time work increases the likelihood of unauthorised absence significantly (Dustmann *et al.* 1997).

As children are displaced between systems – for example, awaiting a school placement as a result of care placement moves or a new school following exclusion – work becomes a much more attractive option. While this may appear preferable to doing nothing constructive, it can create short- and long-term problems. In the first instance, it is doubly difficult to persuade a young person who may have had very unpleasant school experiences to give up earning money and the more adult status to return to school. In any event, Year 11 non-attenders who have entered the employment market early are very likely to be displaced in time by someone else who is younger.

Special education

The third main route by which young people became detached from mainstream education is that of the SEN category EBD.

The formal definition of EBD is so wide as to embrace very many children with multiple problems: 'Emotional and behavioural difficulties lie on the continuum between behaviour which challenges teachers but is within normal, albeit unacceptable, bands and that which is indicative of serious mental illness. They are persistent (if not necessarily permanent) and constitute learning difficulties' (DfEE Circular 9/94: 7).

This definition clearly gives considerable scope for varying and subjective judgements. Given the multiple problems that young people who are excluded have, it is difficult to see why many, if not virtually all, of them do not fit within this category.

Research into the profile of children entering special schools is not abundant, but such similarities to those who are excluded or in the care or criminal justice systems appear to exist that again, to all intents and purposes, they appear to be the same children. In a study of 67 children in residential EBD schools, the following emerged:

- Only half had a statement specifically relating to the admission.
- Half the sample were in contact with social services, one-third being of looked-after status.
- Nine per cent were on the Child Protection Register on admission.
- Twenty-seven per cent of children had undergone a serious illness and the same percentage had at least one health impairment.
- The great majority, 85 per cent, had unacceptable behaviour in school as their educational behaviour difficulty.

The report concluded that 'disconcertingly, there was evidence to suggest that if children had experienced an organised continuum of provision that might have prevented the need for referral. The behavioural difficulties they posed were more frequently described than their personal problems. The process of admission appeared, therefore, to be socially driven rather than planned according to national criteria' (Grimshaw and Berridge 1994: 45). Their schooling history had been complex and unstable with considerable changes of school – over three-quarters had changed school on grounds other than age, and over 10 per cent had experienced four or more school changes.

Even if the concept of EBD as a discrete category of SEN could be sustained, it is currently impossible to be precise about the numbers of children and young people involved. The reasons for this ignorance are an interesting commentary on this whole area. In the first instance, despite the official recognition of their specific needs, these children are far more likely to be excluded from either mainstream or special schools. There is an obvious contradiction here, as considerable amounts of resources are expended to identify these emotional and behavioural problems that the children have to the extent that it impedes their learning and yet the child's learning, self-esteem and perhaps family circumstances are to be jeopardised by exclusion.

The number of children designated EBD and who are within the special school sector has been estimated to be up to 18,000 (Visser 2003). Despite the high cost of these pupils, there is very little assessment of the effectiveness of their segregation into special schools. What studies there are suggest that while behaviour modification in some respects improves within the school, the successful transfer of this through progression post-16 and reintegration into the community is much more limited. Apparently only 39 per cent of children nearing the completion of compulsory schooling in four residential special schools had plans for their post-16 education. As more than half of these involved remaining at the special schools post-16, a small proportion were preparing for further education or training (Grimshaw and Berridge 1994: 122).

Non-participation post-16

It is very likely that prolonged periods of detachment during compulsory schooling increase the chances of non-participation in subsequent years very significantly. The SEU (1999) found that young people excluded from school in the last two years of compulsory schooling were two and a half times more likely not to participate in education, training or employment during the next two years than their peers who were not excluded.

Pearce and Hillman (1998) outlined the following characteristics of young people who do not participate in education, training and employment following compulsory schooling:

- GCSE attainment: attainment at 16 is considered to be the strongest predictor of future participation in education and labour markets. Those who do not participate in education, training or employment are, on average, the least qualified of school leavers.

- Socio-economic group: attainment at 16 is higher for those in higher socio-economic groups, so too is participation in education and training after leaving school.

- Housing: linked to socio-economic background, there is evidence to indicate that young people in council or housing association property are more likely to be out of education, training and employment, than young people in mortgaged housing.

- Family circumstances: young people not in education, training and employment are more likely than their counterparts to live with neither parent, while those with difficult or disrupted family backgrounds, or who moved around a lot, are disproportionately over-represented in non-participation statistics. This is also the case for children in the care system.

- Ethnic background: black and Asian young people are more likely than their white peers to remain in full-time education post-16, although they are more likely to do so at further education colleges than schools. Young white people, on the other hand, are more likely to enter the labour market directly than all other ethnic groups, apart from Bangladeshis, who have been found to be over-represented in the group that does not receive education or training after school.

- Gender: young women are more likely to continue full-time education or training than young men, although the rates converge at age 17.

- Learning difficulties: not surprisingly, young people with learning difficulties are over-represented among those not participating in education and training. This group includes those with SEN, EBD, or physical difficulties (Pearce and Hillman 1998).

Size of the detached population

There are major measurement and definitional problems involved in calculating the size of the detached population. Exclusion and absence from school are highly sensitive political issues, and are the subject of much pressure exerted particularly through targets by central and local government on agencies and schools. In such circumstances, the accuracy of statistical returns tends to be compromised: 'Official figures are widely rejected by researchers as considerable underestimates [...] and the practice of schools and LEAs carefully "laundering" their truancy and exclusions figures has been privately admitted' (Webb and Vulliamy 2004: 9).

It is unknown just how widespread is the practice of informal exclusion or collusion over authorised absence through registering unauthorised as authorised to mask attendance problems. A DfES report quotes one head teacher: '[The system of recording absences as authorised or unauthorised] allows the political administration to say they are cracking the truancy problem. And they are NOT cracking the truancy problem. What the schools are doing on their behalf is cracking the statistics problem' (Malcolm *et al.* 2003: 8). Other pressures which can lead to the distortion of statistical returns are attainment targets on schools and a lack of capacity in segregated education and custodial education in young offender institutions.

With regard to permanent exclusions, the annual number recorded ignores the potential stock of young people permanently excluded from mainstream school. Fixed-term exclusion statistics do not include details on just how long those excluded for more than two weeks spend out of school. The frequency and duration of informal exclusions, including those young people rejected by a school and those not on a school roll, can be estimated only through conjecture and anecdote. Absenteeism is monitored through the numbers of days per pupil body of a school, a measure that does not distinguish between those avoiding, say physical education on a Friday afternoon and those who have not attended at all for many months. The numbers of young people who leave and remain outside mainstream school due to a statement of SEN for EBD appears not to be monitored at all. Where the NEET population is concerned, although it is subject to a much more comprehensive tracking process than the compulsory school age population, it is measured only at certain intervals.

One of the major problems is the failure of most local and central management information to distinguish between full- and part-time provision and, more importantly, between scheduled and received. It is, for example, not unusual for a young person in the youth justice

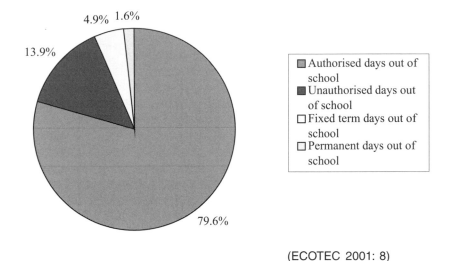

(ECOTEC 2001: 8)

Figure 4.2 Percentages of days out of school for different reasons.

system to be on a school roll but, for all sorts of reasons, not gaining access to a full-time curriculum or indeed any at all.

The greatest proportion of pupils out of school on any given day consists of those with authorised absence. Clear examples of authorised absence include illness, religious observance, study leave, bereavements and public performances. Areas requiring more discerning authorisation on the part of the school include family holidays during term-time and special occasions. What is also unknown is the number of parents who collude in such absence, providing notes of authorisation to satisfy the school's recording processes. Figure 4.2 demonstrates the magnitude of authorised absence compared with the other reasons.

Tim Brighouse's public statement at the Council of Local Education Authorities Conference in 1994 is perhaps the most authoritative estimate of those outside secondary education:

I believe that for everyone officially excluded from secondary school there is another who is voluntarily withdrawn in search of another school, and perhaps three others permanently absent as a result of collusion. If that is right, one way or another there are up to ten percent of youngsters between Year 8 and Year 11 who are finding their secondary education outside secondary schooling altogether (Barber 1997: 72).

[1]Permanently excluded – no access	5,000
[2]Informally excluded – no access	7,500
[3]Not on a school roll	10,000
[4]Long-term non-attenders	100,000
[5]16–18 non-participation [NEET]	220,000
[6]EBD/MLD and specialist care homes	18,000
[7]Custody	3,000
[8]PRUs	10,000
[9]EOTAS	6,500
[10]E2E	25,000
Total	405,000

1 In 2003/4, 12,000 were permanently excluded in England and Wales (ONS 2005), but a certain proportion of those excluded in previous years will not have a placement, so there may be up to 20,000 at any point in time. It is assumed that 25 per cent are without a placement at any point in time (YJB 2006).

2 An illegal practice so difficult to measure with any real accuracy, estimates are approximately 1.5 times the permanently excluded population (Goodall 2005), so there may be up to 30,000 at any point in time. It is assumed that 25 per cent are without a placement at any point in time (YJB 2006).

3 This is a conservative estimate derived from Ofsted (2004). Other estimates are as much as 100,000 (NACRO 2003).

4 Depending on the definition of 'persistence' or 'long term' used this could be as high as 180,000 (Goodall 2005) but is midrange by using the proportions in the Youth Lifestyles Surveys (Graham and Bowling 1995; Flood-Page et al. 2000) and the survey of attendance in Excellence in Cities areas (Morris and Rutt 2004). It also assume that this absence is for more than three months continuously.

5 DfES SFR 21/2006. These figures do not include Wales.

6 DfES website and Visser (2003); DoH/DfES on residential homes with education.

7 This figure includes YOIs, LASCHs, STCs and those young people detained on welfare grounds. This is the average daily population; the throughput in a year is about 8,000.

8 This is based on the answer in the House of Commons (Hansard 2005a) of 12,694 but allowing for joiners and leavers during the year.

9 This includes home tuition, special projects run by voluntary organisations, and Youth Service projects. It assumes that this provision is two-thirds that of PRUs (Daniels et al. 2003).

10 House of Commons (Hansard 2005b). These figures do not include Wales.

Figure 4.3 Detached from mainstream education and training.

Estimating the scale of the detached population is vital from a social policy point of view, given the range of risk factors involved. Clearly, it appears to be highly significant for the strategic aims of the YJB and the other stakeholders at least to be able to measure the sheer number involved and then devise measures to reduce it. This calculation (see Figure 4.3) is an estimate of all those who are outside mainstream education on behavioural or access grounds (they are not on a school roll, have been permanently excluded, are persistent non-attenders, are on a special school roll on behavioural grounds, are registered with a PRU or any other form of education otherwise than at school (EOTAS), are unemployed, are in specialist training provision such as Entry to Employment (E2E), or are in custody.

In making this estimate, relatively conservative assumptions were used, and Tim Brighouse's estimate would be considerably in excess of this equivalent to about 250,000 of secondary school age alone. In addition, there may 'be up to 100,000 children and young people who are in special schools on the basis of a range of disabilities other than "EBD"' (DfES 1997: 45). There also appears to be another shadowy group of young people on 'flexible learning programmes' who may have only a tenuous grip on mainstream education. These young people may be on part-time programmes in an on-site group or unit (often known as learning support units) or out of school placed with various providers. Monitoring is so poor that they may easily be lost to the system (Ofsted 2004). Their numbers may well be growing and could involve many thousands of young people.

Fixed-term exclusions have not been factored into this estimate, although some of these young people could be out of mainstream school for substantial periods of time. The fact that a simple, aggregated snapshot figure for all children and young people who are detached from education, training and employment is so laborious to compile and fraught with assumptions reveals much about the professional and administrative divisions, ineffective management information systems, spurious categorisations and vested interests that do not wish the scale of the problem to be revealed. It is difficult to escape the conclusion that probably well over one-third of a million and perhaps over half a million are detached from the mainstream at any point in time. Of course, during a year, many more may be experiencing episodes of detachment (Hayward *et al.* 2005).

Detachment in youth justice

Detachment from mainstream education appears to be extensive among young people in the youth justice system. There is no national dynamic monitoring but only snapshot studies. Clearly, those young people who have no educational, training or employment provision arranged for them at all can be deemed to be detached and, arguably, so, too, are those in segregated provision, while those on part-time programmes with mainstream schools are at least partly detached. On these definitions, the great majority of those entering and leaving custody are detached from mainstream education, between one-third and a half having no provision at all (ECOTEC 2001).

The most recent and most extensive survey (it collected information on 5,568 young people) of the scale of detachment among young people in the youth justice system found that:

- The Yots in the sample are struggling with very serious issues of access to full-time education, training and employment.
- Under half of the young people in the sample may be in full-time provision at any point in time.
- Young people who are older, have been in the care system, have literacy or numeracy difficulties, have previous convictions and have more serious disposals are all significantly less likely to have full-time education, training and employment provision arranged for them.
- Only around half of those in the sample of statutory school age appear to have full-time education arranged for them. This is a particularly serious issue for those in their final year of compulsory schooling.
- Dubious practices by some schools, coupled with drift and a lack of alternative educational capacity by LEAs, were revealed in the census.
- The quarterly percentage in education, training and employment figures reported to the YJB were significantly higher than the percentages obtained in the census for all Yots in the sample.
- Monitoring by some Yot staff of the education and training of young people in the custodial phase of a detention and training order (DTO) appears to be relatively weak (YJB 2006).

Taking account of non-attendance, as few as 35 per cent of young people in the youth justice system may actually be in full-time education, training or employment on a given day. Delay and drift appear to be relatively common, and practitioners highlighted cases of young people receiving no education for several years and the negative effects on motivation of part-time provision.

These findings are consistent with other surveys of young people in the youth justice system; for example, out of 2211 young people engaged in the youth inclusion programme, almost one-third (695) were not enrolled at a school (YJB 2003b). The extensive analysis of the ASSET data with a sample of 2613 indicates that 21 per cent of young people of statutory school age had no provision arranged (Baker *et al.* 2002).

The situation for those aged 16–18 appears significantly worse, 39 per cent being recorded as unemployed and a further 17 per cent having part-time or casual employment in the ASSET sample of nearly 1200 young people (Baker *et al.* 2002). Looking specifically at those young people who have been more persistently involved in offending and who are placed on an intensive supervision and surveillance programme (ISSP), even greater proportions are completely detached from mainstream education training and employment. For those of statutory school age, out of a sample of 1640, over a quarter had no main source of educational provision, and only 19 per cent were attending a mainstream school. Again, the situation was significantly worse for 16–18 year-olds, 56 per cent being unemployed out of a sample of 1150 (YJB 2006). The levels of non-participation by 16 to 18 year olds is consistently high across different studies of the youth justice system. A survey of Yots in the Greater Manchester area found only 28 per cent of this age group in college or employment (including those with only part-time provision) (Youth Justice Trust 2004).

One study found that between a quarter and a third of young people entering custody had no education, training or employment arranged in the months before they went into custody. Of those who had provision arranged over a third had four or less hours per week and over half had nine hours or less arranged for them. Compared with their peers in mainstream schools only about one third of the total teaching and learning hours were made available to them. When non-participation was taken into account they were receiving only about 15 per cent of the hours received by their peers (ECOTEC 2001).

The best estimates are that the throughput of young people in the youth justice system is at least 150,000 per annum (YJB 2005a).[1]

1   287,883 sentences that resulted in a disposal of some sort were recorded, perhaps representing about 150,000 young people according to the YJB statistics department (personal communication). There is also likely to be a certain number from the previous year's disposals, which would increase this total.

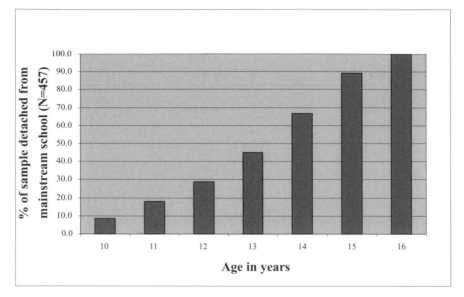

Figure 4.4   Young people in youth justice system detached from mainstream school by age.

Converting the percentages on lack of access and non-attendance from the above studies means that about 100,000 young people are not in full-time education, training or employment, and that of these perhaps 25,000–30,000 have nothing arranged for them at all. Of course, given what is known about the placement instability of the wider population of those not in education, training or employment and particularly for those in the youth justice system, even those young people recorded as being in full-time education at any point in time are likely to have had several episodes without any education or training (ECOTEC 2001; Hayward *et al.* 2005). Allowing for the various assumptions made, it is not unreasonable to conclude that perhaps one-third of those who have become detached from mainstream education are involved in the youth justice system.

Trajectories

The evidence on the trajectories of detachment, particularly for young people in the youth justice system, can be described in outline, although causation and exact sequencing of events are opaque. The most useful evidence is perhaps that provided by combining the data drawn from the YJB and Arts Council England (ACE) studies (ECOTEC 2001; YJB 2002c, 2005b; ACE 2005).

All participants in these studies had been in custody, so they represent those who had offended most persistently or seriously. A higher proportion of other young people in the youth justice system may remain attached. Certain features stand out: detachment accelerates with age and is rarely reversed. It often appears to be the result of cumulative pressures or recurrent events and is accompanied by intensifying professional interventions. This is not to imply a smooth, even trajectory out of mainstream school; rather, it often seems to be a jerky process in which periods of drift or inactivity are punctuated by rapidly occurring events that happen too quickly for rather cumbersome administrative systems.

In broad terms this was confirmed by another study in which out of the 187 young people questioned, only 58 (30 per cent) had remained at school until the statutory-school leaving age. For those young people who were in custody within the sample, 75 per cent had left before they were 16 (Hurry *et al.* 2005).

Some American longitudinal studies support the argument that detachment can be a cumulative process of disengagement that begins early in a school career (Alexander *et al.* 1997). Detachment accelerates by the time young people reach Key Stage 4 at secondary school. This is paralleled by the sharp increase in numbers entering the care and criminal justice systems at this age. Professional interventions increase rapidly but appear not to reattach young people to school; in fact, they may often inadvertently accelerate young people away from mainstream school and hinder their return.

The negative consequences of multiple professional intervention are manifested in two principal ways: drift and amplification. The planning blight that can result when young people enter the care system, so that they spend long periods of time unnecessarily separated from their families, has been extensively documented and provides insight into what appears to happen to many young people when they become separated from mainstream school. This research established that there is a leaving-care curve which slopes sharply upwards at first but then flattens out abruptly. Those who are not returned to their families within six weeks are likely to remain in the care system for a long time (Department of Health 1991). Similarly, those who have become detached from mainstream education through either formal or informal processes appear to be far more likely to be reattached in the first few weeks; otherwise, a long-standing out-of-school career may emerge.

Some studies have found significant time lags in simply convening exclusion case conferences (Mitchell 1996). The Audit Commission suggested that time lags between exclusion and placement typically range from two-thirds of a school term to half a school year (Audit

Commission 1999). Another study found that the average delay between permanent exclusion and an offer of a placement was more than three months, and that one in seven had to wait more than six months for a placement (Daniels *et al.* 2003). Such delays could have serious consequences: 'For these students, the administrative drift which appears to follow many permanent exclusions may contribute significantly to the onset or acceleration of offending careers' (Berridge *et al.* 2001: 49).

The definition of deviant behaviour by those with formal responsibility for controlling such behaviour may in itself exacerbate the problem by isolating the particular young people from their mainstream peers, thus pushing them into closer association with other similarly stigmatised young people. Values and norms of behaviour are therefore likely to be developed that are increasingly at odds with the mainstream values of the school. Deviancy amplification can be created whereby behaviour and official reaction to it spiral towards removal and segregation.

Another related dynamic which has been observed in relation to young people entering the secure accommodation system, and which probably operates more widely, is the tendency of multiagency intervention to locate the problems within the child. Multiple interventions by agencies can blur rather than sharpen the original focus for intervention, as more problems are perceived and the young person is increasingly viewed as the problem. The meaning of the initial behaviour of the young person is thus lost sight of.

The instruments and processes of assessment can conflict between agencies, and information exchange is often poor, a situation that can result in a highly complex and chaotic administrative environment that has powerful inherent exclusionary forces. More professionals tend to be drawn into the network, and the culmination is often the decision to remove the young person to a different and usually more restrictive setting. This is often justified on the grounds of ensuring a thorough assessment, although in effect it may really be buying time for the professionals.

Once removal has occurred, the professional network loses momentum and disperses. When young persons do eventually return to the mainstream, they are not only in more difficult circumstances but also receive a rudimentary support service that has fractured links with the original assessment and intervention work. A paucity of information can reinforce stereotyping of a young person who has been excluded and make attempts at reintegration into a new school more likely to be unsuccessful (Berridge *et al.* 2001).

There are particular effects caused by the interaction of the education and youth justice systems that ratchet young people further away from mainstream schools. Several studies have found that magistrates place considerable emphasis on educational issues and that this can move young people up the sentencing tariff (NACRO 1988; Ball and Connolly 2000). Evidence suggests that young people who are excluded from school are twice as likely to receive a custodial sentence as their peers who are not excluded (Graham 1988; Graham and Bowling 1995). If sentenced to custody, more young people are detached from both mainstream and segregated education, and the stigma of custody may delay the return of those who were already detached (ECOTEC 2001).

Intervention that places young people in segregated or special education, even if the initial intervention is supposed to be temporary, also tends to detach them from mainstream school and may lower participation rates post-16. Reintegration is the ostensible objective of PRUs, according to government guidance (DfES Circular 10/99). Reintegration rates and destinations are not routinely monitored, but what information there is indicates that reintegration is achieved only for a minority of young people with very low rates for those in Year 11 (Parsons and Howlett 2000). The same appears to be true of young people categorised as having EBD. Although the planning process often indicates a return to mainstream school as the objective, removal to a special school is nearly always permanent (Lloyd and Padfield 1996; Farrell and Tsakalidou 1999).

Important lessons can be learned from some of the research in the 1980s into the operation of the care system (Rowe *et al.* 1988). For example, it was established that many young people were 'lost' in care and that planning drift caused them to spend extended periods of time – often years – unnecessarily separated from family life. Clear and consistent patterns of entry into the care system and returns to families were observed across several local authorities. The dynamics of multiagency working often caused delay, leading to inert decision-making and resulting in young people not returning to their families as rapidly as they could. There are strong similarities in the dynamics of the segregated education sector and the care system. It may be helpful to adopt the notion of an out-of-school career for both policymakers and practitioners.

Types of detachment

In analysing exclusionary pressures that tend to detach young people from mainstream education or interrupt their participation in training or employment, it may be useful to distinguish between structural, cyclical and frictional factors.

Secular trends in the youth labour market, demographics, inequalities, and family size and composition will probably influence the resilience or willingness of schools to cope with certain behaviours and their selection practices. For example, the withering of the youth labour market in the 1980s, exacerbated by the restrictions of the National Curriculum, has been seen as breaking the social contract with young people and increasing their alienation. 'Many young people were, until recently, prepared to trade their obedience for qualifications. But once there are very few or no jobs at all available for school leavers and once a few qualifications can no longer guarantee employment ... the existence of these qualifications can no longer be relied upon to secure classroom consent or efforts' (Hargreaves 1989: 54). New legislation, either deliberately or through unintended consequences, has at different times resulted in significant numbers of young people being moved from mainstream education to segregated education (see Chapter 2).

There may also have been a long-term deterioration in the mental health of young people due to changing environmental influences such as significant changes in family composition and breakdown (Collishaw *et al.* 2004).

Some influences may be more cyclical in nature, most obviously through variations in demand for labour according to the business cycle. The trade depression of the 1870s, for example, was linked with an increase in admissions to industrial and reformatory schools (Grigg 2002). However, there may be other cyclical pressures that have an impact on both the education and youth justice systems. General election campaigns may be associated with subsequent spikes in custodial populations, as sentences reflect the heightened scrutiny of law-and-order issues. The recurrent moral panics that periodically appear to sweep across education and youth justice have been well documented (Pearson 1983).

Frictional exclusion could be illustrated by episodic detachment, often associated with multiple professional intervention, which can introduce drift and amplification. Care placement moves are often triggers for educational placement breakdowns or moves (Brodie 2000). Entering and leaving custodial establishments or transient populations are also illustrations of punctuated learning which could lead to complete detachment. Episodic involvement in training and casual employment also appears to be a characteristic of many young people who have become detached from mainstream education and are often in contact with the youth justice system (Baker *et al.* 2002). The Nuffield review of education and training 14–19 (Hayward *et al.* 2005: 101) highlighted the dynamic employment situation of the NEET group, as these 'young people are finding short-term employment, or are being taken on for a trial period and are not showing the necessary qualities for continuous employment with that organisation'.

Offending and detachment

The association between exclusion from school and offending behaviour is referred to throughout the literature (see Daniels *et al.* 2003 for literature review). In response to the increased media coverage and heightened public concern over non-attendance and offending, it was estimated that 40 per cent of school-aged young people sentenced by the youth courts had been excluded and that 23 per cent regularly do not attend school (Cooke 2000). A study of seven LEAs found that rates of offending were higher with excluded students than those non-attending (Malcolm *et al.* 2003).

Similarly, the Audit Commission's report on young people and crime, *Misspent Youth*, concluded:

> Reducing the number of pupils who are not at school for reasons of truancy or exclusion could significantly reduce the number of young offenders in a local area. Half of truants offend, but only one quarter of non-truants do. If half of the truants returned to school, and the returned truants were as likely to offend as the non-truants, the percentage of offenders in the age group could be reduced from 35 to 30 percent. Similarly, three-quarters of excluded pupils offend, but only one-third of those who are not excluded (Audit Commission 1996).

Reid made a similar point (1999: 3) but omitted the simplistic assumption that a return to school of itself could make such a reduction in offending:

> The consequences of truancy are enormous. Consider a few simple facts. Forty per cent of all street robberies in London, a third of car thefts, 25 per cent of burglaries and 20 per cent of criminal damage were committed by 10–16 year-olds in 1997 and were blamed on truants. Truancy is the greatest single predictor of juvenile and adult crime. Two-thirds of young offenders begin their criminal activities while truanting.

The two youth lifestyles surveys of 1992/3 and 1998/9 (Graham and Bowling 1995; Flood-Page *et al.* 2000) examined the correlates of offending, including various school factors. The definitions of truancy appear to be different between the two surveys, as Graham and Bowling used truanting once a week as a measure of persistence, and Flood-Page *et al.* used truanting once a month as a measure of persistence. However, both studies found a significant correlation between detachment in the form of non-attendance and exclusion and offending. In the 1992/3 survey, nearly eight out of ten boys (78 per cent) and just over half of girls (53 per cent) who admitted non-attending once a week or more committed offences, compared with 38 per cent of males and 15 per cent of females who did not admit to non-attendance (Graham and Bowling 1995). In the later survey nearly half of 12–16-year-old boys (47 per cent) and just under a third of 12–16-year-old girls (30 per cent) who were non-attenders at least once a month admitted offending, compared with 10 per cent and 4 per cent respectively for those who did not admit to non-attendance (Flood-Page *et al.* 2000). Both surveys also found that the onset of non-attendance and offending began at a similar age, about 14 for both boys and girls.

Exclusions, both permanent and fixed term, were related strongly to offending. In the 1998/9 survey almost a quarter of boys (24 per cent) who had been excluded had offended, compared with 11 per cent who had not been excluded. With girls, the ratio was similar, 13 per cent of those excluded admitting offending, compared with 6 per cent of those who had not been excluded. The earlier survey analysed the effects of permanent rather than fixed-term exclusions and found an even more marked relationship but from a very small sample.

Two recent Home Office surveys have produced more equivocal results on the relationship between offending and detachment as expressed through truancy, although this may well be a result of their definitions and the nature of the sampling. The On Track Youth Lifestyles Survey found that non-attendance did not appear as a significant correlate with regard to general offending behaviour, although it seemed to be linked to reports of attacking someone (Armstrong *et al.* 2005). This survey was school based and therefore likely to have missed those who were chronic non-attenders, on lengthy fixed-term or permanent exclusions, and contained a very small proportion of those in their final year of compulsory schooling (who are most likely to be completely detached). Analysis of the 2003 Crime and Justice Survey did not find detachment, in the form of exclusion or non-attendance, to be a significant independent risk factor for antisocial behaviour (which included offending) in the model used (Hayward and Sharp 2005). The definition of non-attendance, however, was very wide: having skipped school once in the last 12 months or ever for those above school age, and this may have affected the results.

The strength of the relationship between offending and exclusion is not surprising, as some of the behaviours that lead to exclusion, such as theft, criminal damage and assault, are criminal offences.

People who offend are disproportionately represented in unemployment statistics, but it is difficult to establish a simple causal relationship between unemployment and offending, although it is possible to make links between unemployment, poor basic skills and educational achievement. Employability is not solely determined by literacy or qualifications, and the protective effects of employment from involvement in offending may vary considerably according to age and circumstance.

Mair and May (1997) found that only 21 per cent of their sample of adults serving community sentences were employed. Of those, 79 per cent were in manual occupation. Just over half (51 per cent) of those people in the National Probation Service basic skills pathfinder evaluation were also unemployed, a much higher proportion than the 5 per cent that would be expected in the general population. Analysis of the data revealed strong statistical associations between school attendance, highest level of qualification achieved, basic skills difficulties, substance misuse (particularly drugs misuse), risk of reconviction status and employment (McMahon *et al.* 2003).

Similar levels of unemployment were revealed by an analysis of the pre-custodial education, training or employment status of young people aged 16–18 in custody (ECOTEC 2001).

Transmission

While there is an extensive body of evidence on the association between being out of education, training and employment and offending, the evidence is sparse on causation. The temporal order is not firmly established – are young people who offend more likely to be excluded or stop attending school or does detachment from mainstream school have an independent effect? If there is an independent effect, is it direct or indirect, short or longer term? What might the intervening variables be?

There have been insufficient longitudinal studies that could identify the causal order, and the practical difficulties of tracking an out-of-school population and retrieving sufficient educational, care and criminal justice data are formidable. One study which attempted to look at pre- and post- exclusion offending did find a significant increase when young people were out of school (Berridge *et al.* 2001). Another study noted that in the month after release from custody, none of those who had full-time education immediately available was reconvicted, whereas nearly one-third of those without such provision were reconvicted (ECOTEC 2001).

Despite the problems with establishing the direction of the relationship conclusively, it is still worth reflecting on the potential causes. A variety of explanations could be applicable acting either singly or in concert. Obviously one important factor is the greatly increased amount of time that young people have on their hands. While this affords more time and opportunities for offending, it could also lead to the formation or reinforcement of delinquent peer groups. The chances of being involved in a wider range of risk behaviours, such as substance misuse, may also increase.

Having a teenager out of school or training for a prolonged period of time can also raise the potential for conflict within families already under severe pressure. This could act as a trigger for a care placement or leaving home prematurely, both of which events are likely to depress educational participation and increase other risk factors associated with offending.

It is possible that being out of school will result in greater surveillance by the police, particularly now that there are increased powers regarding being stopped and returned to school. Whether or not offending has occurred, the young person comes to the attention of the police and this could lead to processing bias.

It may not simply be the increased likelihood of joining or remaining in a delinquent peer group but also the removal of the positive socialisation effects of school and pro-social role models. Prolonged absence may well be reinforcing risk perpetuation effects similar to those observed in the unemployed (Gregg 2000).

There is a strong relationship between attainment and detachment through either exclusion or absenteeism. Young people who had experienced a fixed-term or permanent exclusion in year 11 were three times less likely to have achieved five or more GCSEs at grades A–C than their peers (Flood-Page et al. 2000). The gap was even greater for those who were persistently absent where only 10 per cent achieved five or more high grades compared to over half of their peers (58 per cent) (Flood-Page et al. 2000).

Other studies have found that poor school attendance for any reason is associated with lower educational attainment. Those with weak attendance had lower attainment even when IQ, social class and other background factors were controlled for (Hibbett et al. 1990).

While there are reported differences in non-attendance between social groups, with much higher rates among young people from working-class backgrounds, there are differential effects. High levels of absence have a disproportionate impact on young people from more deprived backgrounds. Analysis of the attainment scores for children in the National Child Development Study found that the relationship between non-attendance and attainment reached statistical significance only where the young person came from a working-class family with the father in manual employment (Zhang 2003).

The direction of the relationship may be unknown at the point of detachment; that is, low attainment may well influence behaviours of young persons and those around them that lead to detachment. Clearly, though, their relative attainment will fall further behind that of many of their peers simply by dint of being out of learning for very long periods of time. It can be surmised that this would lower motivation to become reattached to formal learning, but there is no strong evidence on this. Where the evidence is more unequivocal is that, unsurprisingly, detachment from school for whatever reason tends to be reproduced in either no or intermittent participation post-16.

Again, non-participation post-16 would be likely to have similar increased risks associated with being detached from school, but the risks may be heightened, in that these young people are far more likely to undergo very early transitions to independent living, including young people leaving care. Analysing the data from the National Child Development Survey, Gregg (2000) found that youth unemployment carried persistent effects on later unemployment until at least the age of 33. This had a particularly marked effect on young males with low levels of educational attainment.

While nearly 80 per cent of young people who had not experienced periods of detachment progressed from compulsory education to full-time education post-16, only about a quarter of those persistently absent did so (Flood-Page et al. 2000). A much larger proportion went into full- or part-time work, up to a quarter being complete non-participants. The recent study of engagement in education, training and employment for young people in the youth justice system found that about one-third of 16–18-year-olds had no education and training arranged or were unemployed (YJB 2006).

There is a longer-term effect which may increase offending, as non-participation for 16–18-year-olds was the single most important predictor of unemployment at age 21 (SEU 1999), and there is a significant association between offending and unemployment in the literature (Farrington et al. 1986; Rutter et al. 1998). The rising qualification threshold may mean that non-participation is increasingly likely to lead to unemployment or sporadic employment in casual jobs. The lack of positive socialisation effects from school may lead to employment being less sustainable through particular behaviours. Achieving an appropriate stability and quality of employment, which is likely to be affected by academic and vocational qualifications, also appears to be important in reducing reoffending (Harper and Chitty 2005). Possessing a criminal record, particularly having been imprisoned, could act as a barrier to gaining employment.

Unemployment appears to act upon the individual in two ways: a loss in income and a reduction in social interaction and status. Some evidence indicates that offending for personal material gain increases particularly during periods of unemployment. In addition, it may well be that these individuals are more liable to be drawn into delinquent groups and would certainly have more spare time and opportunities for involvement in crime.

Several relevant studies have assessed the impact of unemployment on offending behaviour. The Christchurch longitudinal study (Fergusson *et al.* 1997) examined offending in 17- and 18-year-olds in relation to the length of time they were unemployed when they were 16 and 18. Young people who had been unemployed for six months or more were ten times more likely to have been convicted than those who had never been unemployed (19.7 per cent and 2.2 per cent respectively). However, the independent effect of unemployment on offending appears to be less significant, as unemployment in itself was strongly associated with all major risk factors. Even when these risk factors were taken into account, those who had been unemployed for at least six months were still two to three times more likely to have been convicted than those who remained employed.

Another longitudinal study (Farrington *et al.* 1986) found that young males who offended while unemployed tended to have much higher rates of offending even when employed, suggesting the influence of other risk factors, but that their offending rates increased significantly when they became unemployed. It seems, then, that becoming detached from employment tends to amplify the existing risk factors that an individual may have accumulated. Importantly, though, this study found that unemployment seemed to be a more significant influence on offending for those young people who had just entered the labour market. Reasons for this may be that there were greater expectations held at that age, so failure to gain or sustain employment produced disproportionately higher levels of frustration or boredom, and that younger people may be more susceptible to older negative peer influences.

A suggestion that may also have relevance to children and young people who have become detached from schooling is that unemployment may have a longer-term influence on crime through the delayed and chronic weakening of individuals' ties to society and its values. If this effect was greater on offending than the immediate stresses due to the loss of a job, it would not be expected that increases or decreases in youth crime would coincide directly with changes in levels of employment. Similar time lags may have occurred in the relationship between detachment from school and subsequent offending rates.

Conclusions

The evidence that being detached from mainstream school and non-participation post-16 for lengthy periods of time is associated with delinquency is pretty conclusive but the causal relationship is not. There are major problems both of definition – for example, what constitutes persistent non-attendance? – and of how local authorities and central government record and monitor such events. It may be that the routes taken from mainstream education are less relevant to understanding the risk of offending than the simple fact of becoming completely detached from ordinary schools. Becoming detached from ordinary school may, through a series of indirect effects, increase the likelihood of offending, as through the creation of delinquent peer groups both outside school and in segregated education, the increased opportunity for crime, the loss of any positive socialisation effects of school, the weakening of the levels of supervision, and the increase in the chances of later unemployment through depressed attainment.

There may be trends in the size of the out-of-school population that could be unconnected with any alleged deterioration in the behaviour of young people but might be due to structural economic changes and shifts in public, political and professional opinion. Professional interventions may inadvertently lead to more prolonged detachment for some young people. Restricted access to, and low participation in, mainstream education is a particular feature of the youth justice system, and interactions with the education system may be compounding this. Certainly, entry into institutional care or custody tends to increase educational placement instability and subsequent detachment.

Summary

❑ There is a relatively substantial body of evidence attesting to the association between being out of school and the increased likelihood of being involved in offending.
❑ The evidence is increasing that there may be a causal relationship between becoming detached through exclusion and subsequent offending.
❑ There are no reliable official estimates of the total numbers of children and young people who have become detached from mainstream schooling – it may be over a third of a million.
❑ Detachment from education may act to increase the numbers of young people joining delinquent peer groups, afford greater opportunities for risk behaviours, lead to a bias in processing by

agencies and sentencers towards high tariff disposals and tend to lower the chances of subsequent sustainable employment.

❑ Entry into residential care and custody appears to increase the likelihood of lessening attachment to mainstream school.

❑ African-Caribbean young men are disproportionately represented in those excluded, paralleling their representation in the youth justice population.

❑ The out-of-school career of many young people appears to have the same features as a care career whereby drift in planning can occur and young people do not return to mainstream education from PRUs or special schools.

❑ The notion of the 'truant' is limited and unhelpful and tends to mask very different causes for non-attending, such as caring for siblings, being bullied and mental health issues, behind a quasi-criminal label.

Chapter 5

Low attainment and underachievement

Low educational attainment is 'the most powerful of any childhood precursor' of negative outcomes in adult life (Hobcraft 2002: 477). This is reflected in the failure to acquire qualifications, placing young people at a much higher risk of becoming socially excluded as adults (Sparkes and Glennerster 2002).

Poor educational outcomes are generally associated with young people in the youth justice system, particularly those in custody. This chapter brings together some of the evidence on the prevalence of underachievement by these young people and examines it in the context of the wider population of young people who have low educational attainment. It examines critically some of the explanations for this underachievement, such as the incidence of dyslexia and the alleged existence of particular learning styles, among these young people. The nature of any causal relationship between low attainment and the onset, persistence and desistance of offending is also considered.

The concept of underachievement lacks clarity in the literature, and although it is frequently used, it is uncommon to find it defined precisely. Its use has its critics, too, as for example, when applied to the attainment of young black people, as the notion of 'underachievement' could undermine ethnic minority efforts to succeed and erode the desire to do well (Gillborn 2002). Given the multifaceted nature of the concept, this discussion is restricted to aspects of relative low attainment and the actual or potential linkages with delinquency.

In contrast to young people who are being looked after, there is no real systematic monitoring of the attainment levels and academic or vocational progression of young people in the youth justice system. In the community, the only continuous assessment process in the youth justice system is through ASSET, when the practitioner (often not an educationalist) ticks a box as to whether the young person is 'underachieving'. For those young people in custody, an initial assessment of their literacy and numeracy skill levels is taken on entry but rarely on exit, and it is impossible currently to monitor individual progression (YJB 2004b).

Prevalence of low attainment in the general population

One of the striking features of academic attainment in the whole UK population is the polarisation of outcomes. Gaps in attainment appear early and tend to persist. By 16, the top 10 per cent of pupils achieve an average points score at GCSE almost 20 times those in the lowest 10 per cent. By comparison, internationally, the UK tends to have a much greater range of attainment than many other countries particularly where literacy is concerned. While about half of all pupils gain five A–C grades at GCSE, approximately 6 per cent gain no qualifications at all, although some studies have placed this higher (McIntosh 2003).

The Chief Inspector of Schools has highlighted some specific low-attainment issues. In his report for 2001/2, he emphasised the literacy problems of boys, of whom 25 per cent were not reading at the expected standard by age 11 and half had not gained the expected standard in writing. This relative underperformance increases with age, as less than two-thirds of boys reach the expected level in English at age 16. In his report for 2003/4, he went on to emphasise the attainment gap between schools with different levels of disadvantage (Ofsted 2003; 2005).

Low attainment at school tends to persist as young people attempt to enter the labour market, and it appears very difficult for them to catch up in terms of improving the likelihood of employment and relative remuneration (McIntosh 2003). This study found that 42 per cent of men who left school with no or only low levels of qualifications did not acquire any further qualifications at all after leaving school, 26 per cent gaining at best a Level 1 qualification and 17 per cent gaining at best a Level 2 qualification (McIntosh 2003).

Prevalence of low attainment among young people who offend

Academic failure at school is widely recognised as being endemic among the population of young people who offend. This is particularly true in the American literature: 'School failure and poor reading performance as early as the third grade, truancy, poor achievement, and misbehaviour in elementary school, and the failure to master school skills throughout schooling are among the most reliable predictors of delinquency and other "adolescent rotten outcomes"' (Schorr 1988, cited in Coffey and Gemignani 1994: 16).

In terms of the wider population of young people who offend in England and Wales and are known to Yots, ASSET returns indicated that:

- One in two Yot clients is under-achieving in school.
- One in three needs help with reading and writing.
- One in five has SEN. (Baker *et al.* 2002).

The charity INCLUDE (2000) carried out a small survey for the YJB's Basic Skills Initiative of the literacy and numeracy levels of young people with whom Yots were working. This survey revealed reading ages that were lagging several years behind chronological ages. The educational attainment levels of young people who have been involved in serious and persistent offending are even lower. The average reading age of young people starting ISSP schemes is over five years below their chronological age (Moore *et al.* 2004).

The levels of literacy and numeracy of 10–17-year-olds on their entry into custody is very low. Of those of compulsory school age (15- and 16-year-olds in this sample), about half had literacy and numeracy levels below that expected of an 11-year-old. Almost one-third (31 per cent) had literacy levels at or below that expected of a 7-year-old, while over 40 per cent had numeracy skills at or below this level (ECOTEC 2001). Nine out of ten young offenders in one STC were found to have a reading age well below their real age (SEU 2002). The interim report of a study on improving literacy and numeracy (Hurry *et al.* 2005) among a group of young people aged 15–18 years who were all on a court order, either in the community or in custody, found that about two-thirds were at or below Level 1 (the level expected of the average 11-year-old). Over two-thirds of the respondents (69 per cent) in this study had left school without any qualifications compared with about 6 per cent in the general population (Hurry *et al.* 2005).

It must be borne in mind that the circumstances, that is, just having entered a custodial institution with all the potential fear and confusion involved, might temporarily depress these assessment scores.

Not surprisingly, the levels of attainment in literacy and numeracy are also low among the adult custodial population. While estimates have varied widely on the incidence of low basic skills, probably due to differing methods of assessment and definition, it is clear that these problems are significantly greater for the adult offending population than for their peers (McMahon *et al.* 2004).

Literacy and numeracy

The information from ASSET indicates that many Yot staff underestimate just how far behind the attainment levels of the majority many young people in the youth justice system are. A consistently smaller proportion is deemed to have difficulties with literacy and numeracy through ASSET returns than is demonstrated through actual literacy and numeracy assessment scores. For example, a large sample of literacy and numeracy assessments showed that two-thirds of the custodial population had significant difficulties with literacy (performing at or below the level of an 11-year-old), yet under half of the supervising officers (46 per cent) recognised that there was a difficulty with literacy and numeracy (ECOTEC 2001).

Not surprisingly, awareness of literacy and numeracy problems appears to be higher among the Yot education staff, nearly two-thirds of the staff believing that three-quarters or more of young people in the youth justice system suffered from these difficulties (YJB 2004c). In contrast, only 27 per cent of a large (n = 2514) ASSET sample were identified as having difficulties with literacy and numeracy (Baker *et al.* 2002).

Given what is known about the educational antecedents in terms of missed education of these young people, this seems to be a considerable underestimate. This mismatch may be due to the lack of a screening process for education, inadequate transmission of information from schools, and a lack of confidence on the part of Yot staff that do not have an educational background; more likely, it is a combination of all of these.

Attainment and detachment

Lower attainment is associated with detachment from school. The Youth Cohort Study 2001 report (DfES 2001) has interesting but potentially limited information. These data were collected by postal self-completion questionnaires. While there was a weighting employed to allow for the effect of non-response, the response rate was only 55 per cent and must raise doubts about its validity for young people with low levels of literacy, particularly those detached from mainstream education.

Only 10 per cent of those who were persistent non-attenders achieved five A–C GCSEs, compared with 58 per cent who did not report any unauthorised absence. The gap was even greater where no GCSEs were obtained, one in five of those persistently absent (21 per cent) gaining none, compared with only one in 33 for those who attended full-time.

There was also a disparity in attainment between those who were excluded and those who were not, although this was not as great as for persistent non-attendance, three times as many of those who were not excluded achieving five A–C grades at GCSE (52 per cent and 17 per cent). The gap was similar for leaving school with no GCSEs, 10 per cent of those excluded being without qualifications, compared with 4 per cent of the population who had not been excluded.

The findings by McMahon *et al.* (2004) from the sample in the evaluation of the Basic Skills Pathfinder project also indicate that young adults who offended and had missed significant amounts of schooling were likely to have lower and/or fewer educational qualifications than those who attended regularly. This was found to have a knock-on effect on subsequent employment.

A higher proportion of young people who leave school with no/poor GCSE qualifications are not in education, training and employment than those who leave with some qualifications. While 25 per cent had no qualifications, only 1 per cent had five or more GCSEs A*–C (SEU 1999).

Attainment in the care population

Much greater emphasis has been placed in social policy terms on the educational attainment of young people in the care system. One important aspect has been an improvement in the recording of attainment. Consequently, far more is known about a population that not only shares certain risk factors with those in the youth justice system but also are often one and the same young people. Therefore, the annual figures produced on the attainment of young people who are in the care system arguably provide an approximation of the pattern of attainment of those in the youth justice system.

In 2000–1, just 8 per cent of young people in Year 11 who had spent at least one year in care gained five or more GCSEs graded A*–C, compared with 48 per cent of all young people. Half had no qualifications at all at GCSE level. Data on those achieving 'A' levels and NVQ3 are not collected. However, in 2001–2, just 46 per cent of care leavers were known to be engaged in education, training or employment at the age of 19, compared with 86 per cent of their peers. An estimated 1 percent of young people from care go to university, compared with around 40 per cent of all school leavers (SEU 2003). No one knows the equivalent figure for those in the youth justice system, but it would be surprising if it were higher, particularly where young people had become more involved in offending.

Non-school factors associated with low attainment

For the general population, the literature identifies six key non-school variables associated with educational attainment:

- child's personal characteristics;
- socio-economic influences;
- parental educational attainment and experience;
- family size, structure and institutional care;
- ethnicity/language;
- other: parental interest and involvement; locally based factors (Sparkes and Glennerster 2002).

Clearly, many of these risk factors interact with and amplify one another, so that the total effect is greater than the sum of the separate factors. The relationship between experiencing multiple risk factors and low attainment and poor behaviour increases dramatically. One study found that while only just over 10 per cent (10.8) of those without recognised risk factors fell into the bottom 25 per cent of the age group at age 11 (based on verbal reasoning tests), this rose to over 90 per cent (91.7) for those experiencing multiple risk factors. The proportion deemed to display 'disturbed' behaviour rose correspondingly from 5.6 to 42.3 per cent of those in the bottom 25 per cent as the risk factors increased (Sparkes and Glennerster 2002).

Again, the research base is simply not robust enough to provide detailed analysis against these factors for young people in the youth justice system. It may be that low attainment is a result of a lack of access to, or participation in, appropriate learning opportunities. Equally, it may be that these young people were beset by a significantly higher proportion of acquired or innate learning difficulties that impeded the acquisition of reading, writing and calculating skills. The reality may be a complex interrelationship between the two apparently competing hypotheses. There could be reciprocal effects between being detached for long periods of time and behaviour.

The research evidence is a long way from being able to delineate the boundary between the impact of not being in learning (and thereby excluded from the experiences, and parity of esteem with peers) and so-called learning difficulties. Unfortunately, it may well be that it becomes increasingly difficult to reverse low basic skills, partly because of the negative feedback loops of a diminished attachment to school and increasing involvement with delinquent peer groups. Furthermore, young people who have survived into adolescence with very low attainment levels in literacy and numeracy may not only ostensibly scorn their value but also become adept in hiding these difficulties.

The following five reasons were given for the relatively low educational outcomes for young people in the care system, and the evidence such as it is confirms that they apply to young people in the youth justice system too:

1 Many young people's lives are characterised by instability.
2 Young people in care spend too much time out of school or other place of learning.
3 Children do not have sufficient help with their education if they get behind.
4 Carers are not expected, or equipped, to provide sufficient support and encouragement at home for learning and development.
5 Children in care need more help with their emotional, mental or physical health and well-being (SEU 2003: 20).

Conversely, in a study which contrasted the fortunes of a group of educational high achievers with the majority of those young people in the care system, Jackson and Martin (1998) identified some protective factors associated with educational success. Access to books, which was associated with early reading, was a distinguishing feature between the successful and unsuccessful groups. The high achievers appear to have received more general encouragement from a parent or a significant adult. This appears to have been particularly important in ensuring progression to further education.

It is interesting that the main explanations given for the relatively low attainment of young people in the care system focus on matters external to the young person. In contrast, for young people who offend, the focus is on their individual behaviour, such as exclusion or non-attendance, as contributing to their low attainment. In addition to the above explanations for low attainment, others have been adduced which also concentrate on the inherent deficits of the young person or their parents. These include the incidence of SEN and in particular dyslexia, the attitudes and aspirations of the young people and their parents, and their learning styles.

IQ

Two of the constructs most widely used for providing an explanation of differences in individual learning are intelligence and personality. In everyday language, both constructs lack clear definition and are often value based. Simplistic assumptions about intelligence and personality have influenced many educational discourses. Many educationalists would put far more emphasis on concepts such as multiple intelligences (Barber 1997). Despite this, the high-crime:low IQ association as both causal and predetermined, which is very long-standing, persists (Gould 1996). Certainly, several studies have shown an inverse association between IQ and offending (Rutter et al. 1998). Maguin and Loeber (1996), in their meta-analysis of academic performance and delinquency, concluded that low intelligence functioned as a common cause of both academic performance and delinquency. However, this finding emerged only when a particular study was excluded; otherwise, on the basis of their full sample, intelligence did not appear to act as a common cause.

The mean IQ of young people who offend appears to be well within the average range of the general population and is only slightly below that of young people who do not offend. Unless IQ can be proved to be inherent and unchanging, it is just as reasonable to suppose, given the multiple adversities in the lives of these young people and their probable low self-concept as learners, that their scores could be depressed. In any event, as an explanation of literacy and numeracy levels that are up to 10 years behind their chronological ages, a somewhat lower IQ is likely to provide only a limited explanation.

Lower IQ and a failure to acquire language skills before school have been found to be associated with a later risk of antisocial behaviour. This does not discount the role of educational failure in further depressing attainment but rather emphasises the importance of literacy and oracy skill acquisition in the early years (Parsons and Bynner 1998).

Learning styles and strategies

Apart from the issue of SEN, very different learning outcomes can result for individual young people. This is despite the nature of the topic, the knowledge and skills of the learners, their motivation, their previous experience of learning, and the knowledge and skills of the person facilitating this learning. The gap between the theoretical understanding of such individual differences and a practical application in particular learning circumstances has been bridged by a wide range of style constructs.

Differential learning outcomes despite common contexts has been tackled by several criminologists. Bonta (1996: 31), for instance, asserts that 'offenders differ in motivation, personality, and emotional and cognitive abilities, and these characteristics can influence the offenders' responsiveness to various therapists and treatment modalities'.

Out of the extensive literature that has resulted over many years, academics in both education and criminal justice have adopted learning styles as being useful in understanding and supporting learning. Within education, the concept of learning styles appears to be widely accepted, and various instruments are employed to assign learners to particular categories.

In youth justice, while managers and practitioners may view formal learning as being largely the province of education professionals, there is to some extent a recognition that, for example, interventions that aim to change behaviour depend upon learning. Certainly, academics concerned with the identification of the effectiveness of interventions in preventing offending and reoffending have often embraced the validity of learning styles constructs.

Surveys of the major meta-analytic reviews identify a number of principles relating to the designing and implementation of programmes that are more effective in terms of reducing recidivism (McGuire 1995). The key principle in relation to learning styles is that of 'responsivity'. 'Programmes work best when they are carefully structured and learning styles of individual offenders and the staff working with them are well-matched. The learning styles of offenders tend to require active, participatory methods of working' (McGuire 1995: 15).

There are three key assumptions that can be questioned within this principle: that learning styles can be clearly defined and measured and are relatively unchanging for individuals, that matching this learning style with the respective teaching/instructional styles makes a significant difference; and that young people who offend tend to have an active and participatory learning style.

Even bolder claims have been made for the negative impact of a lack of responsivity in education. It has been argued, for example (Hodges 1982), that the urban poor (in America) and young people who offend are more likely to possess a right-brain dominance and be spatial/ holistic, visual learners. This is contrasted with the assertion that most learners in society possess a left-brain dominance and are verbal/ analytic learners. This chain of reasoning links disruptive behaviour, detachment from school, low attainment and associated offending by so many of the urban poor to their inability to learn effectively due to the verbally based instructional methods that allegedly characterise most American schools.

Although learning styles are meant to be stable psychological constructs, they have been remarkably difficult to assess reliably for any learners, let alone young people who offend. A recent comprehensive literature review commented that despite the weight of material this area was 'opaque, contradictory and controversial' (Coffield *et al.* 2004: 2) with 'very few robust studies which offer ... reliable and valid evidence and clear implications for practice based on empirical findings' (Coffield *et al.* 2004: 1).

This report concluded that most of the psychometric instruments were not only unreliable and lacking in validity but also unsuitable for learners with relatively low levels of literacy, which is a common characteristic of many young people who offend, and their psychometric properties have not been validated.

A more fruitful approach probably needs to take account of the relationship between learners' use of effective learning strategies and their academic attainment (Adey *et al.* 1999: 21). It is possible that children and young people with low academic attainment did not absorb some of the basic learning strategies required for school learning during their primary education.

A recent report on learning styles and young people who offend (YJB 2005b) concluded: 'The evidence does not have sufficient weight to justify claims of the existence of a discrete, stable learning styles construct. Indeed it could be constrictive and unhelpful to rely heavily on such a simplistic approach.'

Dyslexia

One explanation for the low level of literacy and numeracy skills among both younger and older people who offend is that a disproportionate amount of them suffer from dyslexia. The SEU, for example, noted that poor levels of literacy in the youth offending population may be due to a high incidence of previously unidentified specific learning difficulties associated with dyslexia (SEU 1999). The British Dyslexia Association also believes that there is a high rate of dyslexia among young people who offend (Pruden 2005).

These claims have been disputed on a number of grounds. The validity of dyslexia as a concept is not accepted by some researchers (Rice and Brooks 2004). There is considerable variation in definitions among adherents to the concept due to the different theoretical approaches adopted. These range from those who propose a biological origin to those who emphasise the impact of home and school and yet others who see a relationship between the experiential and biological influences. The different standpoint adopted leads to very different assessments of the prevalence rates for dyslexia among both the general population and specific populations such as those who offend.

There appear to be particular problems with the methods of assessment used. Criticisms have been made on the grounds of lack of full validation and failure to distinguish accurately between poor readers and those deemed dyslexic, as well as the fact that utilising an IQ discrepancy approach represents a narrow view of intelligence. The unproven nature of the assessment processes, research methodology flaws and the absence of appropriate control groups may mean simply that a high incidence of poor reading skills is being detected.

Many of the research studies have been criticised on the basis of methodological weaknesses that can lead to overstated claims (Rice and Brooks 2004). The ferocity of the debate indicates that more is at stake than simply the definition of a term and the validity of assessment tools. Indeed, dyslexia has recently been dubbed an 'emotional construct' in that it is used to remove the stigma of supposedly being a poor reader due to deficiencies in intelligence. Elliott has argued that the wide range of competing understandings of dyslexia render the label practically meaningless, and expresses little confidence in anyone's ability to offer a diagnosis of dyslexia (Elliott quoted in Mansell 2005).

Suffering from a condition that requires treatment may improve self-esteem, but what does it do to those who are poor readers but are not deemed to be beset by this condition? One argument is that either all poor readers are dyslexic or no-one is. From an operational perspective, much of the debate may be redundant, as, on the evidence to date, approaches that appear useful for those assessed with dyslexia are equally useful for those who are poor readers.

A study of ISSP using several tests to assess different aspects of young people's intellectual functioning with regard to their educational progress suggested 'the possibility that inadequate exposure to words and their meaning may be contributing to the poor literacy skills of at least some of the young people in the sample. This would be consistent with the socio-economic and educational backgrounds of many of these young people – they have lacked adequate opportunities to learn' (Moore *et al.* 2004: 137).

Special educational needs (SEN)

The findings of the YJB's audit of education and training within the secure estate in relation to SEN concluded: 'It is likely that perhaps as many as three-quarters of the custodial population has special educational needs and if assessed would probably receive a statement' (ECOTEC 2001: 44).

One of the major issues at local level is the poor transmission of information between schools, LEAs and Yots. The difficulty in acquiring significant educational information was highlighted in this audit by the fact that out of 525 ASSET forms collected and analysed, one-quarter of the assessments recorded that they did not know whether SEN had been identified, let alone at what level. While it is reasonable to suppose that there is a very a high incidence of SEN, it may well be that this constitutes a large proportion of those exhibiting behavioural problems (EBD), or it could simply be the consequence of several years without formal education.

The proportion of young people in PRUs in England who have a statement of SEN is much higher than the national average – 18.5 per cent in 2002 compared with 3 per cent across all mainstream schools. At least 35 per cent of those in custody and 15 per cent of those across youth justice had been statemented (ECOTEC 2001; Baker *et al.* 2002). The American literature is more extensive, although different definitions and categories of SEN are used. A meta-analysis found that the incidence of learning disabilities among young people who offend averaged 35.6 per cent, compared with only 1.86 per cent among the general school population (Coffey and Gemignani 1994).

Homework

Homework, although an apparently mundane matter and largely absent from the literature, is perhaps a critical indicator of a young person's educational constraints. It is common for young people in mainstream education to be undertaking the equivalent of an extra day's work a week in their own time. But young people in noisy, crowded, living conditions whose parents' circumstances do not allow sufficient support and supervision are at a considerable disadvantage. The advent of PCs and the Internet also potentially disadvantages those on low incomes. Apart from its contribution to attainment and developing young people as confident learners, homework has also been seen to possess important socialisation qualities. Impulsivity is noted widely in the literature as an individual feature of young people who offend. Homework, it has been argued, is an investment activity that could mitigate this feature, as it develops consideration of today's activities in terms of subsequent consequences (Gottfredson and Hirschi 1990: 106). From a teacher's and peer perspective, the failure to complete homework could also feed into any labelling processes.

The state and its professionals appear to perform poorly in this respect. Homework is seen to be of minimal significance compared with other issues of behaviour. Critics of the effect of entry into the care system on educational performance first drew attention to this. The fact that there has been more provision for smoking than for homework in children's homes is a graphic illustration of this neglect. This is paralleled within the criminal justice system. Televisions and play stations, rather than pens and pencils (banned on security grounds), are often offered as the YOI substitute for homework.

Attainment and socio-economic disadvantage

Studies at both the level of LEA (using dependency on state benefits) and the school level (using eligibility for free school meals) have illustrated a strong link between poverty and attainment (West and Pennell 2003). This appears to be a progressive effect in not only that initial attainment is lower for children eligible for free school meals but also that they make poorer progress than predicted. Parental involvement in issues such as reading and writing appears to be relatively more important, and for those young people who enter institutional care, this could be a double disadvantage.

This strong negative relationship between socio-economic disadvantage and educational attainment is much stronger in the UK than in other European countries (Steedman and Stoney 2004). Lower parental aspirations combined with less confident learning identities appear to establish cycles of low attainment and subsequent socio-economic disadvantage.

The relationship between attainment and the young person's learning identity can create a vicious circle:

> for some pupils the entire experience of their statutory years of schooling is one of failure. Not surprisingly, such pupils may develop a poor self-concept in relation to their academic work, lack of motivation and behavioural problems ... pupils with a higher rate of learning/behavioural difficulties in one year tended to make less progress in reading over the next year. Similarly, pupils with lower reading scores in one year tend to show an increase in behavioural and learning difficulties (Mortimore 1991: 19).

If adversity experienced during childhood becomes persistent, its cumulative effects could tend to amplify both material and psycho-social risks, which continue into adulthood. Schoon (2003), for example, argues that psycho-social adjustment is progressively weakened and that subsequent adversity becomes more and more difficult to cope with. Using the evidence drawn up from the National Child Development Study (NCDS) and the British Cohort Study (BCS70), she emphasises the impact of aggregated risks, particularly during the crucial transition from compulsory schooling to further education and training.

Relationship of low attainment and offending

In their meta-analysis of 118 studies, albeit largely American, Maguin and Loeber (1996: 246) concluded that 'Poor academic performance is related to the prevalence and onset of delinquency and escalation in the frequency and seriousness of offending, while better academic performance is associated with desistance from offending'.

There is very little evidence indicating a direct relationship between low attainment and offending. This does not necessarily detract from the predictive power of early low attainment but does imply that the relationship is possibly spurious, indirect, or delayed. A Swedish study Olweus (1983) cited in Gottfredson (2001) concluded that both attainment and aggressive behaviour that were correlated were influenced by family variables. Indirect effects of low attainment could operate through streaming and lead to the development of antisocial peer groups. Dishion *et al.* (1991) found that attainment levels were significantly inversely related to antisocial peer behaviour two years later, and this relationship was independent of prior antisocial behaviour.

The Youth Lifestyles Survey for 1998/9, although also likely to have missed some young people most likely to be low attainers and involved in offending, found a relationship between attainment and offending. While 6 per cent of males who rated their attainment at school as above average had committed an offence in the previous year, three times as many offences were committed by those who rated themselves average or below the level of their peers. For those who had left school without any qualifications, the ratio was again close to three to one (29 per cent of males without who offended and 11 per cent with qualifications who did not). The lowest rates of offending were among those who continued in education post-18 (Flood-Page *et al.* 2000). The corresponding survey in 1995, however, did not find a relationship between attainment and offending (Graham and Bowling 1995).

In a wide-ranging review, mainly of evidence from studies in the USA, Gottfredson found an association between poor performance academically and drug use and other adolescent problem behaviours. Attainment levels in school in America have been shown to be moderately related to delinquency.

Another indirect effect could be through weak attainment decreasing attachment to school and reducing pro-social attitudes and beliefs. In an analysis of their findings from the Rochester Youth Development Study, Thornberry *et al.* (2003) concluded that poor academic performance weakened school commitment, which was related to involvement in delinquency. They also found that the converse was true: higher attainment was associated with resilience.

Both positive and negative delayed effects have been found. Tremblay *et al.* (2003) found that academic performance at ages 12 and 14 was a robust and consistent predictor of offending during early adulthood. This effect of low attainment persisted independently of adolescent delinquency. Several studies have shown linkages between difficulties in reading and behavioural problems but a greater association with inattention and hyperactivity (Rutter *et al.* 1998).

Disentangling the relationship between low attainment and offending is difficult. It may be that the association is derived from the psycho-social consequences of perceived educational failure rather than low attainment in itself. For example, Maughan *et al.* (1996) concluded in a longitudinal study that children with significant reading problems were far more likely to be non-attenders. Their increased risk of offending arose largely through their non-attendance. Early problems with language and reading appear to be more associated with children who begin antisocial behaviour and offending early rather than in adolescence. Equally, behavioural problems can precede literacy difficulties. The Christchurch longitudinal study found that conduct problems at age six were associated with reading difficulties at age eight (Fergusson *et al.* 1997).

A meta-analysis also found that higher attainment was related to desistance from offending (Maguin and Loeber 1996). The odds of delinquency were estimated to be about twice as high for low-attaining young people as for their peers with high attainment. Low levels of attainment were linked to both a higher frequency of offences and more serious, particularly violent, offences. Some of the evidence indicated that low attainment is related to the early onset of offending and all of the findings applied more strongly to boys than girls, and to white than to black young people.

The evaluation of the YJB-funded education, training and employment projects (YJB 2003a) detected a link between attainment in literacy and numeracy, gaining qualifications and positive outcomes (such as progression to employment, education or training), and reduced recidivism.

Conclusions

The evidence base regarding the educational attainment of young people in the youth justice system is very limited, particularly in terms of UK evidence. This subject is both under-researched and weakly monitored by local authorities and central government. Far less is known than about young people being looked after. While underachievement does seem prevalent within the youth justice system, it is only part of a much wider problem affecting many more young people who do not get involved in offending. While low attainment at a young age may be predictive of later offending, this could well be a reflection of other adversities rather than any direct effect being involved. This does not, of course, preclude indirect effects acting through deteriorating behaviour within the classroom and subsequent detachment from school. Lowered self-esteem as a learner coupled with reinforcement through labelling by staff and falling further behind peers through missed schooling could continue this negative feedback loop.

What part underachievement plays in the persistence of offending in the teenage years is much more difficult to establish. Currently, there is not the empirical evidence to disentangle the effects of being detached from school from those of being an underachiever. It may be that there is a stronger association between failing academically and offending for young people, given how central school is to their lives, compared with adults, who can call on a range of other skills to succeed in the workplace. Some emerging evidence suggests both that higher attainment can act as protective factor and that literacy and numeracy gains may influence desistance (Hurry *et al.* in press).

Summary

❑ Low attainment is a significant predictor of offending and is a highly prevalent risk factor, but there is little evidence to demonstrate that it acts to transmit risk directly, although it may act indirectly.

❑ Information is not routinely collected (except on entry to custodial institutions) on the attainment levels of young people in the youth justice system, in contrast to their peers in the care system.

❑ While the evidence is not robust and some of the constructs are questionable there appears to be a very high incidence of SEN among young people who offend.

❑ Learning styles figure prominently in education and also in the tenets of effective practice for youth justice through the responsivity principle. Their existence as a discrete, unchanging construct, however, appears to be unsupported by the evidence.

❑ There are several possible transmission mechanisms between low attainment and offending. Low self-esteem as a learner may be expressed through aggressive behaviour, leading to exclusion or complete disengagement due to lowering motivation. In addition, low attainment at school-leaving age is associated with subsequent non-participation and unemployment, which is a significant risk factor.

Chapter 6

The influence of the school

Let us reform our schools, and we shall find little reform needed in our prisons.

John Ruskin

Having examined the evidence for the relationship between low attainment and detachment from mainstream education and offending, we must ask what part educational institutions play in this. Despite the weight of evidence regarding the association between educational difficulties and current and subsequent offending, there are very varied views on the role of schools. It could be that schools have few direct or indirect effects other than providing an arena where children and young people predisposed to delinquent behaviour act this out. In contrast, schools could be either effective or ineffective agents of social control whose success or failure is implicated in the incidence of antisocial and offending behaviour. This chapter will survey the evidence and the possible ways in which schools and other educational institutions might affect offending.

Theoretical background

The influence or otherwise of schooling on delinquent behaviour is part of a wider debate on the causes of crime. Theories that emphasise the importance of stable characteristics formed early in life, particularly the absence of self-control, attribute little or no causal role to the school. According to this analysis, if people have a high propensity towards delinquency, that is, their traits include a strong tendency towards impulsiveness, risk taking, and thrill seeking, then school-related factors are spurious because they, too, are dependent on self-control. Low attainment and weak attachment to school are simply symptomatic of low self-control, as schoolwork is seen as boring, and they would have great difficulty meeting the expectations of teachers to be attentive, obedient and quiet. Similarly, young people with low self-control are seen as less likely to form lasting relationships with others. Delinquent peer groups therefore do not accelerate offending behaviour but simply represent the grouping together of those rejected by their more conventional peers.

Such theories have been seen as unduly deterministic, while developmental theories of offending causation, in contrast, place emphasis on the different causal factors that have an impact during the life course. Some developmental theorists have postulated that there are two types of offenders – 'life-course-persistent' and 'adolescent-limited' with different correlates and causes of offending (Moffitt 1993).

While there are very different theoretical perspectives, there is also common ground. Even theorists who stress the primacy of stable individual characteristics see the school as having at least a potentially significant socialising role even if it is only up to about the age of eight and is restricted by uncooperative families. Equally, most theories recognise the importance of the absence of self-control, its early occurrence, and its relative stability through the life course.

The most comprehensive review to date of the evidence adopted a middle ground, recognising that there are early personality dispositions and 'although not very stable, these early differences resemble major personality dimensions known to be related to crime later in life' (Gottfredson 2001: 59). These predispositions are presented as being malleable by both family and school, but by early adolescence 'social controls in the form of attachment and commitment to school ... and peers exert causal influence at this developmental stage' (Gottfredson 2001: 60).

As noted above, low levels of educational attainment and high levels of detachment constitute important risk factors for offending, and it may be that school effects on non-attendance and attainment could therefore provide indirect risk mechanisms for offending.

During the last 15 years, there has been a much greater focus on the school itself and the impact of it as an institution on academic attainment. Non-attendance has also been studied in the context of issues such as whole-school behaviour policy, incentives and sanction systems, curriculum and pastoral care systems, and home school links. Although the detailed pattern of non-attendance is unclear, it appears that, as with formal exclusion, there is a wide variation between schools with exactly the same intake. It may be that it is not any one factor that can be isolated that leads to the success of a school in this area, but it seems there is something about the prevailing ethos in the school which appears to be strongly linked with effective leadership from the head teacher and senior managers.

The importance of school intakes

While the literature makes clear that there are observed differences among schools, it is important to assess how far these are a reflection of the influence of schools. An alternative explanation often put forward by teaching unions is that differences simply represent variations in pupil admissions to schools. If the differences in attachment, attainment and behaviour between young people at the end of their schooling are simply a continuation of the intake differences, it is unlikely there is a significant independent school effect.

Several leading educationalists have taken issue with this argument. Marland (quoted in Shah 2001: 34) summed up this approach as creating

> an over-simplified kind of 'determinism', which is allowed to trap pupils in their current plight: 'You can't expect high literacy standards. Look at their homes', or 'There's nothing relevant in the curriculum for them, so naturally they aren't motivated to do homework.' Such attitudes ... are dangerous if they lead us to treat pupils as if school had nothing but sympathy to offer.

It is interesting that both academics and teaching staff who downplay the independent role of schools in influencing the behaviour of young people see the role of parents and the family as being overwhelmingly important. This not only denies the potential impact of teachers and schools on life outcomes but also ignores the similarity in socialisation processes.

From the age of four or five, the school starts to share with the family the responsibility for moulding the behaviour and disposition of the child. In punishing misbehaviour and rewarding good behaviour, setting out rules, emphasising diligence on task, and requiring cooperative and conscientious behaviour, school staff act *in loco parentis*. It is as unrealistic to expect all teachers to be equally effective in this socialisation process as it is to expect that of parents. If families can become dysfunctional in this respect, it is reasonable to assume that institutions can too. If ineffective parenting, characterised by such features as harsh and inconsistent disciplining, weak supervision and monitoring, and limited positive involvement, has been found to be closely related to the development of antisocial behaviour, then it is a reasonable supposition that equivalent practices within schools could have similar negative outcomes. School staff can exacerbate antisocial behaviour by children, and this process can be amplified by peers who start to reject those identified as troublesome, and in time the child may be formally isolated from the rest of the class. In these circumstances, the continued interactions could result in academic failure and detachment.

There is no doubt that there are significant differences in school intakes. While some schools will have forms of selection both formal and covert related to attainment and behaviour, others will have catchment areas that include significant numbers of young people from disadvantaged backgrounds, and may in addition have to take a disproportionate share of young people who have been excluded from other schools on behavioural grounds.

The longitudinal studies which cover the school careers of young people and thereafter are perhaps the most informative in this context. As Rutter *et al.* (1998: 231) have emphasised, there are three essential issues that must be verified before causal effects can be attributed to schools:

> the variations in outcome must remain after taking into account differences in pupil intake; the outcome variations must be systematically related to the qualities of the schools; the outcome variations must show a closer association with the school qualities than do the intake variations.

Not only do school processes have to be distinguished from compositional effects but also account has to be taken of the fact that schools are embedded within local communities. Disentangling school effectiveness from community effectiveness is not easy. Within the context of social disorganisation theory, all the principal socialising institutions – families, schools and churches – are less effective in particular areas. Disadvantaged communities may well be much less likely to attract high-quality staff to their schools and less able to give support or raise funds for their schools. Similar effects in these areas may also be felt in the support services that are more necessary given the greater needs of the young people (Ballas *et al.* 2005). Consequently, weaker educational practices can evolve, such as low expectations of young people or reliance on supply staff. Such factors may increase the likelihood of detachment and thereby delinquency.

School effects

Few UK longitudinal studies give insights into education and offending. Two such studies stand out – West and Farrington's Cambridge study (1973) and Rutter *et al.*'s *Fifteen Thousand Hours* in 1979. Whereas the Cambridge Study of Delinquent Development indicated that school effects on delinquency were relatively unimportant compared with intake differences, Rutter *et al.* identified independent school effects in terms of four measures of school outcome: attendance, behaviour in school, academic attainment and delinquency out of school – those who went to less effective schools were twice as likely to display poor attendance, and these poor attendees were twice as likely to leave school before sitting examinations.

This work was subject to much questioning of the methodological and statistical approach adopted, and the theoretical stance and interpretation of the data were also criticised. While some of the criticisms have been answered (Maughan *et al.* 1980; Rutter 1983) those remaining are interesting in that they highlight significant research challenges.

In order to isolate the effects of a school (which is usually a secondary school), it is essential to have early and detailed intake measures pre-school (parental interest, literacy and numeracy, etc.) but also adequate information on primary school experiences. There are two other fundamental problems which beset this work and potentially any other such studies. If we control for intake variables such as pre-school behavioural problems or parental attitudes to education, then, by definition, there is no allowance for the potential interaction between these intake variables and any independent effects of the school (Graham 1988). Equally importantly, difficulties arise when aggregated data from schools are used in tandem with individual outcomes to assess the existence of school-level effects. This omits the potential importance of, for example, classroom-level effects.

Another potential problem relating to intake variables for either primary or particularly secondary school is the potential effects of labelling. Troublesome behaviour in the home and at school is often seen as a precursor to delinquency, and it is seen as a significant variable. The definition, classification and reinforcement of this behaviour by teachers, other staff and other children, according to labelling theory, could influence this behaviour. While cohort studies by Stott and Wilson (1977) and West and Farrington (1973 and 1977) have found a significant association between the behaviour of children defined as 'troublesome' and their later involvement in delinquency, they ignore some potential school influences by using ratings of behaviour by teachers to predict subsequent delinquency.

There was no consideration of the possibility of the schools actively inhibiting or reinforcing individual predispositions to troublesome behaviour. The Cambridge study therefore contains an implicit assumption that primary schools do not affect the tendency to or away from delinquency. It would not be unreasonable to suggest that poor attendance and low attainment, which partly constituted the measure of 'inadequate performance at primary school' that was found to predict delinquency, could result in part from being at a failing school. As regards 'troublesome' behaviour as defined by primary schoolteachers, there is some evidence to indicate that this is partly the result of the particular primary school attended (Heal 1978; ILEA 1986). There is also evidence that teachers' assessments of 'troublesomeness' may not necessarily be reliable (although these assessments could potentially still be self-fulfilling) (Rutter *et al.* 1970).

It could be argued that this approach underplays the potential for labelling by both teachers and peers from an early age with a consequent negative impact on learner identity. Teacher identification of problem behaviour is not necessarily robust enough to draw conclusions about supposedly stable personality traits. Certain children could be selected into weakly attached groups, which then become self-reinforcing. The potential role for institutional and professional categorisation and amplification often appears to be ignored.

Other research approaches have included assessing the impact on a failing school of the appointment of a new head teacher, or of measures taken to improve the quality of schooling and consequent effects on attainment and behaviour. The major limitation of this type of research evidence is that it tends to focus on school effects on attainment and attendance with little on challenging behaviour or delinquency. The evidence on attainment and detachment indicates strong indirect effects. To the extent that challenging or difficult behaviour within school can be the precursor of delinquent and antisocial behaviour outside schools, there may be direct school effects. Again, there is evidence that schools with very similar intakes have very different rates of disciplinary exclusions and while this may be a differential response to similar behaviour, it may also indicate differential school effects on behaviour.

The evidence that exists on the direct impact of schools on behaviour indicates that this operates through at least two mechanisms:

• The ethos of the school (combining both pedagogic and social) at the general, departmental and classroom level, displayed through such positive qualities as leadership style, differentiated teaching styles and an orderly atmosphere with high-quality, non-coercive classroom management. The school ethos also expresses itself crucially through effective relationships with parents, particularly those whose children are most at risk of detachment from the educational process. This is often treated in the literature as a non-school variable, assuming that schools cannot secure greater levels of parental participation (Bradshaw *et al.* 2004).

• The intake balance. Adverse or positive effects have been noted through the peer groups formed in schools, which can extend beyond circles of friends to have a more pervasive effect on the norms of the school. Admissions policies and incentives that result in some schools having high concentrations of vulnerable children and children experiencing multiple adversities can increase exclusion across communities. The more inclusive the intake of a school, therefore, the greater the positive influence at an aggregate level (Rutter *et al.* 1998).

While the evidence does not sustain the argument that the composition of the student body completely determines outcomes such as attainment, attendance and good behaviour, it is clearly extremely influential. Rutter's original work (1979) found that the profile of the pupil intake had more influence on the delinquency levels in schools than did the organisational features of the schools. Schools having a large majority of low-attaining students face increased risks of offending. This effect is over and above the role of a young person's low attainment in increasing the risks of their antisocial behaviour and offending. There appears to be a potential peer-group aggregate effect created by the predominance of other low-attaining young people (West and Pennell 2003).

Bullying and being bullied also appear to be risk factors that schools can influence. The importance of bullying as a school risk factor is not clear. It does appear to be a school-related risk factor for violence. As a form of aggression, it has been found to be linked with later adult offending (Farrington 1993). More research is needed to clarify the relationship between victimisation through bullying and subsequent offending. A strong relationship has been found between other forms of violent victimisation and violent offending (Howell 2003). There appear to be different levels of bullying between schools, and some programmes appear to have been effective in reducing the incidence of bullying.

The level and range of school effects have tended to be identified, as progressively more sensitive and sophisticated research techniques have been applied. Aggregated data at the school level can obscure within-school variation. Important features of school organisation can be correlated with school compositional characteristics, so examining the residual variations after controlling for intake appears to have underestimated the effect of school organisation on the outcomes for young people.

The great majority of multilevel studies have demonstrated independent school effects on a wide range of outcomes, including offending (see Gottfredson 2001 for a summary). Large-scale studies in the UK found both specific school process and compositional effects (over and above the intake) on the outcomes for young people (Mortimore *et al.* 1988; Smith and Tomlinson 1989). Multilevel studies have demonstrated effects on delinquent activities and also on contributory factors such as attainment, detachment and substance misuse. As Gottfredson (2001: 81) concludes:

> School effects have been demonstrated for students at the elementary and secondary levels of education, and for students in different countries. These effects cannot be attributed solely to the grouping of individuals with different propensities and prognoses in schools. School effects persist after outcomes are adjusted for the effects of individual-level demographic and other predictors.

It is important, though, not to minimise the impact of multiple social disadvantage on depressing school performance. Various studies have concluded that between 66 per cent and 85 per cent of school variation in attainment at GCSE is associated with pupil intake factors (Bradshaw *et al.* 2004).

However, the magnitude of school effects is moderate rather than small, and Gottfredson argues that the effect sizes identified in multilevel studies imply that an effective school might increase the success rates of its young people from 29 to 42 percentage points above those of similar young people in less effective schools (Gottfredson 2001). These school effects compare favourably with many criminal justice and other interventions, raising the possibility that investing in school organisation and management may yield a greater return than the provision of some targeted prevention and intervention services.

Schools and the youth justice system

Schools can also have an influence on the operation of the youth justice system. Reports from schools appear to have had a disproportionate significance with different players within the sentencing process ranging from interagency panels at the pre-prosecution stage through to magistrates and judges. Negative school reports may also have influenced custodial sentencing, and certainly perceived school status, such as being excluded, is given considerable weight by magistrates.

Individual schools may have a differential impact depending on the strengths or weaknesses of their linkages with the youth justice system, as for example, in their willingness to supply timely and accurate educational information to Yots (Ball and Connolly 2000). For young people receiving a custodial sentence, schools may increase or decrease the risk factors for future offending by, in the first instance, deciding whether or not to remove young persons from their school roll, and subsequently by the effectiveness of their contact with the young persons in custody and their reintegration arrangements thereafter.

Schools and resilience

The concept of resilience has started to attract more attention in research studies of antisocial behaviour. This is because, throughout all the studies on the multiple adversities experienced by children and young people that are associated with antisocial behaviour, there is enormous variation in young people's responses. The evidence so far is sparse. Research on protective factors has not been as abundant as on risk factors. There is little consensus on what they are, let alone how they operate to prevent or reduce antisocial behaviour (Gottfredson 2001; Armstrong *et al.* 2005).

It is possible that schools have an important influence in the development of this resilience. Several studies have found, for example, that schools can help young people to acquire, through positive experiences, a greater ability to plan their lives. Young people from high-risk backgrounds who were enabled to adopt this approach were less likely to join peer groups with antisocial behaviour, and this had a beneficial effect on their life choices, such as employment (Rutter *et al.* 1998).

It may well be that resilience is more likely to be developed in normal settings such as mainstream schools. While behaviour can be modified in a segregated setting, it is the transfer to the everyday world that appears to create the real challenge. Reintegration models such as PRUs that group together young people on the basis of their antisocial behaviour and encourage them to form a group – in an environment that is very different from mainstream school – would appear to have a limited chance of success in terms of equipping them for a return to mainstream school. Even positive behaviour, when it is learned in 'abnormal' environments, will not easily survive the challenge of transferring to a school, college or workplace (Galloway *et al.* 1985).

Teacher effects

Teacher attitudes and behaviour may well have a significant impact not just on educational attainment as measured by qualifications but also on the acquisition of softer generic skills linked to employability. Analysis of the National Child Development Study data has shown that the more experienced teachers as measured by their salaries were linked to increases in future earnings of pupils. This effect was over and above that on the achievement of formal qualifications, suggesting that the more experienced teachers were more effective in helping young people acquire skills valued by employers.

It may be that young people with fewer out-of-school resources have a greater reliance on schools and teachers to assist their development through support and guidance. Using data from the American National Longitudinal Study, Croninger and Lee (2001) examined whether or not teachers increased the social capital of students at risk of not completing high school. They measured social capital through the opinions of young people about how much their teachers supported their efforts to succeed in school and by the reports of teachers on the guidance they dispensed about school and personal matters.

There was a strong relationship found between the levels of social capital and detaching from school irrespective of risk factors. Although this teacher-derived social capital was apparently beneficial for all young people in school, it was of most benefit to those at greatest risk of detachment.

Given that schools gather together large numbers of young boys, many approaching the peak age for offending, it is a legitimate question as to whether schools are criminogenic places. Various national surveys in the USA indicate that a disproportionate amount of crime occurs in schools. For example, 37 per cent of violent offences and 81 per cent of thefts against younger teenagers occurred at school (Gottfredson 2001). Similarly, there appear to be adjacency effects for particular offences where proximity to a school increases the likelihood of property crimes and some kinds of assaults. Despite this, data on the timing of criminal events indicate that offending is lower when young people are in school, at least compared with when they are unsupervised in the community. Being unsupervised for extended periods of time – for instance, between the end of school and the return of a parent in the evening – appears to raise the risks of involvement in risk behaviours such as substance misuse. The supervisory influence of school for certain young people who may be at risk of offending appears to be significant, at least in the American studies.

Engagement and attachment

The concept of school engagement has received more attention recently as potentially providing a more useful construct in understanding motivation, commitment and attainment (Fredericks *et al.* 2004).

There are three potential explanations of the relationship between engagement and attainment:

- Disengagement precedes lower attainment.
- Failure to succeed in academic work lowers engagement.
- Other factors (including family and individual) jointly influence both attainment and engagement outcomes.

The Programme for International Student Assessment (PISA) looked across the OECD countries and using a large dataset (224,000 young people in 8300 schools across 42 countries) attempted to analyse student engagement at school from the two dimensions of a sense of belonging and of participation (Willms 2003). The definition of engagement used was 'a *disposition* towards learning, working with others and functioning in a social institution' (Willms 2003: 8), which is expressed in students' feelings that they belong at school, and in their participation in school activities. It is not clear that the questions used in the survey were directly relevant to 'working with others' and 'functioning in a social institution'. Nevertheless, this definition has a more positive point of departure than 'disaffection' or 'alienation'. It also avoids the lack of clarity introduced by treating motivation and engagement as synonyms (Fredericks *et al.* 2004; Steedman and Stoney 2004).

Young people who were detached from compulsory education were not covered in the survey, an important omission. In a cross-sectional study, age effects are obviously omitted, as is a fuller discussion of the possible causal relationship between engagement and the acquisition of literacy and numeracy skills. In addition, such a large-scale international study of necessity tends to obscure cultural components and the effects of local contexts. The measure of participation used understandably focused on absenteeism, whereas a broader measure, including homework, extra-curricular activities, sport and the arts, could have provided more insight.

This study attempted to provide an indication of the strength of the relationships between attainment outcomes and engagement at age 15. It also examined the strength of these relationships to both family and school factors.

Interestingly, a student's sense of belonging was not always strongly related to participation or to any of the attainment measures used. By these measures, the sense of belonging was found to be quite low for some young people that had relatively high academic attainment as well as for those that had very low levels of attainment. While those with the most sense of belonging tended to have a wide range of socio-economic status poor literacy performance was strongly associated with lower socio-economic status.

In common with the measures of attainment across the OECD countries, the results indicate significant effects associated with school context on engagement. One of the main findings was that young people from low socio-economic status families are more likely to have lower levels of engagement, but that this is exacerbated by the fact that they are also more likely to attend schools that have a high percentage of students from such backgrounds. This mirrored the double-jeopardy finding in relation to analyses of student attainment where young people from a low socio-economic status background and who also attended schools with a higher proportion of young people from such backgrounds had a heightened risk of poor attainment due to the two factors working against them. Measures of engagement were correlated with school factors, including a high average socio-economic status, high expectations by teachers of young people, a strong disciplinary culture and good student–teacher relationships. Interestingly, the linkages appeared to be more to do with the culture of the school than the levels of school resources, although young people were less susceptible to low participation in schools with a smaller pupil:teacher ratio. These findings do not support the one-dimensional approach of disaffection, which often assumes that those least likely to succeed academically are more prone to disengagement, as school offers few rewards.

Post-compulsory participation

It may be that the weakening of attachment that appears relatively common at age 15 or 16 is a normal part of adolescent development, and that most young people still go on to participate in education and training after compulsory schooling. For some young people, a weakening of attachment to school, accompanied by decreased participation, can become a progressive process, ending in detachment through either exclusion or non-attendance, which are significant risk factors for offending. Another area of risk linked to disengagement is the critical transition from compulsory schooling to further education or training. A failure to enter the labour market at a sustainable level or not being in education or training between 16 and 18 increases the chances of persistence in offending. It may be that a successful transition to post-compulsory schooling is linked to levels of engagement in the last two years of schooling, given that success at school during this period, or at least the perception of it, appears to be related to participation in post-compulsory education and training.

Relatively little is known about young people's decision-making processes regarding the transition to further education, training and employment while they are at secondary school. One of the few longitudinal studies of relevance to this issue concluded that these important decisions had been influenced over several years and that there were direct school effects. Ryrie (1981: 105) emphasised 'the power of the schooling process, its organisation and the assumptions that it comes with, to shape the decisions and therewith the lives of those who pass through it'.

Given the changes that have occurred in staying on rates post-16 and a substantial increase in the proportion of young people gaining A–C grades at GCSE, it has been argued that the nature of the decision-making process for some young people may have changed. There is no reason to think that the conclusions regarding the influence of the school should be any less applicable to young people who are at risk and still have some level of attachment to compulsory schooling:

> Decisions of the young people arose fairly directly from the structure and organisation of the schooling process, and beyond that, from the perceptions and assumptions which lie behind that structure, and not from the individual choice and free decision-making of the students themselves ... the controlling concept underlying the whole process is that of 'ability' (Ryrie 1981: 64).

Substantial differences in staying on rates between individual schools have been found after controlling for attainment, socio-economic status and other relevant factors (Payne 2002). A study of 34 inner-city schools also supports this contention, as young people reported significant differences between schools in attitudes towards education (Hagell and Shaw 1996). If schools can affect staying-on rates this is possibly a relatively immediate risk factor but also one that can have significant longer-term effects in terms of restricting access to the labour market and consequent unemployment.

In the context of offending behaviour, increased attachment and participation could be considered important schooling outcomes in their own right. The PISA findings support the argument that behaviours and attitudes can be significantly affected by teachers and parents and moulded by individual school policies and practices.

Treating increased attachment and participation in both academic and non-academic activities within school as important protective outcomes, coupled with the evidence regarding the risk effect of unbalanced socio-economic intakes, points clearly towards the potential role of inclusion in the prevention of offending. There are also other protective spin-offs from higher levels of engagement in the feelings of being included and involved in social pursuits correlated to young people's health and sense of well-being (Putnam 2000).

In an attempt to unify the diverse definitions of engagement and draw generalised findings from the varied research methodologies employed, a recent review proposed three components of engagement – behaviour, emotion and cognition – that were all dynamically related within the individual young person. In considering engagement as a multidimensional construct, the following definition was proposed:

- Behavioural engagement draws on the idea of participation; it includes involvement in academic and social or extra-curricular activities and is considered crucial for achieving positive academic outcomes and preventing dropping out.

- Emotional engagement encompasses positive and negative reactions to teachers, classmates, academics, and school and is presumed to create ties to an institution and influence willingness to work.

- Finally, cognitive engagement draws on the idea of investment; it incorporates thoughtfulness and willingness to exert the effort necessary to comprehend complex ideas and master difficult skills (Fredericks *et al.* 2004: 60)

Although most of the evidence is American, there were outcome correlations in relation to both attainment and detachment and school-level effects in terms of the antecedents of engagement. Positive correlations were found in several studies between behavioural engagement and attainment across all ages. There were significant differences in behavioural engagement measures between academically successful groups, less academically successful groups that remained within school, and those who became detached. Early onset of difficulties with behavioural engagement was a predictor of later low attainment and becoming detached from school (Alexander *et al.* 1993; 1997).

There was significantly less research information found on the relationship between emotional and cognitive engagement and attainment. This may be partly due to the fact that many different definitions of engagement, often combining elements of both emotional and behavioural engagement, have been used (Fredericks *et al.* 2004).

There appears to be a strong and progressive correlation between behavioural disengagement and becoming detached from school. Young people who do become detached often experience this as the end of a process where less homework was completed, and participation was reduced in school activities along with an increase in disciplinary difficulties. Conversely, participation in extra-curricular activities has been associated with a reduced risk of becoming detached, and it has been suggested that this may be particularly important for those at risk of low attainment (Fredericks *et al.* 2004).

Early school engagement behaviour appears to be a critical mediator in the detachment process. The failure of some young people to gain early behavioural engagement appears to be compounded by lower attainment and often culminates in detachment.

The picture that emerges is that the failure to secure an early attachment to school in tandem with poor participation can set up a reciprocal process between low participation and weak attachment. Once a child starts to become unsuccessful at school, this further weakens attachment, and this in turn, can lower participation, resulting in even lower attainment. The concept of attachment also includes the relationship of the young person with their peers and the parental relationship with the school.

In terms of school-level effects, teacher support has been demonstrated to have an influence on behavioural, emotional and cognitive engagement. This support can be either academic or interpersonal, as the majority of studies do not make this distinction. Behavioural engagement may have a reciprocal influence on the relationship with the teacher. The extensive literature indicates that young people who conform, take responsibility and are academically able are preferred to young people who are more aggressive and disruptive (Battistich *et al.* 1997). In American studies, teacher support and caring has been associated with various aspects of behavioural engagement, including increased participation, less disruptive behaviour and lower probability of detachment (Croninger and Lee 2001; Ryan and Patrick 2001).

Segregated education

While much remains to be learned about the effects of mainstream schools on antisocial behaviour and the development or prevention of offending behaviour, many of the young people involved in offending are receiving their formal education in other ways. Only a minority of young people in the youth justice system, particularly those over the age of 14, may be receiving their education in mainstream schools (YJB 2006). Special schools, PRUs, FE colleges, home tuition and a range of alternative education projects provide for many of those of compulsory school age. Evidence relating to educational outcomes, let alone effects on behaviour and offending, is extremely limited. This diversity of provision could range from a few hours taught at home to living in a residential special school or being taught in small classes in a PRU of 20 students, compared with attending vocational courses at a FE college with 2000 students.

The most important issue is the compositional effects. The segregated education population is a distillation of all those characteristics that are associated with a high incidence of offending: the subjects exhibit socio-economic disadvantage expressed through the incidence of free school meals (Berridge *et al.* 2001), fractured family backgrounds and experiences in the care system; are older, as the majority are 15 and 16; have low attainment; have missed significant amounts of mainstream schooling; have a greater involvement in substance misuse; and possess a criminal record.

If school effects acting largely through the additional negative impact of unbalanced intakes have been observed, it is reasonable to contend that these could be intensified in such environments. Berridge *et al.* cite a literacy project where those who had offended were mixed with those who had not done so previously, but who commenced offending on the project. Similarly, several American studies have found unintentional negative effects by aggregating at-risk youth in projects (Tremblay *et al.* 2003). These compositional effects could be magnified through their effect on staffing. It is likely that recruitment of the most effective teachers may be more difficult; staff themselves may become marginalised from changes in mainstream teaching and expectations (Ballas *et al.* 2005).

One of the complicating issues is that of dosage – many young people in segregated education appear to be on part-time timetables, so increases in offending may be related to this rather than any direct effects of the educational institutions. Berridge *et al.* did record apparent increases in offending for young people following exclusion, but there may be two other causes. The effects of rejection by mainstream school in terms of depression, risk taking, or resorting to substance and alcohol misuse may increase the likelihood of offending. This may be compounded by professional drift, as there is evidence that there is a considerable time lag between the breakdown of a school placement and recommencing full-time education (Mitchell 1996; Berridge *et al.* 2001; Daniels *et al.* 2003). In fact, for many young people who are involved in, or at risk of involvement in, offending, no new education placement is arranged at all – exclusion from school effectively becomes exclusion from education.

It could be argued that the much smaller class sizes of PRUs could be more effective in social control and behaviour modification, offsetting the delinquent peer group effects. While some studies have found improved behaviour, there is no evidence that this successfully transfers to mainstream environments such as FE colleges or employment, and it may represent effective containment rather than socialisation (Galloway 1985). There is very little evidence on patterns of offending within segregated education provision (see Chapter 9).

Conclusions

There is no conclusive evidence that schools can have a direct influence on delinquency. However, there is a considerable amount of evidence that schools exercise an independent influence on academic attainment and detachment from school, which are closely associated with delinquency. It also seems likely that schools can affect transitions, particularly that to post-compulsory education and training. If some schools are able to increase engagement, the converse would also seem to be true whereby school processes and teachers can lead to disengagement and ultimately detachment. Rigorous research and evaluation evidence has not kept pace with the many educational initiatives of the past 20 years.

One of the reasons has been the growth of segregated education, where a significant proportion of young people who offend are supposed to receive their education. Despite this growth, these institutions remain under-evaluated, but what evidence there is does not suggest that they are able to meet their ostensible aim – the reintegration of young people into mainstream secondary education or post-compulsory education and training. Some of the risk factors for delinquency may actually be increased through, for example, creating more antisocial peer groups.

Summary

❑ The empirical evidence on a causal role for schools on offending is limited, but what does exist shows that the qualities of schools as social institutions are important.

❑ The make-up of the pupil body is important, as the presence of male delinquent role models and a high incidence of bullying can create significant compositional effects. These can be intensified by not attracting the highest quality teaching and support services staff.

❑ Schools appear to be able to affect both attainment and detachment over and above the nature of their intake, and both these factors may affect offending behaviour indirectly rather than directly.

❑ Many young people in the youth justice system are supposed to receive their education in segregated institutions, but very little is known about the institutional effects of, for example, special schools or PRUs on delinquency.

❑ The concept of engagement at school is becoming more clearly defined and could be a useful tool to explore further the links with delinquency and attitudes towards school and learning.

❑ Mainstream schools may have the potential to foster the development of resilience, so that young people are more able to overcome the adversities that may face them.

❑ The attitudes of schools towards particular young people, as expressed via court reports, can influence sentencing practice, sometimes leading to higher-tariff sentences.

Chapter 7

Custody and custodial education

The only School provided in Great Britain by the State for children, is
– THE GAOL!

Mary Carpenter (1851) [1968: 26]

Education and training have often purported to be at the centre of the regimes of those institutions to which young people have been removed on either criminal-justice or care grounds since at least the mid-nineteenth century. Indeed, one of the strong and pervasive arguments in favour of custodial institutions for young people who offend or display antisocial behaviour is the provision of highly structured, compulsory education with an emphasis on basic skills. It appears to be eminently sensible that, for young people whose lives have been characterised by low participation and attainment, a custodial experience with formal and informal education at its centre would be beneficial. However, given the very substantial rise in custody for young people during the last 15 years and the apparently weak effects in terms of recidivism, it is worth re-examining the evidence that underpins such beliefs.

Given the high rate of recidivism that prevails among young people released from such establishments (70 per cent and 68 per cent reconviction within two years for young people sentenced to custody in 2001 and 2002) (Home Office 2004), it is important to assess the role of education and training. Does it mitigate the educational risk factors that young people bring with them on entry into such institutions? Does it have no discernible impact or could it even in some ways be involved in increasing the risk factors for reoffending? In trying to answer these questions, it is instructive to examine the evidence for the educational antecedents of young people entering such institutions, their experiences therein and the educational outcomes on transition to the community.

Structural problems

Reviewing the American evidence, Howell (2003: 134) concluded that:

> Large, congregate, custodial juvenile corrections facilities are not effective in rehabilitating juvenile offenders. Whether confinement in juvenile reformatories halts or accelerates juvenile criminal behaviour is a question that has not yet been resolved; this issue has been debated since the mid-19th century. Post release recidivism rates for correctional populations range from about 55 percent to 90 percent and prior placement in a juvenile correctional facility is one of the strongest predictors of returning. It is clear that housing juvenile offenders in large reformatories is not an effective way to prevent or reduce juvenile offending.

In discussing the recent problems of overcrowding in American custodial institutions, which have been paralleled by those in the UK, he went on to assert: 'Studies have shown that in large, overcrowded correctional facilities, both treatment opportunities and effectiveness of service delivery are diminished. Custodial concerns tend to override concerns about the delivery of treatment services and program quality suffers' (Howell 2003: 135).

These difficulties are further compounded by institutional issues relating to the operation of secure facilities themselves and the weaknesses of multiagency working, including:

- weak case management and supervision structures;
- the lack of integration between separate planning systems and the wider sentence planning process, coupled with the poor transmission of key information relating to need and progress made by young people between custodial and community providers;
- difficulties in establishing stable learning groups within custodial establishments due to population churn resulting from a large number of short sentences and the transfer of young people between establishments;

- the high turnover rate of staff working in custodial establishments;

- lack of continuity between custodial-based services and those provided (if at all) in the community;

- overcrowding in large secure establishments has also been shown to have a deleterious effect on recidivism. The impact of large numbers of young people in confined spaces coupled with low staffing levels is likely to result in an overemphasis on regime security and the greater use of punitive sanctions, overriding the effective delivery of services (Howell 2003). The net result of this is to make regimes more akin to boot camps, shown in research to have no impact on recidivism (Lipsey *et al.* 2000; ECOTEC 2001; Howell 2003).

Despite the lengthy and significant history of the education of young people in various forms of custodial institutions, the evidence base is relatively meagre. This appears to be equally true in the USA, even with its very large custodial population (Coffey and Gemignani 1994).

Key to this discussion is whether or not custody is intrinsically damaging to a young person's development in terms of subsequent access to, and participation and progression in, mainstream education, or whether the problem is ineffective management and under-resourcing. Certainly, custodial environments have inherent limitations, as Sutton (1992: 6) points out: 'The coercive environment of prison makes it an especially difficult setting for educational services that aim to enable people to make decisions and have some control over their lives.'

The sheer geographical distance between young people placed in custodial establishments and their home communities is another significant barrier to resettlement and access to mainstream education. The relatively low number of secure establishments for juveniles means that young people are often placed far from home, reducing the capacity for contact with family members and carers. Research from social care indicates that where young people who are looked after lack positive family support, they are more likely to have poor post-care outcomes and greater difficulty making and sustaining relationships with others (Biehal *et al.* 1992). It would seem reasonable to assume that the same is likely to be true for young people who are taken very suddenly from their communities on a custodial sentence and then returned fairly abruptly with little interim support or contact. Geographical distance also appears to exacerbate difficulties of communication between Yots and secure establishments and continues to be an issue raised by practitioners as a barrier to cooperative working to ensure a seamless resettlement process from custody (YJB 2006).

The population in the juvenile secure estate is turbulent, the average length of stay for a DTO being around four months and a significant proportion serving even shorter sentences. This immediately limits the effectiveness of any intervention, since proper assessment and meaningful learning gains are not achieved easily in these circumstances. Short sentences also have a direct impact on administrative processing and the logistical demands on operational staff.

The large number of interestablishment moves further compromises consistency of provision during the custodial phase of the sentence. It has been estimated that a young person stands a more than one in four chance of being moved in the custodial phase of a DTO (YJB 2004b). Population churn has been identified as one of the most significant factors determining the quality of learning experience that a young person has while in custody (LoBuglio 2001; YJB 2002a). The formation of stable learning groups becomes extremely difficult, if not impossible, in these circumstances. This affects the quality of lesson planning and the necessary differentiation of work for young people. It also begs significant questions about the nature of the curriculum (defined in its broadest sense as being vocational training, offence-related work, substance misuse programmes, and enrichment as well as what has traditionally been regarded as 'education') that should be offered within the custodial part of a sentence.

The reasons given for the high number of midsentence moves vary but primarily fall into four categories:

- population pressures and overcrowding;
- proximity to home and family visits;
- 'discipline' and behavioural issues;
- the availability of specific programmes.

Population instability can be transmitted to and among groups of staff. For example, the pressures of such a rapid turnover of young people could be reflected in the turnover of educational staff and their sickness rates. Equally, the absence of prison officers can have a serious impact on whether education is available or not. Instances were noted, in a YJB report (2004c), where the absence of a prison officer determined when PE took place, which in turn removed young people from scheduled lessons.

The operational pressures that YOIs work under are often intense, and in the face of such unstable populations, the provision of education becomes fragile. Education shutdowns can occur at very short notice in establishments, and late starts to lessons appear to be perennial.

Education in LASCHs and STCs

These establishments are usually fundamentally different from YOIs largely due to their much higher levels of funding and significantly smaller size. In addition, they tend to cater for a younger age group primarily 14 and 15 years old. The LASCHs are also perhaps influenced by their welfare origins and often have a stronger attachment to a social-work rather than security ethos. STCs are a relatively recent creation, and their operation is governed by extremely detailed contracts which give education a high priority. Initially, these were 40-bed units, but out of the four sites, three are now 80-bed. Although larger than most of the LASCHs, they are still only one-third of the size of the average YOI in accommodation that is largely purpose built.

These factors mean that, in general, education plays a much more central role in the life of these establishments and for the young people. There is a significantly higher ratio of teaching staff that tend to be qualified and to have access to a much wider range of facilities, including information and computing technology (ICT). Although there appears to be more contact for young people outside their establishments, in the STCs at least education is set as such a high priority that no visits are allowed to interrupt lessons. Management information systems, covering such essentials as assessment, attendance and, in some instances, learning gains from the custodial phase of the sentence, are commonplace.

It is undeniable that the educational experience of the majority of young people in these establishments is significantly better than those in YOIs. But in terms of the effectiveness of education in reducing those risk factors associated with offending, the impact of LASCHs and STCs must also be questioned. They face many of the same systemic problems as YOIs.

Within the establishments, even those with much higher levels of funding, the curriculum is necessarily much more restricted due to lack of facilities than would be a secondary school or FE college. Vocational facilities and science laboratories both tend to be inadequate. The educational information that accompanies a young person into LASCHs and STCs is often as limited as for those young people entering YOIs. While there is a greater emphasis on educational assessment, no standard approach is used which renders comparative analysis difficult. Effective joint planning with Yots can also be difficult. Ensuring a smooth transition from a learning environment of the LASCH or STC into a school, PRU or college in the community remains a considerable challenge. No matter what the learning gains in custody may be, ensuring continuity of subjects and courses without a damaging hiatus between the custodial and community phases of the DTO seems to be almost impossible for the majority of young people.

The secure college?

The YJB launched a series of initiatives in its attempt to reform the quality and quantity of education provided in custody particularly in YOIs. In recognition particularly of the importance of learning and skills in relation to preventing offending, the YJB introduced a major reform programme to transform secure establishments into secure colleges. The aim of this was to counter the negative impact of custody. Its vision was to establish high-quality centres of learning where the young people are held in secure conditions – 'secure learning centres'.

The 'secure learning centre' vision is enshrined in the YJB National Specification for Learning and Skills:

> It is axiomatic that each establishment's vision for its work must embrace the philosophy that learning is the most important component of the rehabilitative process and must be the centrepiece of each young person's institutional experience. [The National] Specification is therefore designed to expand learning from the classroom into the entire fabric of the establishment and to provide the framework for education and to enable all institutional staff to support learning and influence behaviour positively.
>
> The two most important functions of a secure establishment, after welfare issues are dealt with, are therefore:
>
> • The promotion of learning;
> • Managing the successful transition of young people into mainstream education and training. (YJB 2002a: 6).

The YJB's aspirations were that the education and training that are provided at all stages of a sentence should:

• reach the standards provided for young people in mainstream schools and colleges;
• operate as a coherent and integrated programme across the sentence (custody and community);
• be targeted closely at the particular needs of the young person.

This is perhaps one of the most prescriptive approaches to custodial education ever adopted and was an attempt to achieve a cultural transformation within YOIs. Implementation has fallen short of these aims according to recurrent progress reviews commissioned by the YJB and supported by inspection findings which indicate limited progress, with much of this national specification remaining aspirational. The reasons for this probably include continued significant underfunding, difficulties in recruitment and retention of education staff, and the fact that there is no truly separate juvenile secure estate within the prison service. Arguably, though, there are fundamental systemic problems that are bound up with the public's attitude to sentencing young people and compounded by the very different professional cultures in the prison service, education and Yots.

What is custodial education for?

The wider debate in regard to the overt and hidden purposes of education is reflected in consideration of the purpose of custodial education. It may be that the objectives of imprisonment – removal of choice, deprivation of freedom and the external imposition of order and control – are potentially at odds with both the objectives and practical delivery of education.

Views on the purpose of custodial education are perhaps closely allied to the beliefs of individuals and groups of staff in the causes of crime. Thus staff who believe that parents, communities and schools have failed to exert sufficient control and sanctions on young people may see education as a reward to be earned rather separate from disciplined and rote activities. In contrast, others may perceive education as an escape route from a life of adversities, including a miserable and failed experience of school. In reality, such a division may be somewhat simplistic, as, for example, the acquisition of basic skills can appeal equally to both punitive and progressive instincts (Stephenson 2004).

There are perhaps four main explicit themes within custodial education:

* reconnecting to education training or employment;
* acquiring basic skills;
* vocational training;
* changing behaviour.

Obviously, these interventions are closely allied, and arguably all are necessary, but none appears to be sufficient to ensure the prevention of reoffending.

Equipping young people with the knowledge and skills necessary to return to or commence school, college, a training provider or employment is attempted through their gaining qualifications, by reacquainting them with classroom routines and disciplines, and by providing information, advice and guidance so that they can make appropriate choices.

Acquiring the skills of literacy and numeracy necessary to function effectively in society, let alone at the level which enables young persons to fulfil their potential, has often been seen as fundamental to the provision of education in custody. While there is some evidence to indicate that prison officers, for example, may not always be well disposed towards education, certainly for adults who offend (Wilson and Reuss 2000), illiteracy in particular can evoke more sympathetic responses.

It is in the nature of large institutions to evolve bureaucratic, rather rigid and repetitive practices. The regular control and movement of significant numbers of prisoners shape the management practices of establishments and create a particular self-reinforcing culture – a regime. The acquisition of basic skills by rote, traditional classroom layout and didactic pedagogy understandably all fit comfortably within the quasi-military approach that has characterised prison service establishments. Basic skills qualifications also have an ostensible appeal in that they are easily counted.

Offending behaviour programmes have in recent times been promoted as the main mechanism of individual change to prevent reoffending. Their popularity and rapid adoption may lie in the fact that their apparent connection with the desired result of reducing reoffending appears much more direct than that of gaining qualifications or improving literacy and numeracy, and their organisation (through accredited programmes) fits neatly with the running of an establishment. An almost medical model has been adopted whereby the carefully regulated administration of a clearly prescribed treatment at an appropriate dosage with positive and predictable results has proved seductive to the prison service. Interestingly, although this process shares many of the features of traditional educational learning, it is managed and perceived very separately by both its practitioners and its participants.

Education within custody can also be seen as a medium for pro-social modelling, particularly given the fact that educators may be seen as separate from the disciplinary aspects of the regime. It can also be seen as a way in which young people can gain more effective thinking, planning and organisational skills as a by-product of their studies.

Vocational training has a long history within custodial establishments from the nineteenth century onwards. While, historically, there was a significant demand for relatively unskilled labour, so preparing young people for the rudiments of particular trades could be seen to be beneficial to employment prospects, there was also an important overlap with the day-to-day running needs of establishments such as cooking and cleaning.

Depending on which of these four objectives is given priority, the shape, staffing, resources and culture of an establishment may vary considerably. Some of these objectives may in fact be incompatible with certain kinds of sentences: can significant qualifications be gained in just a matter of weeks, for example? More fundamental questions are begged: can new behaviours be readily acquired in a tightly controlled environment and then subsequently applied in a far less controlled one? Can reconnection with education and training be readily achieved after disconnection through removal to a custodial institution?

The rationale for custodial education

In the nineteenth century, the new school classrooms where the 'teacher became the precept and model for the pupil' (Copeland 1999: 20) provided the apparatus for the instilling of moral principles that would protect the 'perishing and dangerous classes' from becoming involved in crime, and they, in turn, would relinquish their 'vicious and degraded' ways and become useful members of society. From this perspective, then, concern for the custodial education of young people was the point of departure for shaping the education system for all young people.

Modern conceptions of the role of custodial education for young people contain echoes of this earlier discourse. The emphasis of the prison service on 'purposeful activity' with its overtones of useful works could just as easily sit in a Victorian moral tract. Within the current context of 'what works', two complementary rationales have been put forward for custodial education (Wilson and Reuss 2000), although, in the first instance, it has been queried as to whether it should be 'prison' or 'prisoner' education. The importance of this distinction is that 'prisoner education' emphasises the learning of people within a specific environment – the prison – and from this perspective education provision in custody could be viewed as offering benefits and opportunities to learners as individuals. This personalises judgements about the effectiveness of education and training provision, so the focus is on the benefits to the individual rather than the requirements of the establishment or other policymakers. This approach, though, does run the risk of placing imprisoned people within a special educational category, that of particular intellectual and cognitive deficits.

An 'education for empowerment' model emphasises the value of learning to people, and this assists them to 'retain a degree of choice and control in what they do whilst in prison' (Reuss 1999: 125). Under this model, judgements as to the effectiveness of custodial education would be derived from assessing the ability of education to enable individuals to make more informed and responsible decisions about their futures. Education here is not simply the process of knowledge acquisition; rather, it involves the development of positive personal identity as a counterweight to a negative sense of self. What works here is all about the individual and not necessarily the establishment, as there will be considerable variability between individuals. The emphasis within the definition of empowerment is on 'giving ability to' and 'enabling'. This provision of opportunities through education to enable individuals to change their attitudes positively is contrasted with an approach to education by prison management that is all about meeting key performance indicators. This 'pile it high, and sell it cheap' mentality by the prison service is exemplified by the emphasis on counting the literacy and numeracy qualifications achieved.

The distinctiveness of 'juvenile' education

The literature on the education of prisoners is limited, and most of it relates to the education of adults. There are distinctive features relating to the education of children and young people under the age of 18. Most importantly, perhaps, for approximately one-quarter and one-third of all those receiving custodial sentences, education is compulsory on grounds of age. This immediately poses a series of problems for those charged with educating young people in custody and equally for those providing for them in the community. The impact of the school-leaving age can be considerable in that young people in the same custodial establishment have different rules applying to their attendance at education. The prevalence of short sentences for young people also has particular educational implications.

In contrast to adults, therefore, education for many young people in custody is not an elective opportunity to be pursued over a significant period of time, but it must follow many of the prescriptive elements of compulsory education, yet it often is compressed into just a few weeks.

Profile of young people in custody

The very low levels of attainment in literacy and numeracy recorded on reception into custody were noted in Chapter 5.

In addition, such key features as severely interrupted patterns of formal learning, low expectations of educational attainment by significant adults, and a weakening of family ties are also common for young people in custody. While the focus of this discussion is on education and training, there are significant health factors, including risk behaviours, that can hinder a young person's learning.

It is clear, for example, that many young people (between 46 per cent and 81 per cent) entering custody are experiencing some kind of mental health problem (ONS 2000). Similarly, the risk behaviours in relation to drug and alcohol misuse are significantly higher than for the general population, although the effects of some of these may be more limited in a custodial setting on a young person's learning (YJB 2004b).

A significant number will have experienced being in the care of the local authority at some point. Her Majesty's Chief Inspector of Prisons has found that 'a staggering proportion of these young people had a history of care or Social Services contact (over half of the under 18s)' (Her Majesty's Chief Inspector of Prisons 1997: 24). Hazel *et al.* (2002) put the figure at 41 per cent taken from a subsample of 336 young people.

Educational information

One report described the flow of basic educational information into and out of YOIs as a trickle (ECOTEC 2001). Given the shortness of the custodial phase of the DTO, the timely arrangement of education in custody is crucially important. In most cases, it seems that individual education plans, SEN statements and care plans (which should contain a considerable amount of information on a young person's education and training needs) rarely accompany a young person into custody. While estimates of that portion of the custodial population that could require a statement of SEN remain somewhat speculative, it is not unreasonable to assume this may be about one-half, yet perhaps less than 1 per cent are represented by statements arriving at YOIs. The main source of information is ASSET. However, as a predictive instrument, it is of somewhat limited educational assessment use. There are often significant gaps in its compilation and delay in its arrival at establishments. Most young people receive a literacy and numeracy assessment. This, of course, represents only a first step, but even so it can take up to two weeks to arrange. It would not be unusual for young people with complex educational needs to complete the custodial phase of a DTO without anything resembling a complete educational assessment to occur, let alone services provided to meet these needs.

These difficulties tend to be greater in YOIs due to their sheer size and population turnover, but there is undoubtedly a widespread problem in providing relevant, accurate and timely educational information to all custodial providers.

Detention and training order

The responsibility for ensuring the coherence of the DTO and the effective transition between custody and the community lies with the designated supervising officer of a Yot. Many of these staff become very frustrated with the continual struggles with the current educational infrastructure and the attitudes of its professionals. A sample of supervising officers recently identified three key areas that caused particular problems:

- Timing – current pace of planning, communication and arrangement of learning opportunities is simply too slow.

- Flexible provision – current educational providers, particularly schools and, to a lesser extent, colleges, are not structured flexibly enough to offer opportunities throughout the year, so that young people can access them immediately on release from custody.

- Recognition of risk – it was felt strongly that many of the agencies involved in education did not see the need of these young people as a priority (ECOTEC 2001; YJB 2006).

One supervising officer spoke for many in describing the operation of the DTO as follows: 'The pattern is community STOP custody STOP community STOP' (ECOTEC 2001: 54).

The supervising officers surveyed in this study were critical of the role of LEAs but were much more negative about the attitudes of school staff, as many felt that these young people had been abandoned by mainstream education:

'Schools take no responsibility and dump the young person on other agencies.'
'There is a huge distance between social services and schools.'
'Schools' attitudes to young people is the main blockage ...'

'Head teachers need to be more accountable – schools have a responsibility to follow up the young person' (ECOTEC 2001: 57).

The positive and negative impact of custody on young people

Several studies (for example, Hobbs and Hook 2001) have identified positive changes in young people's attitudes within custodial institutions. Another study produced very similar findings, although these positive changes may be seen as ephemeral when judged in terms of post-release reintegration into the community and reductions in reoffending. On balance, there appears to have been a positive impact on these young people's attitudes towards education and training as a result of their custodial experience. However, it is unknown how much of this positive shift is a reflection of the very restricted positive experiences in custody and thereby likely to be short-lived (ECOTEC 2001).

There has been some systematic comparison work carried out for institutions providing custody for young people who offend. One such study compared the reconviction outcomes for young people who had committed grave crimes and who were accommodated in YOIs compared with LASCHs. The main differences between the approaches of the two types of institution were that the LASCHs ensured stronger ties with the families (39 per cent received family visits at least three times a month, compared with 1 per cent of those in YOIs), more contact with the external community (over two-thirds of those in the LASCHs had weekly trips away from the institution, compared with 1 per cent of those in YOI), and a wider range and higher volume of education and training. The emphasis on education was highlighted by the fact that a much higher proportion attained educational qualifications in the LASCHs.

Reconviction rates were significantly higher after two years for those leaving YOIs (53 per cent) than those leaving LASCHs (40 per cent). There was also a much higher incidence of reconviction for violent offences for those in YOIs. While these young people form a small minority of even the custodial population, let alone the wider population of young people who offend, these findings do suggest that an approach that maintains ties with family, community, and education and training can have a positive effect on later outcomes (Ditchfield and Catan 1992).

The most negative consequence appears to be greater detachment from education, training and employment as a direct result of custody.

While between a quarter and a third of young people had no education, training or employment arranged in the period before they entered custody this had risen to 60 per cent one month after their release. For those where provision had been arranged a greater proportion was part-time and there was a significant discontinuity in the courses and materials they followed compared to those undertaken in custody (ECOTEC 2001).

Educational outcomes

Assessment of the effectiveness of custodial education presents an immediate paradox, in that, despite being such a controlled and highly visible set of institutions, surrounded by a constellation of targets and performance indicators and regularly visited by inspectors and monitors, they can provide so little robust evidence on outcomes. The unique nature of prison culture tends to lead people into working practices that would bemuse lay people and do confuse researchers. Starved of resources and often concentrating on security, yet having to meet apparently unrealistic targets are factors that combine, either deliberately or unconsciously, to produce a rather surreal approach to measuring educational success.

The Chief Inspector of Prison's recent report (2006) produced a series of examples illustrating how the hours of 'purposeful activity' (which include education) were greatly exaggerated in half of the local prisons inspected. The inspector observed that 'There is little evidence that these misleading returns are queried either within or outside the prison. Such practices merely serve to disguise the scale of the problem' (HM Inspectorate of Prisons 2006: 6). With Soviet-style creativity, the prison ship *Weare* even had preprinted forms containing hours out of cell prepared in advance.

Perhaps the most useful remedy is not to make allowances for these difficult circumstances but rather to approach the educational practices and outcomes of these institutions as reasonable parents might approach their mainstream school. Two of the most basic and reasonable questions would be how much learning does an individual young person participate in and to what effect? Reframing these questions in terms of access, we may ask, what is on offer to all young people entering custody? In terms of participation, we may ask, how often do young persons attend, how punctual are they and how interrupted is their learning? In terms of progression, we may ask, what learning gains have been made, particularly with regard to literacy and numeracy;

have there been positive changes in motivation; and are these learning gains built upon in a progressive educational experience in the second half of the DTO? Currently, neither the prison service nor the YJB can answer these basic questions.

Access and participation

There appears to be, on the available evidence, a considerable problem for many young people in YOIs gaining access to full-time education. The latest published YJB report (YJB 2004b) concluded that there was evidence to suggest that a significant number of young people were receiving less than three hours' education a day in custody. In fact, this whole area is cloudy, with unreliable statistics and estimates, and difficulties with semantics.

Historically, since education was contracted out in 1992, the prison service has focused on how many hours of education were being made available. This of course ignores the much more important questions of how much education was needed and how much actually received by each young person. Apparently, 'it is clearly still the case that in many establishments reporting systems are not sophisticated enough to provide information on the actual take-up of learning and skills as opposed to what is on offer' (YJB 2004b). Whether this remarkable emphasis on the arrangement of education, rather than its receipt, is the result of a contract culture, rudimentary information systems, the disguising of the inadequacy of the amount of education available, or a combination of all three is impossible to tell. What is perhaps more explicable is the likely reaction of an individual parent or groups of parents to being told proudly by a school that despite the fact that their particular children had had no or limited access to it, the school had in fact arranged abundant lessons and thereby met its government targets.

A further twist is that each YOI calculates and reports on simply the average number of hours of education offered per week. This of course means that, depending on the distribution of the values, there could be a significant number of young people receiving virtually no education, while a number of young people might have a relatively high number of hours made available to them.

In social policy terms, the influence of such distortions can be damaging. While ministers may have required in 1999 that all 16- and 17-year-olds in custody participate in 30 hours per week of education, personal development and work activity by 2005, this is not only far from being achieved but also the evidence adduced is insufficient to indicate much, if any, progress (SEU 1999). In terms of 'what works?', this situation makes it impossible for research to be undertaken to examine the nature and volume of education and training received in custody and its impact in terms of re-engagement in education in the community and subsequent offending.

What is astonishing about the situation is that these institutions are a fraction of the size of modern secondary schools (in fact, the total juvenile YOI population barely exceeds that of a large secondary school), all of whom have systems that enable detailed and timely monitoring of the education available and received by all children on an individual basis. In 2001, the YJB published recommendations that included the introduction of electronic attendance monitoring. In 2003, it published a report recommending the introduction of a paper-based registration system, but by 2004 all mention had been dropped of monitoring attendance through individual registration, and it has still not been introduced (ECOTEC 2001; YJB 2003c, 2004b).

This is a serious issue, as it goes to the heart of public and professional expectations of just what is being done with those young people who are committing offences of such seriousness or with such frequency that they are deprived of their liberty. Even with the underfunding of the secure estate, considerable sums of public money are involved. At one level, this is apparently a relatively simple management problem. Yet, the fact that it has defeated the requirements of ministers and the best efforts of the YJB is perhaps indicative of deeper and more intractable problems. Arguably, it is symptomatic of the fundamental culture clash between a security-focused prison service and the requirements of an institution that focuses on learning. The Crime and Disorder Act 1998 did not create a coherent framework for the creation of a juvenile secure estate. This was left to a political battle of wills between a non-executive departmental public body (the YJB) and Home Office civil servants and prison service management.

If sentencers are to make judgements as to the balance between community and custodial sentences, they will need far more information that is accurate and timely as to the effectiveness of custodial institutions in regard to education. Sooner or later, it is likely that the combination of a relatively large and very costly custodial population and a general increase in the transparency and accountability of public services will mean that sentencers will need information to judge the relative effectiveness of different custodial institutions.

Attainment and progression

Similar problems face the measurement of learning gains in that the only individual information generally gathered on young persons is their initial literacy and numeracy assessment on entry to the YOI. Learning gains as expressed through qualifications achieved or improvements in literacy and numeracy for each individual during the custodial episode are not currently systematically measured. Instead, a rather peculiar educational approach has emerged where the YOI is given a target number of qualifications to be achieved at different levels. However, achievement of this is not expressed as it would be with a secondary school by a percentage of pupils reaching different levels but rather against an apparently arbitrary target set for the institution (although it is claimed that these emerge from a process of negotiation between the YJB, the prison service, and offenders' learning and skills units (YJB 2004b)). So, for example, the target for 13 YOIs in 2003/2004 was 3534 qualifications; in the event, 4448 were achieved, exceeding the target by 25 per cent, 'an apparently encouraging performance against targets on literacy and numeracy gains' (YJB 2004b). But does this represent educational gains in any meaningful sense? In the first instance, it is not known how many individuals achieved these qualifications. Equally, these figures could simply represent a relatively small proportion of the population being entered for lots of qualifications in order to hit the target. There is no means of knowing whether the attainment of these qualifications represents any increase in academic level; in fact, the pressure of the target could well have a perverse effect if young people are entered for qualifications they can achieve relatively easily at or below their existing attainment level.

The National Specification for Learning and Skills requires that all young people be retested prior to release in order to assess any literacy and numeracy gains. This retesting appears not to be occurring. Despite the potential limitations of the assessment tool, this could have provided some indication of progression during the custodial episode.

One area where educational outcomes often appear to be particularly poor is in relation to the small minority of young people who have been relatively successful in education or at least are still in mainstream school or college. One report found that 'For these young people, custody has the potential to be an educational disaster' (ECOTEC 2001: 62). This finding was corroborated by a study of school-age young men in YOIs, which found that significant numbers were capable of taking GCSE or GNVQ examinations but were denied the opportunity in custody (Howard League 2001). Even with relatively short custodial episodes, young people often lost a whole academic year, particularly if entrance or examination dates coincided with custody. YOIs are simply not equipped to provide the necessary breadth of curriculum to offer continuity in mainstream examinations such as GCSEs.

Conclusions

Removing young people by force or circumstance from their immediate communities appears to have a significant negative impact on their education, training and employment prospects. Custody means that the most delinquent and damaged peer groups live together. Institutional life may lessen the resilience of a young person by weakening or preventing the growth of those protective factors that enable some young people to surmount adversities that defeat others. The stifling of autonomy in custodial institutions could have such an effect.

Custody appears to have three innate weaknesses that weaken protective factors and increase risks. It curtails decision-making and planning skills in those who require them the most. Learning is provided in such an abnormal environment that the subsequent application of this learning in the community is extremely limited. This has long been recognised. The Rev J. Turner, who established the Philanthropic Society, in his evidence to the parliamentary committee in 1850, asserted that 'the best prisoner makes the worst free boy ... because he has been so accustomed to depend upon the mere mechanical arrangements about him, that he finds self-action almost impossible' (Carpenter 1968: 339). Removing young people who have only a tenuous attachment to formal education (even if only a PRU with part-time provision) causes further dislocation for them, their parents or carers, and the relevant professionals.

The custodial experience, then, through the further stigma now attached to the young person, means that the chances of reintegration into a mainstream school are remote, as most schools are very reluctant to accept a young person, probably in the final year of schooling, with a criminal record that involved custody. This is further compounded by a lack of information about any gains made while the young person was in custody or any portfolio of work done. This criminal record may also, of course, restrict the young person's chances of employment, and family ties have probably been weakened further.

Summary

❑ Regimes focused on control may weaken resilience, further limiting the capability of young people to deal with the apparently commonplace dislocations relating to accommodation and education and training when they return to the community.

❑ Entry into the custodial systems (as with the care system) often tends to weaken attachment to particular educational providers and may also independently depress attainment.

❑ Custodial education has a long history as a tool for the moral reclamation of young people who offend. Christian precepts have been replaced by YJB learning objectives, but the prison service emphasis on purposeful activity echoes the Victorian tracts.

❑ The evidence base on custodial education is thin, but this has been augmented in recent years by increased inspection activity and the YJB's series of reports.

❑ On balance, as currently constructed, custodial educational experiences tend to be just another episode in a much interrupted educational experience. Entry into custody tends to increase risk factors by increasing detachment rather more than it ameliorates through enhancing attainment.

❑ A secure learning centre constructed around education may well be antithetical to the requirements of a security regime and thus is likely to remain rhetorical.

Section III

Chapter 8

Stakeholders: public opinion, magistrates, Yots and young people

It is far too easy for schools to exclude ... Our system has its emphasis on the greater good of the school being realised by abandoning the young person when they are most in need.

Tad Kubisa, President of the Association of
Directors of Social Services (1995)

Typical nonsense from social workers who deal with clients on a one to one basis and have no idea what it is like to deal with a class of thirty.

Nigel De Gruchy, General Secretary of the NASUWT

Public opinion is being given greater prominence in constructing social policy, and increasing public confidence in youth justice is a key objective of the YJB. In addition to public opinion, the youth justice system has several stakeholders, principally magistrates and Yots, but educators also have a statutory duty to prevent offending and can have a significant influence on both sentencing and the outcome of sentencing (Ball and Connolly 2000). Young people are not often treated as stakeholders in the youth justice system, but given that assumptions are often made about their disaffection from education, their attitudes towards both mainstream and the different forms of segregated education are worth examining.

This chapter, then, is primarily about the attitudes of the key players towards education specifically in the context of youth justice. It attempts to make a start on answering some basic questions: is education perceived as having an important part to play as part of the purpose of the youth justice system? Could compulsory education become a more explicit part of sentencing? Are the attitudes of educators consistent with the inclusion of young people who offend within mainstream education? How do young people in the youth justice system perceive education in the context of their experiences?

Public opinion

It is apparent that taking account of public opinion in policy formulation is becoming more common. This is certainly true in relation to criminal justice, where increasing public confidence has become an explicit policy objective. This is partly because the justice system cannot function without certain levels of acceptance and cooperation from the public but also because public opinion sets the limits of political permission. So, for example, sentencing policy is attempting to become more sensitive to public opinion, as evidenced in the report of the sentencing review in England and Wales (Home Office 2001), and the YJB has increasing public confidence as one of its core aims (YJB 2004a). It has been suggested 'that in some cases, judges sentence offenders with one eye on the dock and the other on the reaction of the community' (Roberts 2002: 34), and there is a considerable body of evidence indicating that public opinion both directly and indirectly has a significant impact on sentencing policy (Roberts and Hough 2002). Nearly one-half of magistrates who responded to an Audit Commission survey (2004) took account of public opinion in coming to their sentencing decision.

Politicians are often not content with simply taking account of public opinion but also seek actively to change it. One high-profile example is the pressure on resources exerted by rising prison populations and the attempts by government to alleviate this through promoting community interventions. The need for better understanding on how to influence public opinion is illustrated in this instance by the often widespread hostility towards punishment in the community which constrains such initiatives. This was drawn attention to by the Lord Chief Justice in his comment that it was a 'regrettable fact that neither the public nor sentencers have confidence in the community alternative' (Roberts 2002: 34).

Given the historical overlap between the youth justice system and the education system, it is interesting to examine the views of the public in relation to both. Do similar groups of people hold similar views and how, for example, do more punitive views on justice issues manifest themselves in relation to education?

National opinion polling across many countries has revealed some consistent patterns. These include a belief that courts are too lenient in their sentencing, and there are strong doubts about the capability of sentencers (Roberts and Stalans 1997). Another consistent feature is that the public's ignorance in regard to offending and justice tends to be both wide-ranging and systematic. For example, despite the evidence to the contrary, many members of the public in different countries believe that their courts are using imprisonment less and that crime is getting more serious.

Although there are consistent patterns across countries, there is a significant variation in how punitive public opinion is between countries. The UK, for example, has been found in some studies to be markedly more punitive than many other countries with the exception of the USA. The congruence between public opinion and sentencing practice is underlined by the fact those countries which had the highest rates of imprisonment also had the highest levels of public support for incarceration (Roberts *et al.* 2002).

Within these cross-national studies, 'One of the firmest findings is that the less educated hold more punitive views. Many studies also indicate that the elderly have more repressive views ... Men are usually found to be more punitive than women ... There is no consistent evidence that experience of victimisation increases punitiveness' (Mayhew and Van Kesteren 2002: 76). Other distinguishing features included the fact that tabloid readers tended to be more punitive and authoritarian than broadsheet readers, while those with educational qualifications of A-level and upwards tended to be less punitive. Limited knowledge of crime and justice is also associated with very negative views of both sentences and the justice system. Those living in cities also tended to have more punitive attitudes. All of these factors appear to have greater or lesser independent effects (Hough and Park 2002).

Superficially, it might appear that there is a dichotomy between punishment and rehabilitation and that public opinion is attracted towards either pole. The reality, however, appears to be much more complicated, in that large sections of the public are apparently able to hold simultaneously contradictory views. Even in the USA, where punitive views are prevalent, surveys have found strong public support for community sentences coexisting in public opinion with more punitive attitudes (Doble 2002). Various studies have revealed that attitudes on crime and punishment are layered rather than simply inconsistent (Stalans 2002).

Given that public opinion appears able to impel social policy in general, and sentencing practice in particular, down more punitive routes, it is not unreasonable to suppose that similar pressures could operate in respect of educational institutions. Indermaur and Hough (2002: 210) have stressed this: 'Whether we like it or not, it is often public emotions that define public debates and political initiative in the field of penal policy, not public information. Anyone who wants to improve public debate about crime needs to be attuned to this emotional dimension.' As noted earlier in Chapter 3, school exclusions and custodial sentences for young people both rose rapidly during the mid-1990s. Bearing in mind how entwined are public attitudes over discipline in schools and antisocial behaviour and offending by young people, we may learn useful lessons from research on changing public attitudes towards offending.

Research sponsored by the Rethinking Crime and Punishment Initiative looked at public and professional attitudes towards education and young people who offend through a series of surveys (Stephenson 2004). The opinion poll of 1,332 members of the public documented many attitudes in line with other research. For example, public knowledge of the youth justice system appeared to be limited, nearly half admitting not to know very much. Interestingly, public opinion appeared to see a greater role for education and training in terms of preventing reoffending rather than preventing offending in the first place. While being unable to read and write was seen as the least important reason for young people beginning to commit crimes, it was rated as one of the most important factors in reducing reoffending.

Questions on the influence of the culture and organisation of schools on the likelihood of young people offending revealed that teachers and schools were seen by the public as more important than any other professional group (including the police) and far more important than custodial institutions or the courts. They believed very strongly that mainstream schools should teach about the causes and consequences of committing crimes. A clear majority (60 per cent) thought that children and young people should be treated differently by the courts than adults.

Those in favour of custodial rather than community sentences tended to be older men of lower socio-economic status and no qualifications, who read tabloids and had little confidence in the youth justice system. Interestingly, when findings about the low educational attainment levels both pre- and post-custody for young people were presented, support for the custodial option was nearly halved. Either reflection on the poor educational experiences of these young people evoked greater sympathy for their plight, or education in the community, particularly if compulsory, was seen as providing a more effective form of punishment.

While many of the respondents appeared to hold attitudes that exaggerated the extent of offending by young people and were negative about the response of the courts to offending, another nationally representative opinion poll indicated that a significant proportion of the public would be prepared to volunteer to help with the literacy and numeracy of young people who offend (YJB 2005d).

Causes of crime

The general public, magistrates and educators (teachers, teaching assistants, head teachers, and principals and vice-principals in FE colleges) ranked the same top three reasons for young people committing crime. Not necessarily in rank order, the three most important factors identified by sentencers, the public and educators in secondary schools were poor parental supervision/discipline; drug, alcohol and other substance misuse; and having criminal friends or siblings. Though not in the top three choices, all groups thought non-attendance at school was an important factor in causing crime.

Magistrates gave a great deal of weight to educational factors: non-attendance at school, academic underachievement and lack of qualifications, and illiteracy. In fact, the magistrates' perceptions of the reasons for offending by young people were probably in closer accord with the research evidence on the factors most associated with offending than was the case with either the general public or the educators.

As might be expected from educators, considerable weighting was given to those educational factors that are implicated in offending by young people. Low attainment, for example, was generally seen as being notably important as a cause of offending except by teachers, who in common with members of the public, rated it of less importance than did managers in FE and secondary education and magistrates.

Although educational failure was not generally picked by respondents as a cause of crime, in terms of the most important factors in preventing reoffending, FE principals and head teachers alike thought that getting a job, receiving support/supervision from family members and carers, and being able to read and write were the most significant factors. Other staff in secondary schools, as with causing criminal behaviour initially, perceived alcohol and drug treatment programmes to be of more importance to reoffending rates than educational factors.

Purpose of the youth justice system

Background knowledge of the youth justice system was not extensive, particularly among teachers and teaching assistants, whose knowledge was apparently no higher than that of the general public. While most educational managers agreed that children and young people aged 10–17 should be treated differently from adults within the criminal justice system, only half of teachers took this view and almost a third disagreed.

There were major differences between the punitive nature of views of educators and the general public with regard to the purpose of the youth justice system. While, for example, under half of the general public respondents thought the purpose of the youth justice system should be rehabilitation, this rose to between two-thirds (68 per cent) and three-quarters (78 per cent) among educators. Only 9 per cent of head teachers and FE managers saw the purpose of the youth justice system as being 'to punish that young person'; educators were more likely to perceive the purpose of the youth justice system as the discouragement of young people from committing further crimes and the rehabilitation of young people rather than their punishment.

Custody

Attitudes towards punishment were mirrored with some variations in the attitude of educators towards custody, only 5 per cent of head teachers and FE managers believing such sentences to be beneficial to young people, while this was favoured by 30 per cent of the general public. Similarly, very large majorities of educators believed that placing young people who offend in custody could disrupt their education (compared with just over half of the general public). The underlying pattern for the educators, as for members of the public, was that those who had a less sympathetic outlook were those people who admitted least knowledge of the system – namely, teaching staff and learning support assistants. However, in contrast to respondents from the general public, the overwhelming majority of all educators wanted to know more about the youth justice system.

Closer inspection of the results, however, does indicate that teaching staff seemed much less committed to their views than head teachers, favouring the 'tend to' options rather than the 'strongly' agree or disagree choices. This particularly applied in relation to the removal from education as punishment, where all groups were in overall opposition to this, but only 1 per cent of teachers disagreed 'strongly' with the statement, compared with 74 per cent of head teachers.

Magistrates' views differed markedly from those of the general public regarding the relative benefits to education and training of a custodial as opposed to a community sentence. While 30 per cent of the public believed a custodial sentence to be more beneficial to a young person's education and training, only 7 per cent of magistrates shared this view; nearly three-quarters of magistrates supported a community sentence as being of the greatest benefit.

Magistrates often did not appear to be any more aware than the general public of the disruptive effect on education almost inevitably caused by a custodial sentence. They were, however, far more concerned (perhaps because of their greater knowledge of the realities) that there should be provision for young people who offend to continue with their education upon their release from custody.

Educational information and the courts

It is apparently rare for magistrates to request or receive a separate report from a school, local education authority (LEA), college or training provider. This is despite the fact that 60 per cent of magistrates believed that access to, and participation in, education, training and employment were an important factor as part of the young person's welfare needs when deciding on an appropriate sentence.

This underlined the finding by Ball and Connolly (2000: 601): 'In contrast to the wealth of information on family background, educational information in the majority of reports, whether in PSRs or coming directly from schools, although present in some form in most (96 per cent), was sparse and often uninformative.'

Given that two-thirds of the magistrates reported that they did not know enough about the range of education and training placements available to young people who receive a community order, this information gap could be encouraging magistrates to make custodial disposals, because they appear to assume that education and training programmes are more likely to be available in secure establishments. This finding was supported by that of the Audit Commission survey (2004) that three-quarters of magistrates take education into account when sentencing, but a large majority believed they did not have adequate information about the education that sentenced young people received, especially those sentenced to secure facilities.

Nearly one-third of magistrates stated that they never receive feedback on the education and training received by young people during their sentence; over three-quarters of magistrates would welcome individual reports on education, training and employment of those young people whom they have sentenced. This interest also extended to the post-sentence period.

Many magistrates were deeply concerned about the role of school exclusions in terms of offending, some rejecting even the notion of schools having the power to exclude. Their experience of the length of time taken to arrange placements and the limited number of hours made available to young persons if they had a placement aroused the strongest feelings.

However, providing magistrates with more information on educational issues such as poor behaviour in school or non-attendance could have a negative impact on sentencing. In discussing potential processing bias, Graham (1988: 19) quotes the findings of a small unpublished study: 'Among those defendants who get a custodial penalty, the proportion of those whose educational status was problematic was twice as high as in the overall sample.'

Schools and inclusion

One of the critical issues is the extent to which educators considered mainstream schools and colleges to be suitable for young people who offend, which could be interpreted as indicative of their commitment to social inclusion. There was a marked difference found between the outlook of FE managers and that of teachers and others in secondary education. Almost two-thirds (62 per cent) of FE principals and vice-principals believed colleges to be a suitable option for 10–17-year-olds on release from custody; only 14 per cent disagreed. Within secondary education, in contrast, although 40 per cent of head teachers considered mainstream secondary school to be appropriate, almost one-quarter disagreed. The situation was reversed among teachers; just over one-quarter were in favour and almost 40 per cent were against. The views of many respondents in secondary education were not based on actual experience, as fewer than one in five schools could be certain that they had been involved in the reintegration of young people on release from custody in the last three years. FE colleges appear to have far more experience in this respect; over three-quarters of FE colleges had been involved in the reintegration of young people on release from custody.

Respondents identified a list of the critical barriers to the reintegration of young people into mainstream education. The majority of secondary school educators perceived young people's attitudes to be the most significant barrier to re-integration. Although FE college principals perceived that young people's attitudes were a more significant problem than other factors, only 38 per cent identified it as a barrier to reintegration.

Higher numbers of teaching staff than head teachers or learning support staff recognised their lack of appropriate knowledge and skills in meeting the needs of these young people and their lack of time as difficulties for the young people. This echoed the findings that head teachers appeared to recognise the salience of educational factors in relation to offending behaviour, in contrast to the teachers whose focus was on other aspects of the young person's life, including the attitudes of parents.

Other significant barriers identified were a lack of suitable learning materials and a young person's previous experience of education. The availability of school or college places was perceived to be relatively much less significant. FE colleges also identified a lack of suitable support systems and funding.

As might be expected, while head teachers dealt with more policy-based issues, demonstrating knowledge of the potential links between education and crime, teaching staff showed concerns regarding the practicalities of reintegration. More specific issues for teachers and classroom assistants included concerns about the potential effect on peers, support in class, confidentiality and the safety of other pupils.

Yots and schools

In contrast to the views of education staff, particularly those in secondary education, there is apparently a pervasive belief among Yot managers and practitioners that there is either a lack of suitable provision or an unwillingness by schools, colleges and training providers to accept young people who have offended. The findings of a survey by the Audit Commission (2004) were supported by YJB (2006) research into the barriers to engagement in education, training and employment. The most important factor in their view affecting the engagement of young people both above and below school-leaving age in education and training was access to suitable provision (YJB 2006).

Education staff within Yots reinforced these concerns, fewer than one in five considering educational provision for young people who offend to be good or very good and almost half considering it to be poor or worse (YJB 2004c).

Other problems identified by YOT managers included:

- Financial – these was seen as particularly significant, as many of these young people may have no or limited family support, and this could be exacerbated by low financial rewards for participating in training, allied to the loss of benefits in commencing training or education.

- Exclusion – including the apparent ease of permanent exclusion. They also perceived an overuse of fixed-term exclusions and particular frustration with over 'informal' exclusions.

- Inflexible admissions – school and college admissions and the commencement of courses tend to be at set dates, whereas sentences and interventions designed to re-engage young people can occur at any point in the year (YJB 2006).

It is clear that links with Yots appear weak; only one in three head teachers knew the name of their Yot's education practitioner, as did fewer than one in ten teaching staff. The exchange of information appears limited, but there was an apparent widespread desire to improve the situation (Stephenson 2004).

Young people

There is a dearth of information on the attitudes of young people who have become detached from education and involved in the criminal justice system. This has come about for a variety of reasons. Understandably, public and professional opinion is not always concerned with the opinions of those who perpetrate antisocial or criminal behaviour. Relatively little attention has been paid to the views of children and young people in either education or youth justice arenas. Children and young people have traditionally not been perceived as the 'stakeholders' in education or youth justice, given the close association with issues of social control and the inculcation of moral values.

More work has been undertaken in this respect on behalf of children and young people in the care system, who often have difficulty gaining access to mainstream services and are limited in other ways in participating and progressing within them. Yet, these young people are disproportionately represented in the at-risk population, those who enter the youth justice system, and particularly those in custody. Part of the reason for this disparity of approach is the very different emotions aroused by the labels of care and crime in both professionals and the public. These attitudes, which may be more rooted in prejudice and stereotypes than professionals and policymakers care to admit, have an unfortunate influence on social policy.

In the first instance, the focus tends to be on individuals, not on their circumstances regarding their schooling. Rather than identifying weaknesses in education and support services, the prevailing assumption is that both the low attainment and the perceived weak attachment to education of these young people means they are not suited to academic work and to the alleged chalk-and-talk approach that this necessitates in mainstream schools. Both those who would take a more punitive approach instinctively and many of those who tend towards a treatment model of intervention tend to unite in the belief that these young people simply cannot fit into mainstream schools.

In addition to reinforcing the view that this is about the pathology of the young person, the indiscriminate use of the elastic term 'disaffection' conceals the enormous variation between individuals and also obscures the complexity and ambivalence of attitudes towards schooling held by young people.

Even if it were helpful to use such terminology, the following important questions would remain:

- Who or what is doing the disaffecting as far as the young people are concerned?
- Are some young people disaffected from the whole notion of learning?
- Are some young people disaffected from particular aspects of their school experience?
- Are the attitudes of educators and others towards the education of young people who offend significantly different from that of the general population?

Systematic analysis of the perceptions of their educational experiences by young people in the criminal justice system, particularly those who have entered custody and who have become detached from education and suffer from low attainment, could help in understanding how educational risk factors are translated into delinquency.

There is hardly any evidence from the perspective of the young people who have failed educationally on their experience of mainstream, or segregated education. Very little is known of their perception of what went wrong with their education and their aspirations with regard to learning. The main surveys tend to miss them, and research studies struggle with high rates of attrition. There have been a few small-scale qualitative studies, from which it is not possible to generalise (Kinder *et al.* 1996; Cullingford 1999). Care must be used in the very negative responses of some young people looking back on their failed school careers when they have become involved in criminality. As the large-scale Keele University study underlines, significant proportions of teenagers who are surviving in mainstream school also express negative feelings such as rejection, disappointment and anger at their experience of education (Barber 1997).

Cullingford (1999) emphasises the informal aspects of school, the 'hidden curriculum' where what happens outside the classroom is at least as important as what happens within it. Analysing what occurs within schools from the perspective of young people can often provide a mirror image. From a professional standpoint, immersion of young people in the formal curriculum may be punctuated by the necessity of breaks, lunchtimes and the ferrying of large groups of young people around school sites, but from young person's perspective, it is the complex interaction of relationships with both adults and peers that can dominate their time. To many young people, schools are primarily social centres and occasionally centres of violence (Cullingford 1999).

From a labour market analysis perspective, concerns have been expressed that a minority of young people undergo a progressive disenchantment with and consequent disengagement from secondary school. This is further reflected in a failure to enter and remain in post-16 education (National Commission on Education 1993).

Croll and Moses (2003) used data from the British Household Panel Survey to examine various aspects of young people's attitudes to secondary school and the outcomes in terms of qualifications at 16 and remaining in post-16 education. As with most mainstream surveys, it is likely that young people already completely detached from schools or from birth families may be under-represented. Nevertheless, it is very interesting in that it sets the educational trajectories followed by young people in the context of their attitudes towards school.

Their key finding is that 'young people overwhelmingly believe that doing well at school is important to them'. What is clear is that the results do not support the concern that a substantial minority of young people lack interest in education and demonstrate hostility to school, or support a very negative picture of young people's experiences of secondary education (Cullingford 2002). While they may not have identified progressive disenchantment, they did find that strongly positive views towards teachers decreased with age and 'for a minority of young people some strongly negative attitudes [towards teachers] have developed' (Croll and Moses 2003: 9).The weakening commitment to school as young people progressed through secondary school was also observed in the On Track Lifestyle Survey (Armstrong et al. 2005). Given that complete detachment appears to be strongly age-related, young people with the most negative feelings towards teachers may not have participated in the survey.

The results of the survey also showed a very strong relationship between parents' educational achievements and those of their children. The survey, however, omitted non-resident parents, who are much more common for those young people in the youth justice system and those who are detached from education. Early intention to stay in post-compulsory education was found to be strongly related to actual behaviour five years later.

While this study focused mainly on attitudes towards teachers, its emphasis on the social transmission of decisions about staying on being decided early and on the influence of the educational status of parents could give important clues regarding educational attainment and detachment for young people who offend. For these young people, the chances of periods of institutional care are much higher, and that may diminish positive influences towards education. The fact that decisions have been made so early also points to links with low learner self-esteem, particularly among those who were relatively low attainers at primary school.

A series of reports commissioned by the YJB used a similar methodology in getting young people in custody to rate different aspects of their experience of schooling (ECOTEC 2001; YJB 2002c, 2005b; ACE 2005). Combining these data provides some insight into young people's perception of mainstream school, segregated educational placements and custodial education, as shown by a total sample of 500 young people. The main aspects that young people rated were teachers, lessons, individual support (for reading, writing, mathematics and ICT), other students, and overall score. These ratings were provided for their last mainstream school, their last educational placement before entering custody, and their custodial education. They also assessed their own performance relative to their peers in reading, writing, mathematics and ICT.

What emerges is an interesting and complex picture of their ties to schooling. Nearly 40 per cent of young people rated their overall experience of mainstream school as very good or excellent, which seems relatively high given that this is probably the most estranged group of young people in our society. However, the distribution of their scores indicates a significant minority for whom school was an unrewarding experience. But this overall rating is certainly not indicative of wholesale 'disaffection' with mainstream schooling.

Lessons – the balance of subjects, their content and other aspects – did not draw out significant feelings in terms of either very low or very high scoring. There was little evidence of widespread feelings that subjects taught were not regarded as relevant. Responses in interviews generally indicated a high level of awareness of the connection between qualifications and employment.

With regard to teachers, there was clearly a group of young people who had had difficult relationships with some teachers, as nearly a quarter of the sample rated them as 'poor'. This does not seem to have been such an issue for the majority (57 per cent), who rated their teachers in mainstream school as 'good', 'very good' or 'excellent'. The evidence from the review of young people's views appears consistent with the Ofsted finding that the majority of exclusions within a school are associated with the interactions of students with a relatively small proportion of teachers (Ofsted 1996). In explaining their absence from school, poor relationships with teachers was the second most cited reason by young people (Kinder *et al.* 1996). American studies of detachment have found a consistent correlation between beliefs about teachers and early departures (Croninger and Lee 2001).

Not unexpectedly, the most positive aspect of mainstream school for these young people was their relationship with other students. Over a third rated this aspect as 'very good' or 'excellent'. In contrast, the area that received the most negative ratings was that of individual support for learning. Nearly a quarter of the sample rated this as 'poor'. Many young people expressed themselves very strongly on this issue. Support for literacy was seen to be the most deficient area, compared with support for numeracy and ICT.

Even where young people rated some aspects of their mainstream schooling very highly, it had clearly been an extremely painful experience because of their learning failures and consequent feelings of humiliation. As so many had such severe literacy and numeracy deficits, it is hardly surprising that mainstream schooling was so difficult for them:

'No one knew about me, I kept myself to myself.'
'I didn't want to feel as thick as I am.'
'You wouldn't catch me reading for nothing' (ECOTEC 2001: 41).

These findings are at odds with the views of many of the Yot staff completing ASSET, who tend to ascribe a low level of attachment to school or education (Baker *et al.* 2002). Part of the reason for this anomaly may be that Yot staff may be basing their judgements partly on the reality of detachment in terms of the young people's attendance. It may also reflect the Yot staff's lack of understanding and confidence in relation to educational issues. The negative framing of many of the questions of the ASSET form in this area (understandable in that the approach focuses on risk) may well also distort responses.

Even here there were mixed feelings, as the ASSET forms tend to show that Yot staff felt that a majority of young people had positive attitudes towards FE or training (or rather that they did not have negative attitudes). A much larger proportion of ASSET forms indicated a lack of negative attitudes among these young people towards employment.

According to these ASSET returns, a significant majority of parents/carers did not have negative attitudes towards the education and schooling of their children. This argues against the stereotypical view of disaffected young people, whose parents are also seen as unsupportive on educational matters.

Segregated education

Young people's attitudes towards the various educational and training placements that they had experienced outside mainstream education, such as PRUs or home tuition, were very varied, since they had experienced a diversity of provision. The sample is also significantly reduced in size compared with those giving their views of mainstream and custodial education. Virtually all of the sample had experience of both of those, while a significant number of young people had no provision at all and so could not score on alternative provision.

The most interesting finding regarding young people's experiences of alternative educational placements was that they scored very highly in relation to individual support. This aspect contrasted strongly with both mainstream educational experiences and to a lesser extent with custodial educational experiences. This finding is not necessarily a function of teacher–student ratios, as class sizes in custody can often be under ten young people, although some alternative educational placements, such as home tuition, are highly individualised.

Attitudes to education in custody

Young people's overall attitude towards their experience of education or training in custody was broadly similar to that of mainstream school, 45 per cent assessing the provision as very good or excellent. Perhaps understandably, a less favourable view was taken of other students – only a third rated them as very good or excellent. Individual support was rated more highly than for mainstream school, which again is understandably given class sizes that tend to be about 1–8 students. But significant levels of dissatisfaction were also recorded, almost one in five being very dissatisfied with their individual support. Teaching staff tended to be viewed very positively; almost half of the young people assessed their teachers as very good or excellent.

It may be that the favourable ratings for aspects of custodial education were influenced by the context, in that education may be viewed as the most positive and constructive activity undertaken within the overall regime. Nevertheless, in conjunction with these positive ratings, the young people tended to be very critical of the teaching staff and the learning environment, particularly in relation to disruption of classes and not being able to attend as a result of staff shortages of both teachers and prison officers. Clearly, their opinions were discriminating and varied according to other experiences of the difficult dimensions of their educational provision.

One of the studies incorporated a scale to measure the attitude to learning of young people, and nearly two-thirds of those (64 per cent) on DTOs scored themselves 'highly' or 'very highly' (YJB 2005b). In contrast, those on ISSP in the community scored themselves significantly lower in terms of their attitude to learning only a quarter scoring themselves 'highly' or 'very highly'. The attitude to learning was strongly statistically associated with the levels of support that young people felt they received within mainstream schools.

When the scores for different aspects of the mainstream school experience are compared, an interesting picture emerges. Clearly, a significant minority of these young people were very dissatisfied with aspects of their mainstream school, particularly the amount of individual support they received and their view of certain teachers. However, it was comparatively rare for these young people who registered dissatisfaction with these particular areas to extend this to all aspects of their educational experience. For example, nearly half (46 per cent) of the young people who rated support as being low rated their perception of other students as high. Similarly, their rating of teachers did not necessarily depress their views of other students. A similar, although lesser, effect was seen in regard to the rating for lessons, over half of young people who felt that support was low nevertheless giving a medium rating to lessons. In fact, one in five young people who felt that support was low rated lessons highly. Less than a quarter of young people (23 per cent) rated both lessons and other students as low.

An analysis of these aggregated studies reveals some consistent patterns and trends over the aspects of education scored by these young people. The patterns are consistent across mainstream education, segregated education and custodial education. Despite the chaotic and challenging educational careers these young people have experienced, the evidence does not support a simplistic notion of disaffection. Rather, there appears to be an array of positive and negative attitudes held simultaneously about the different environments in which they have experienced education. Some studies in America have detected positive and optimistic attitudes about future participation and achievement in education among young people who have offended and become disengaged from mainstream education (Coffey and Gemignani 1994).

The perception of whether or not they received sufficient individual support in relation to literacy and numeracy does, however, appear to be influential in their overall feelings towards education.

Conclusions

Even this brief survey of opinions and attitudes reveals a complex picture. Public opinion contains potentially contradictory stances and the punish:rehabilitate dichotomy probably oversimplifies the situation. While there is clearly a strong punitive undercurrent – juvenile crime is getting worse, courts are becoming more and too lenient – at the same time many believed that young people should be treated differently from adults, and that rehabilitation was more important than punishment. Schooling was given the highest priority in preventing offending within the criminal justice system. The reasons for delinquency tended to be attributed to negative individual choices and poor parenting, but education was given considerable weight in preventing reoffending. Education appeared to bridge punitive and rehabilitative opinions, attracting strong support for it to be compulsory in the community as an alternative to custodial sentences.

Magistrates echoed the views of the general public regarding the perceived causes of crime but differed markedly about the appropriateness of custody and placed much more emphasis on education. Most magistrates reported that they received little information on the educational antecedents of young people before sentence, knew little of the education and training options in the community or of the educational facilities in custody, and felt particularly ill-informed about post-sentence educational progress. There was considerable criticism of exclusions from school and delay by LEAs in arranging placements. However, increased information for magistrates could have unintended effects. Currently, some magistrates may be making custodial disposals in the possibly mistaken belief that this will ensure access to an appropriate education. Conversely, there is evidence that information from schools to magistrates can move young people up the sentencing tariff and increase the use of custody.

There was a considerable disparity in views between the different groups of educators. Senior managers in both schools and FE colleges tended to express less punitive attitudes than the general public, but these were not always shared by teachers and teaching assistants. School staff did not appear to have extensive knowledge of the youth justice system, and links with Yots were not well developed. A significant minority of teachers were against the admission into mainstream schools of young people who were leaving custody. More emphasis was placed on the behaviour of individual young people as a barrier to their re-entry to mainstream school than on any scarcity of places. FE college principals and vice principals, in contrast, appeared much more experienced in accepting young people leaving custody, and most believed FE to be a suitable place for them.

In contrast, there was evidence that lack of access to suitable education and training provision was seen as one of the major challenges for Yot staff. From their perspective, links often appeared to be weak with schools, LEAs and local Learning and Skills Councils (LSCs). There seems to be a cultural and structural mismatch between the youth justice and education systems; cultural in that educators often perceive the problems to centre on the behaviour of the individual while Yots see access as the key issue, and structural in that, for example, sentences and course admissions are not synchronised.

The views of young people on schools and other educational institutions they had attended appear to be a web of both formal and informal relationships, the strands of which can be of very different strengths such as strong friendships but hostility towards some teachers. Many young people distinguished between the quality of the different aspects both positive and negative that educational institutions offered them. The beliefs and perceptions of the role of formal learning for young people who offend held by the general public, magistrates and different groups of educators defy easy categorisation yet are potentially powerful in shaping the cultures and structures of education and youth justice.

Summary

❏ Public opinion is complex regarding the education of young people who offend, but the majority of the public believe that they should be treated differently from adults with a much greater emphasis on education.

❏ The education and training status of young people brought before the courts was seen by magistrates as potentially significant in informing sentencing practice, but there was a dearth of information available to them both pre- and post-sentence.

❏ Multiagency working appears relatively underdeveloped with limited links between schools and Yots, although many schools would apparently welcome much more joint working.

❏ FE appears to be much more experienced as a sector, over three-quarters of colleges having been involved in the reintegration of young people from custody, compared with only one in five secondary schools.

❏ Head teachers and senior managers in FE appeared to be much more positive towards a community-based approach than did many teaching staff, who appeared more resistant to the inclusion of young people who offend in mainstream education.

❏ The great majority of youth justice managers and practitioners view access to, and participation and progression in, education and training as both a priority and one of their main challenges.

❏ 'Disaffection' is an ill-defined and probably inaccurate term to describe the complex nature of young people's relationship with their school. Many young people who have become completely detached from mainstream secondary schooling still retain positive attitudes about certain aspects of their experience.

❏ The quality of individual support in relation to literacy and numeracy appears to be influential in affecting attitudes towards other aspects of school.

Chapter 9

What works in youth justice and education

Great store has been set by central government in reforming public services through a 'what works?' approach. The YJB has enthusiastically endorsed this by developing an effective practice strategy for Yots and custody underpinned by a comprehensive human resources and learning strategy. This chapter assesses how far this approach is justified in the context of education and examines the effectiveness of the various educational programmes.

Effectiveness is usually defined as the degree to which intended outcomes are achieved. Understandably, most educators would deem an educational programme or intervention to be effective if it achieved the requisite educational goals irrespective of any later delinquency committed by the participants. Judging effectiveness in this context, then, has to have a dual focus. The evidence is reviewed particularly with regard to interventions in the two key areas of risk: detachment from mainstream school and attainment particularly in segregated education. The potential for effective interventions through schools and custodial institutions is also explored. Immediate difficulties arise in such discussions; if, for example, custody intrinsically tends to increase risks, then, how far can its effectiveness be judged for preventing reoffending? Given that a majority of young people in the youth justice system appear to receive their education, if any at all, in segregated institutions, what is the evidence for their effectiveness? It is also interesting to examine the retention of approaches that have been found to be ineffective and the possible underlying reasons for this.

The expression 'what works?' is derived from the title of an article (1974) by Martinson, which concluded, on the basis of a survey of research evidence, that there was 'no clear pattern to indicate the efficacy of any particular method of treatment' (Martinson 1974: 49). This included various educational programmes in custodial settings.

The 'nothing works' era in youth justice was paralleled in education, in American studies at least, as variations in outcomes between schools were ascribed primarily to differences in student backgrounds – 'schools don't make a difference' (Gray *et al.* 1983: 274). The family was seen as determining the different educational outcomes according to social class and ethnic background. These pessimistic findings were also used to justify approaches in youth justice that became known as 'radical non-intervention'. Similarly, some educators espoused the notion of spontaneous remission, whereby most young people grew out of their difficult behaviour or delinquency (Topping 1983).

The conclusion that changing school policies and practices would make little difference led to more sophisticated research, which, as in youth justice, identified some differences in effects between schools. Similarly, from the mid-1980s onwards, a consensus has developed among researchers that some approaches to working with young people do seem to help prevent offending and reoffending. This was derived by using meta-analysis to review a large number of research programmes, which, in combination, confirmed a positive overall effect. Clear trends have been detected concerning the ingredients of programmes with higher or lower levels of effectiveness in reducing offending. 'What works?' is used to refer to that body of research knowledge and the principles deriving from it.

The emergence of evidence-based practice in the development of health care and policy has been hailed as one of the success stories of the 1990s (Trinder 2000). This approach rapidly developed into an international movement. Evidence-based practice has spread across most areas of health care such as mental health, dentistry, nursing and physiotherapy. Other disciplines and professions to varying degrees have adopted this organisational framework. In criminal justice, it has converged with the 'what works?' movement.

Like all such movements, evidence-based practice is a product of its time. It is derived partly from wider social influences, developments in public services, changing notions of professionalism and practitioner concerns with their effectiveness. Much of the attraction of an evidence-based approach to practice lies in the fact that it is an ostensibly neat and coherent approach to the messy and ill-defined complexities of practice. Politically, it is the epitome of managerialism and purports to be value-free as the application of proven methods to treat the particular social ill. After all, who could possibly argue in favour of what does not work? Perhaps, too, the language of 'dosage' and 'treatment' has been borrowed so readily from medicine because it conveniently supports the idea of offending as a symptom of individual pathology.

According to the YJB, the definition and application of effective practice are rooted in the wider concept of evidence-based practice. The term 'effective practice', as used currently in youth justice, is not a synonym for evidence-based practice but rather for those programmes, processes or ways of working that have the highest level of validation from research and evaluation. Evidence-based practice refers to the wider, cross-disciplinary approach to delivering those products and services that has been validated according to the accepted criteria. Effective practice, then, in this context, comprises those interventions that are most likely to result in the prevention of offending and reoffending.

Evidence-based practice in education

The value of evidence-based practice within education, in contrast to criminal justice, is more hotly debated. Some educators have been zealous in their promotion of evidence-based practice:

> The most important reason for the extraordinary advances in medicine, agriculture, and other fields is the acceptance by practitioners of evidence as the basis for practice. In particular, it is the randomised clinical trial – more than any single medical breakthrough – that has transformed medicine (Slavin cited in Thomas and Pring 2004: 10).

Others contest what should count as evidence and debate the extent to which the scientific rigour that may be applicable in medicine is equally applicable to educational policy and practice (Pring 2004). Equally, it would be a distortion to claim that evidence-based practice is accepted by all in youth justice but rejected in education. The claim by the YJB that 'A considerable body of research has been identified demonstrating clearly that a firmly evidence-based approach to the prevention of youth crime is both a realistic proposition and a strategy that can be confidently expected to be successful' (YJB 2001: 121) has its critics (Bateman and Pitts 2005). Similarly, the assertion by a leading educator that 'there are few areas which have yielded a corpus of research evidence regarded as scientifically sound and as a worthwhile resource to guide professional action (in education)' (Hargreaves 1996: 2) has been strongly contested (Thomas and Pring 2004).

Now, while the 'what works?' movement has swept all before it in fields such as medicine, agricultural science and, to a lesser extent, criminal justice work with adults, it has been argued that it has significant limitations when applied to education. The gold standard within the 'what works?' movement for evaluation is the straightforward methodological approach known as the randomised, controlled trial (RCT). It has been argued that this approach is much more effective where singular treatments are applied to a well-defined set of subjects with specific outcome targets. This could be deemed simplistic when applied to the complexity of educational research. In the context of evaluating the education of prisoners, Pawson (2000: 66) emphasised a series of complexities that undermines an RCT approach:

(a) education is not a 'treatment' applied in dosages but a multi-faceted and prolonged social encounter involving a range of ideas, curricula, and personnel

(b) the 'subjects', namely inmates, are hardly uniform and whilst they do not represent an exact cross-section of society, they do present a mighty range of social backgrounds, a positive jumble of prior educational experience and, indeed, an unfortunate array of offences

(c) the rehabilitative 'outcome' of prisoner education is rarely perceived in simple, therapeutic terms but is considered to work *indirectly* via building character, raising self-confidence, acquiring competence, gaining credentials, promoting self-reflection, creating moral standards, improving social skills, enlarging cultural aspirations and so on.

While Pawson dismisses such an approach to answering the question, 'Does prisoner education work?' as a 'dangerous over-simplification', he does not abandon attempts to answer it.

'What works?' is a seductively simple approach to both policymaking and practice. Its appeal lies in its promise to cut through value-laden arguments, to bind different professionals and agencies together and provide the treatment. While it has been argued that this is a simplistic approach, neither is it as apolitical as it purports to be. In view of the multifaceted nature of education acting on individuals in such chaotic circumstances, it is arguably much more sensible to ask 'why' the education of young people who offend might work, and go on to enquire 'for whom', and 'in what circumstances' and 'in what respects' it appears to work (Pawson 2000). Increasingly, there are challenges to some of the assumptions underlying the 'What works?' approach in youth justice (Smith 2006). It has to be seriously questioned whether the RCT is actually practicable in the youth justice field, at least at present. There are ethical problems in denying potentially helpful interventions, no guarantee that random selection will produce comparable groups, imperfect data-gathering and transmission systems, and, perhaps most importantly, strong vested interests. Few managers would go to all the extra work involved in exposing their existing interventions as ineffective when used as a comparison group. Despite the problems of this approach, the Home Office reaction has been to call for greater methodological rigour in its pursuit of policy certainties (Chitty and Harper 2005). One basic problem is that the implementation of new initiatives and interventions rarely follows the precepts of policymakers, and this tends to invalidate the research design. This, in turn, can lead to potentially erroneous inferences by policymakers. The enormous attrition involved in the Basic Skills Pathfinders programme, for example, meant that the original research intention to judge the impact of improvements in basic skills on offending could not be measured, and this has led some civil servants to query whether there is any effect rather than challenge the model of implementation used (McMahon *et al.* 2004). Equally, where criminal justice is concerned, it must always be borne in mind what it is the public, politicians and professionals actually want to work. Just as custody has a powerful intuitive attraction despite evidence that, in some important respects, it does not work, so if incontrovertible evidence was discovered that safari holidays for young people who had offended reduced the likelihood of their reoffending significantly, it is highly unlikely that they would be adopted as a national initiative. In fact, it may well be that it is the persistence of approaches and practices that appear not to work that poses a greater challenge.

Detachment and attainment

Detachment from mainstream education and attainment were discussed in detail in Chapters 4 and 5 as potential risk factors. But what is the evidence for effective interventions that prevent or reverse detachment or low attainment? Not surprisingly, the immediate answer is that much of it applies to pre-school or primary age children and is often of American origin.

In his meta-analysis of nearly 400 studies that used control or comparison groups representing over 40,000 young people aged 12–21, Lipsey (1995) detected an average overall net 10 per cent reduction in reoffending. This modest but significant effect varied significantly according to the type and amount of intervention. Both school participation and academic performance were also seen to improve on average as a result of interventions. The average effect on school participation was a 12 per cent improvement across the 93 studies reviewed. Academic performance improved by 14 per cent on average across the 42 studies reviewed. School participation outcomes were significantly and relatively highly correlated with delinquency outcomes compared with any other outcome category.

Turning from this large-scale (and mainly American) work to more detailed UK-based studies is largely unrewarding. A recent Home Office report that examined the findings from four studies on education and offending highlighted this problem, as they 'showed the difficulties of providing robust, "evidence-based" findings to inform national policy and practice' (Home Office 2004: 19). The short duration of the programmes combined with other complexities meant that there was little insight gained into issues of causality and attribution, and other potential influencing factors could not be screened out.

Those interventions that have had the most rigorous evaluations in the UK include pre-school education, family literacy schemes, reading schemes (for primary age children), and reasoning and social skills education. These often appear to protect against both detachment and low attainment. Other interventions which satisfy rigorous evaluation requirements but were outside the UK include after-school clubs, mentoring and youth employment with education.

When it comes to research into the effectiveness of UK interventions designed to help lower-achieving children and young people catch up, there is a significant gap for those aged 12–18. For children at primary school, there is a certain number of high-quality evaluations that have been reviewed (Brooks 2002). In the absence of specific interventions, ordinary teaching did not enable children with literacy difficulties to catch up. Brooks (2002) concluded that it was reasonable to expect a doubling of the rate of progress with specific interventions, and that these gains were maintained in most of the schemes where progress was followed up.

A systematic review of literacy and numeracy interventions for adults 'found just enough evidence (all of it from the USA) to demonstrate rigorously in a meta-analysis that receiving adult literacy and numeracy tuition does produce more progress than not receiving it' (Torgerson *et al.* 2004: 13). One reading programme accompanied by a 'community-building group process' for adults in a US prison achieved positive results.

An interesting and challenging area of overlap between the findings of literacy interventions and youth justice interventions is that of 'dosage'. While learners usually need to attend at least 100 hours of instruction to make progress equivalent to one grade level (Torgerson *et al.* 2004), a high dosage in youth justice for any intervention is also deemed to be more than 100 hours (Lipsey 1995).

173

Involvement of parents

Involving parents or carers in their children's education has been found to be a significant factor in strengthening attachment to school and to learning in general (Bynner 2001). This has been demonstrated through evaluation of family literacy projects and usually involves younger children rather than teenagers.

A recent review of the research established a clear and consistent finding that spontaneous parental involvement in education has a large, positive and independent effect on the outcomes of schooling (Desforges and Abouchaar 2003). The research base where planned parental intervention is concerned is flimsy, with findings restricted to participant satisfaction rather than increases in attainment. As with so much of the 'What works?' evidence, there is a significant gap in understanding how to make it work (Desforges and Abouchaar 2003).

Pre-school education

Typically, most initiatives that have been relatively rigorously evaluated tend to be from the USA. The best known of these is perhaps the High/Scope Perry project, which followed up the children involved to the age of 27. This programme was characterised by a focus on a group of families beset with high-risk factors, with a relatively high dosage and substantial length (special classes for two and a half hours daily over 30 weeks supplemented by a weekly home visit from a teacher). Considerable attention was paid to enhancing the academic performance of the children through emphasising active learning, problem solving and concentration on task. Home–school links were emphasised. Teaching staff received specific training and dealt with small groups of children. A number of positive outcomes were found, including a large reduction in the number of lifetime arrests, lower teenage pregnancy rates and large increases in graduation rates. This programme was, however, classified as promising rather than effective (Mihalic *et al.* 2001).

School improvement

The emphasis on school effectiveness in recent years has generated some relevant evidence. Many interventions that have been evaluated have not had the reduction of crime as their main aim, although these interventions may directly or indirectly have reduced risk factors associated with offending (Home Office 2004). A constant theme that runs very strongly, particularly through school organisation work, is that, although there may be a strong indication of 'what works?', there is a real gap in knowing 'how to make it work'.

Research findings on what makes an effective school consistently emphasise the importance of leadership, systematic approaches to monitoring attendance and progress, high expectations of young people in relation to both their learning and behaviour, a balanced use of rewards and incentives, high parental involvement, opportunities for young people to exercise responsibility within the school, and a positive ethos within the school (Rutter *et al.* 1998; Home Office 2004). This is in contrast to ineffective schools, which 'tend to categorise pupils who behave poorly or persistently truant as deviants, and shift responsibility for their behaviour and welfare to other agencies or institutions' (Home Office 2004: 19).

One example of an American school-based prevention programme that focused across the school on key organisational issues and has had a relatively rigorous evaluation is the Program Development Evaluation method, which is a multimodal organisational intervention implemented by school improvement teams comprising parents, teachers and school officials. This was found to be an effective method of improving classroom management and school discipline, leading to significant decreases in disruption in classrooms (Howell 2003).

Being able to describe what works in a successful school is, however, some way from being able to prescribe how to achieve this with all schools. Changing the culture within any institution remains one of the stiffest management challenges, even if systematic evaluations had made clear exactly how this can be achieved – and they have not. The matter is not simply one of the discrete reorganisation of a given school, as, particularly where young people at high risk are concerned, there are all the variable relationships with the other agencies and their professionals to be considered as well as the resources available to the community.

School-wide programmes

Three American programmes for primary age children that offer a school-based, multimodal approach have been evaluated and deemed to be effective or at least to be a promising approach. They are Fast Track, the Seattle Social Development Project, and the Child Development Project.

The Fast Track programme targets children in their early years of schooling that are from low-income, high-crime communities and are displaying particular behavioural problems at home and school. The programme has six integrated components which match six domains of intervention.

The evaluation of the programme involved the random assignment of schools to treatment and control groups. Recipients of the programme displayed decreases in aggression and disruptive behaviour both at school and at home. In addition, their relationships with peers improved, as did a range of social skills.

The Crime Reduction Initiative in Secondary Schools (CRISS) programme in the UK comprised a series of school-focused development projects from which it was hoped to identify measures to reduce actual and potential offending by young people. There is a marked contrast in the nature of this initiative with some of the American examples. The CRISS programme was relatively short-term (two years) and contained a very wide range of rather disparate initiatives (38 projects involving over 100 schools, each school implementing between five and ten separate interventions), and there was a much less rigorous evaluation methodology with considerable emphasis on qualitative research. Not surprisingly, although a central objective of this programme was the collection of robust evidence, the best that could be achieved was recommendations for promising approaches (Home Office 2004).

Bullying in school has been linked to an increased risk of offending. A Norwegian programme designed to reduce bullying in schools through establishing behavioural boundaries with the consistent application of sanctions for rule breaking and fostering cooperative working with teachers and parents reduced the incidence of bullying, and there were indirect effects such as a reduction in absenteeism, vandalism and theft (Olweus 1993). This programme was also reported to have been implemented successfully in England (YJB 2001). However, both these evaluations have been criticised as not being particularly rigorous, and replication in the USA was reported to be unsuccessful (Howell 2003). Antibullying programmes operated in Sheffield across 23 primary and secondary schools. In line with evaluations of most school-based interventions, greater effect was found in the reduction of bullying in primary schools with relatively small effects in secondary schools (Home Office 2004).

Individually targeted interventions

These tend to focus on the reduction of anger, disruptive and violent behaviour by particular individuals. The Social Competence Promotion Program for Young Adolescents in America is a violence-prevention approach that promotes a range of social competencies such as decision-making, social problem-solving, self-control, stress management and communication skills. An evaluation found that the participants were more engaged with school and less likely to be involved in absenteeism, suspensions and minor delinquent behaviour than controls (Weissberg and Caplan 1998).

Basing probation officers in schools has a long history in certain parts of America. This has become a popular approach operating in both a preventative way and intervening directly in delinquent behaviour. In addition to carrying out probation supervision, probation staff in some instances train teachers and deliver law-related education classes. Studies indicate that attainment and attendance may be increased, and antisocial behaviour in the school and also of those on probation is improved (Griffin 1999).

The Safer Schools Partnership (SSP) programme aims to promote the safety of schools and the young people attending them. These programmes vary considerably in structure but generally have active police involvement in schools, often in collaboration with other support staff. The objectives are to improve key behavioural issues in such schools, including non-attendance, bullying, antisocial behaviour and offending. The evaluation of the programme (YJB 2005e) was later supplemented by an extension of the study to over 1,000 schools (Bowles *et al.* 2006). They researchers found a significant reduction in rates of absence (both authorised and unauthorised) in the SSP schools relative to those experienced in the comparison schools. GCSE performance also improved relative to the comparison schools. Difficulties with the data prevented much examination of changes in levels of bullying and antisocial behaviour in schools. Similarly, the data were inadequate to support school-level analysis of convictions or arrest, making it impossible to present any robust findings of the impact of this approach on offending.

Gottfredson's comprehensive review of the evidence for effective school interventions concluded that:

> considerable evidence of positive effects for prevention programmes can be found in the available research, but that implementation, quality and quantity qualify the positive findings. Schools can be a site for effective intervention, or a site for non-intervention or ineffective intervention. Schools have the potential to contribute to the positive socialization of youth. But the range of conditions under which they have been demonstrated to realize this potential is narrow. (Gottfredson 2001: 258).

Further education (FE) colleges

There are a number of promising practice indicators for FE colleges planning to work with young people at risk (Utting 1999), and these include:

- collaborative bridging/access programmes developed with local schools, education authorities and Learning and Skills Councils (LSCs) to create education and training opportunities;

- a student-centred approach with the emphasis on learning as opposed to assessment – sufficiently flexible curriculum and teaching methods to take account of individual student needs;

- occupational guidance and work experience as an integral part of each course;

- effective support for learning being made available, such as one-to-one tutoring and pastoral support;

- students following a curriculum that is not only relevant to their current and future needs, but also shows them how they are progressing;

- other support services such as help with transport or childcare being made available;

- joint training for school and college staff on working with young people at risk.

Employment

As being unemployed seems to be an independent risk factor, schemes that increase employment or at least employability might seem likely to be effective, but again the evidence is sparse and largely confined to adults. For young people who have completed compulsory schooling but have no or few qualifications and will thus struggle to enter the labour markets, gaining post-school qualifications can have a significant impact. One study found that young people with few or no school qualifications who went on to gain Level 2 qualifications saw a dramatic effect on their employment prospects. By the time they had acquired Level 3 qualifications, they were on a par in terms of finding employment with young people who went on to achieve A levels via the academic route (McIntosh 2003).

Previous studies of the efficacy of employment interventions with adults who offend have shown promising results, although these may not always be applicable to young people. Bridges' study in 1998 found that adults who were unemployed at the beginning of their probation supervision, but who had an employment intervention while on supervision, found employment before the end of their community sentences at twice the rate of those who had no intervention. Reconviction studies suggest that employment interventions can potentially reduce reoffending rates (May 1999; Sarno *et al.* 2000). It is not simply having a job that is associated with reductions in offending but the quality and stability of that employment coupled with levels of satisfaction (Harper and Chitty 2005).

The research challenges are highlighted by the Basic Skills Pathfinder evaluation, which sought to measure the progress of adults on basic skills programmes in terms of their basic skills improvements and increased employability, but high attrition rates made this impossible (McMahon *et al.* 2004).

Effectiveness of custodial education

Asking the bald question, 'what works?', of custodial education for young people is simplistic and arguably counter-intuitive, given that the evidence suggests that, for perhaps the majority of young people, custody increases educational risk factors and may reduce protective factors. The best that can be done is to try to assess whether educational programmes within custody have a positive effect within that experience and whether certain approaches can be more effective than others after release.

A number of research studies have been undertaken to measure the effectiveness of custodial educational intervention programmes. However, these are bedevilled by relatively weak research design and are usually focused on adults.

Tolbert (2002: 19) identifies the following as being major limitations of studies investigating the relationship between educational intervention and recidivism:

- Most do not take into account other services and factors inside and outside prison that may affect recidivism rates, such as drug treatment programs, post-release services, and family support.
- Most of the results are vulnerable to self-selection bias; the methodologies do not adequately account for participant characteristics.

- Most do not follow released inmates for a long enough period of time.

- Most vary in their definitions of recidivism – a nationally [U.S.] recognised definition of recidivism does not exist.

- Most are unable to measure various levels of improvement in inmates' behaviours.

- Most are based on correctional educational records that are often poorly kept by institutions.

A few studies, however, do provide some evidence of a positive link between educational intervention and reduction in recidivism, and provide insights into the characteristics of programmes that do seem to be effective, although the studies are North American and deal with adults.

From three studies that employed a random or matched comparison group design, Porporino and Robinson (1992) concluded that the recidivism rate of participants in the Canadian Adult Basic Education programme was significantly lower than that of the comparison group. Other positive results were achieved in studies in the USA. One longitudinal study involving 3,400 imprisoned adults found that participation in educational programmes reduced the chances of reimprisonment by 29 per cent (Steurer *et al.* 2001). Similarly, there was a reduction in recidivism of a third among adult prisoners who participated in vocational and apprenticeship training as part of the Post-Release Employment Project (Saylor and Gaes 1997).

According to Tolbert (2002: 1–2), 'These programs lead to lower recidivism rates, according to advocates, because they provide inmates with the knowledge, skills, attitudes, and values needed to succeed in society and to avoid future criminal activity'.

Considerable caution should be exercised in extending these more positive findings to younger groups in the UK, as they may not be applicable. Not only are they from different countries but also the sentence length for adults is much greater, and the effects of maturation, stable learning groups and greater dosage of education could be considerable.

Resettlement

'Resettlement' is the relatively new term used for processes that have historically been referred to as 'aftercare' (also used widely in the USA although lately superseded by 're-entry') and 'throughcare', terms current until the late 1990s. 'Throughcare' clearly refers to a single rehabilitative process that starts with sentence planning and continues into the community, the 'seamless approach' as envisaged in the Criminal Justice Act 1991 (Raynor 2004).

One of the difficulties in defining what is effective in relation to resettlement is that there is little in the way of specific programme evaluation. What little research exists has either focused solely on custodial interventions, or been based on outcomes for adults rather than juveniles or is methodologically flawed (Altschuler and Armstrong 2002; Howell 2003).

Research that only focuses on custodial interventions often overemphasises the positive change in young people's attitudes within an institutional context even when there is minimal hard evidence of effectiveness in terms of promoting community reintegration and reducing recidivism (Hobbs and Hook 2001).

For example, recent interim evaluation of the Intensive Aftercare Program in the USA has shown less than promising results in relation to recidivism, although the significance of this finding is called into question because the three sites evaluated had small sample sizes and the control group in one of the sites received some aspects of the intervention that should have been received only by the treatment group (Howell 2003).

There is one aftercare programme in the USA that has produced positive short-term effects (Josi and Sechrest 1999). Called the Lifeskills '95 Program, it was designed to reinforce progress made while helping young people confront the fears of the communities they were returning to. Data were collected and analysed on experimental and control groups of young people released on parole in 1995. Individuals assigned to the control group were twice as likely as those assigned to the experimental group to have been arrested, to be unemployed, to lack the necessary resources to gain and maintain employment, to have a poor attitude about working, and to have abused drugs and alcohol frequently after release.

Meta-analysis of resettlement or aftercare programmes has also produced contradictory outcomes. Altschuler *et al.* (1999) found that the few well-designed evaluations of aftercare programmes that have been completed have shown mixed results. Lipsey (1999), by contrast, found through meta-analysis that resettlement programmes that included intensive supervision or a reduced caseload produce significant reductions in recidivism. The reasons for this discrepancy are not entirely clear, although it may be that Altschuler *et al.* focused on programmes that emphasised a more punitive approach, whereas

Lipsey's study was based on programmes that were more practical and developmentally oriented (Howell 2003).

Vocational education

It is striking that many discussions by educators or non-educators turn to the need for more vocational training for young people who offend or are seen to be academically under-achieving. This may be derived from observations of other countries whose education systems place more emphasis on a vocational education and appear to have fewer problems with engagement and possibly more highly skilled workforces. It can also be driven by a belief that traditional 'chalk and talk' teaching methods have alienated these young people. This issue has been thrown into relief as the virtually automatic transition from school to labour market has withered away. The UK, unlike countries such as Germany and Denmark, does not offer a high-status vocational training route as an alternative to continuing with academic studies. Given the popularity of the vocational remedy reiterated recently by the Audit Commission (2004) and by the Tomlinson review of 14–19 education it is worth examining the evidence base.

The underlying hypothesis is that learning that is more obviously associated with the world of work will provide much greater motivation to young people with low attainment and limited or no attachment to school. Vocational subjects could also offer greater opportunities to link to their out-of-school interests and hobbies than the academic subjects. Accordingly, there has been a range of experimental educational programmes from the early 1990s onwards targeted at 14–16-year-olds to improve motivation and engagement through an emphasis on work-related learning. The evaluation of these initiatives lacked RCTs, had limited comparison groups, and struggled to find an appropriate and consistent approach to measuring progress (Steedman and Stoney 2004).

A review of evaluations of a range of initiatives, including those arising from the disapplication of the national curriculum at Key Stage 4, GNVQs, vocational GCSEs, the Connexions Service, the Increased Flexibilities Programme and other work-related initiatives, found that for those who were disengaged:

- There was little effect on attainment.

- Motivation may have increased but was not necessarily translated into greater attainment.

- Careers guidance and information appear to be a major weakness.

- Contact with the workplace could sometimes reduce the likelihood of remaining in education and training (Steedman and Stoney 2004).

The evidence so far does not indicate better outcomes for a vocational route post-16 for these young people. Drawing on extensive Labour Force Survey data McIntosh (2003: 14) concluded: 'It does not appear that post-school vocational qualifications have been at all successful in raising those who failed at school to the generally accepted desirable level (levels 3), or even, for that matter, to level 2.'

It may be that some of the commonly held assumptions about the potential role of vocational learning for those who have low attainment and are becoming detached from mainstream education are flawed. Unlike other European countries, there is a much higher association between low socio-economic status and attainment, particularly literacy, in the UK; therefore, promoting a vocational route for this group runs the risk of creating a two-tier service. It is difficult to avoid the suspicion that under the guise of the 'disaffected pupil' some rather old-fashioned and discredited notions are being given renewed currency. In the present state of the evidence, it is at least as valid a hypothesis that the problems around engagement and attainment are connected with the qualities of pedagogy and individual support within the context of a broader-based curriculum.

Segregated education and training

The history of the education of young people who offend is inextricably bound up with segregated educational provision. This provision is for those young people who through their antisocial or offending behaviour, or perceived differences in their learning needs, are deemed candidates for removal from mainstream school. They are seen as being more appropriately placed in 'specialist' environments.

Without wanting to make the nature and distribution of provision for the education and training of young people outside mainstream school seem more consistent, planned and orderly than it is, we may say that there are four broad and overlapping categories of segregated education. There are separate facilities on the school site, more recently termed 'learning support units' (LSUs); special schools; and PRUs; and often linked to these is a constellation of initiatives offering formal and informal learning, including home tuition. While it is widely acknowledged by LEAs, and practitioners in youth justice, and in segregated education, that such provision potentially caters for many young people who are involved in offending, reducing their delinquency is not usually seen as being an educational objective. In contrast, for those of post-compulsory school age, segregated provision has tended to be a variety of training schemes often run by providers whose explicit brief has been provision for young people who offend.

Given the concentration of young people at risk or actually involved in offending who are attached formally to such provision, or where it remains their only realistic prospect of education, it is important to assess the effectiveness of such provision in meeting its stated aims and also in terms of possible direct and indirect effects on delinquency. For the purposes of assessment of effectiveness, one of the advantages of the increasing size of the out-of-school sector is the greater emphasis placed on definition of provision and its objectives through government guidance.

Learning support units (LSUs)

Special groups or units within schools for young people who are seen to pose behavioural problems in mainstream classes have a lengthy history, but they have seen a significant expansion in recent years through initiatives such as Education Action Zones and the Excellence in Cities programmes. Despite this, the evaluation evidence on their effectiveness is very limited. Their main stated objectives include bringing about behavioural changes so that young people can be reintegrated into mainstream classes, thereby reducing exclusions, increasing attainment and improving attendance.

A study of seven units in Sheffield found no effect on exclusion rates, or on the numbers transferred to special schools, and found that the focus tended to be on the perceived problems of the young person rather than the context in which it occurred – 'the halfway house fallacy' (Galloway 1985: 162). Reintegration rates into mainstream classes were also found to be low in Inner London units (Mortimore et al. 1983).

There is a range of relatively systematic American studies. In reviewing these, Topping (1983) found that in certain circumstances both primary and secondary age groups could show substantial academic gains and behavioural improvement, although many results were disappointing. Gains appeared to dissipate over the long term when young people were returned to mainstream classes.

The evaluation of LSUs in the Excellence in Cities programme was largely qualitative, and there was no systematic evaluation of attainment or behaviour gains (Wilkin et al. 2003). While there were abundant positive comments from staff and small samples of young people, only about 22 per cent were fully reintegrated, and the majority of these were younger pupils with very few Year 10 and no Year 11 students returning to mainstream classes. This provision often was not full-time for all young people. Ofsted (2003) found that a quarter of the LSUs they inspected were not doing sufficient work to help the young people learn more effectively. Other criticisms included 'the use of units simply as "remove rooms" where disruptive pupils were sent at random, weak monitoring and evaluation and a lack of emphasis on staff training and ensuring they were an integral part of the teaching team' (Ofsted 2003: 60).

These units potentially share the weaknesses identified in off-site units – the formation of negative or delinquent peer groups, trying to change behaviour out of the original context and marginalisation of staff. There is no rigorous evidence as yet that this approach is reducing the population of those detached from schools. There is a real risk in some circumstances of net widening, with a growth in the numbers of young people attending both on-site and off-site units.

Pupil referral units (PRUs)

Many young people who have offended, particularly if they continue to offend, will end up being referred to off-site provision, usually a PRU. Despite the fact that the use of small segregated units for a range of young people has a long history and very high unit costs, there is very little evidence on its outcomes. The evidence that does exist is often limited on two counts: there are rarely follow-up data and the evidence is characterised by differing educational expectations of the young people with respect to, for example, curriculum, attainment and attendance. One key issue in assessing the effectiveness of PRUs is agreeing success criteria. There is a lack of clarity about whether this should be progression post-16, qualifications achieved, reintegration into mainstream schooling, desistance from offending, reductions in the behaviours that cause them to be detached from mainstream, and a range of softer outcomes such as increases in self-esteem.

Most studies have tended to be critical, yet this kind of provision has expanded as a corollary to the increased displacement of young people from mainstream secondary school. Perhaps not surprisingly, there is little reference in most studies to the impact of segregated education on offending, but there are several inherent characteristics which could lead it to be less effective in terms of reducing risk factors and increasing protective factors. Given that delinquent peer groups are a significant risk factor for adolescents, a concentration in a PRU is likely to be counterproductive. In the same way that it is suggested that learning in such an abnormal environment as custody does not transfer easily to everyday life in the community, similar difficulties may be posed for young people in small units. Positive changes in behaviour or attitudes to learning may well not survive the dramatic shift from a small highly protected environment to the hurly-burly of educational life in a FE college or the workplace.

Defining successful outcomes is divided between those who argue for clear measurable outcomes as a measure (Topping 1983), those who believe this is too narrow (Munn *et al.* 2000), and those who recognise a progression of 'small steps' (Hustler *et al.* 1998; Kendall *et al.* 2002). Views on the measurement of effectiveness appear to lie on a continuum from a reliance on the positive attitudes of practitioners from segregated education (Kinder *et al.* 2000) through to the argument that effectiveness should be based on studies that that can be generalised to produce hard, objectively measurable evidence with a success rate of over 66 per cent (Topping 1983). Partly due to this lack of a consensus over the aims and purposes of segregated education, very little attention has been paid to the effects either positive or negative on offending (Munn *et al.* 2000).

Research and inspections have revealed serious weaknesses in segregated, particularly unit-based provision:

- Reintegration is the ostensible objective of PRUs, according to guidance issued (DfES Circular 10/99). Each pupil should have reintegration targets for a return to mainstream or special education, FE or employment. The evidence shows that this is achieved for only a minority of children and young people (Parsons and Howlett 2000).

- The curriculum tends to be narrow, and the quality of teaching can be lowered by the lack of specialist subject teachers (Ofsted 1995).

- Academic achievement and progression into FE, training and employment are often low (Ofsted 1995, 2003; Munn *et al.* 2000).

- There is often a wide range of ages in a single unit. This can mean inappropriate role models for younger pupils and long-term exposure to an out-of-school culture that hinders their reintegration.

- The cost is at least three times that of mainstream provision (Audit Commission 1999; Parsons and Howlett 2000)

- There are concerns over the quality of peer group relationships, particularly for the small number of young women (John 1996).

- It contributes to a 'double jeopardy' for young people in residential care, who find themselves at a crucial stage in their development outside both family and school environments. This could restrict their ability to acquire the skills to function in normal group settings.

Alternative education initiatives

In addition to the definition and formalisation of the status of the unit, another symptom of the revitalisation of segregated education is the growth of a wide range of out-of-school educational provision, some of which is delivered by voluntary sector providers. This offers a very diverse mix of formal and informal learning, often with an emphasis on basic skills, personal and social development activities, and work experience. While it very rarely takes place on school premises, sometimes separate centres will be used, training premises or youth centres, and there may be access to FE colleges.

A relatively large-scale evaluation was recently conducted for these alternative education projects (Kendall *et al.* 2002). The overall aim of the evaluation was to 'examine the effectiveness of intervention programmes for permanently excluded pupils. Effectiveness is measured in terms of their success in returning pupils to mainstream education, educational attainment, post 16 outcomes and reducing antisocial behaviour, including offending' (Kendall *et al.* 2002: 2).

Despite the fact that the six initiatives studied in this research were selected because they displayed some success in the re-engagement of young people, weaknesses in the baseline information on young people, and the very diverse characteristics of young people referred and of the projects themselves, coupled with the relatively limited nature of the evaluation, restricted the findings.

Although there is no reference to it in the executive summary or in the key findings, the reintegration rates into mainstream appear to be low, only eight (5 per cent) out of 162 young people in the study apparently returning to secondary school.

Analysis of educational attainment was curtailed in that there was apparently no baseline information on the young people, and in the absence of assessment of their literacy and numeracy levels on entry and exit, the evaluation provided lists of qualifications achieved as indicative of progression. There were real problems relating to the information on attendance that effectively prevented any attempt to compare particular educational or behavioural outputs, in relation to inputs.

This study is unusual in that it did look at offending. In total, there was not a particularly high incidence of young people with a criminal record on referral to these projects compared with some out-of-school projects (approximately 50 per cent), but there was a total of 694 offences committed during their time on the projects. While the number of young people (for whom there was detailed information) involved in offending fell by 11 per cent, the number of offences they committed increased by 22 per cent in the intervention year. The study found that young people with undesirable destinations were 20 per cent more likely to offend, and on average committed 32 per cent more crime than those with desirable destinations.

A recent evaluation of Mentoring Plus (mentoring run in conjunction with a structured education and careers programme) examined changes in social exclusion/social inclusion and offending, and, unusually, incorporated a comparison group (Newburn and Shiner 2005). Social inclusion was defined as changes in engagement in education, training or employment. The proportion of young people who participated in education, training or employment increased substantially during the course of the programme. There was no such increase evident among the comparison group.

There were marked reductions in both the frequency and gravity of offending among those on the programme. These reductions, however, could not readily be attributed directly to the programme, as offending decreased even more among the comparison group. There was no apparent relationship either between social inclusion and reductions in offending, although it was suggested that there might be longer-term effects. Similarly, changes in self-esteem appeared unrelated to changes in both social inclusion and offending.

From an educational perspective, there were important gaps in the evidence. The degrees of engagement could not be measured – commencing a very limited part-time programme apparently counted as much as full-time participation. Following on from this, the amount of education, training or employment received – the dosage – is unknown; it could have varied widely as a result of how much was actually arranged and differential attendance. Any effects of changes in social inclusion as defined here could therefore have been masked. There was no assessment either of learning gains, so it is impossible to examine the relationship between improvements in literacy, numeracy and subsequent social inclusion and with offending.

Special schools

As discussed in Chapter 4, another formal route out of mainstream education is for young people labelled as having EBD. For the overwhelming majority (95 per cent), of children and young people categorised as having EBD, a placement in a special school is in effect permanent, whatever the intentions recorded in the individual educational planning process. Reintegration rates are very low (see Chapter 4). There are very few studies of residential special schools that can yield information on outcomes relating to attainment, detachment and offending. One study of several residential special schools for pupils with EBD found it difficult to collect data there on basic educational skills, and the outcomes in terms of progression to FE and training appear limited. Offending rates appear to have increased significantly following prolonged stays in the schools, but this also may have been due to an age effect (Grimshaw and Berridge 1994).

Post-16 training providers

For many young people who offend and are detached from mainstream education, centre-based provision from specialist trainers is one of their main options. This tends to suffer from the same fundamental weaknesses as PRUs but has additional problems related to the length of the programmes and funding regimes. On the other hand, the young people receive a training allowance.

Evidence on outcomes is very limited, and where it exists, it is not encouraging. The National E2E Young Offender's Pilot was an attempt to provide a route into mainstream provision for those young people on DTOs and ISSPs. Despite being partly funded by the YJB, its explicit aims did not include a reduction in reoffending, and the evaluation consequently makes no attempt to assess this. The very limited nature of the data means that it is impossible to judge the intensity and duration of participation and educational progression. The attrition rates appear high, 41 per cent of those who commenced in custody not continuing on release, and out of the remainder 38 per cent were recorded as having a positive leave from the pilot. Although the evaluators acknowledge that the figures 'are not necessarily reliable or robust', they indicate that only 83 young people out of 340 (24 per cent) who started this programme had a positive leave (Youth Justice Trust 2004b).

Keeping young people engaged (KYPE)

The main aim of the YJB-funded project KYPE was to 'improve education, training and employment provision for all young offenders, but particularly for those subject to intensive supervision and surveillance programmes (ISSPs) and Detention and Training Orders (DTOs)' (YJB 2005f: 4).

In the event, the project appears to have concentrated on the provision of additional personnel deployed as personal advisers/mentors. The implicit assumption that the support role of personal advisers/mentors could be the major determinant of engagement is questionable. There is widespread evidence of a shortfall in the quantity of provision available (Audit Commission 2004), and this is apparently supported by a majority of managers and practitioners in this project (YJB 2005f). Given the relatively small numbers involved in a given Yot area, it would not need much of an expansion or contraction in LEA- or LSC-funded provision or the local demand for labour to have potentially a much more significant impact on the numbers of young people participating in education, training or the labour market, irrespective of the impact of this initiative.

The apparent withdrawal of support for this project by the Connexions Service National Unit (CSNU) may have affected the outcomes, but, in any event, they appear overall to have been at best inconclusive. The evaluation report used a comparison in YJB quarterly returns between participating and non-participating clusters of Yots. The first cluster of Yots in this initiative recorded a 2 percentage point increase in participation rates compared with a 1.9 percentage point increase in non-participating Yots. In the subsequent six months, non-participating Yots increased their numbers in education, training or employment by 1 percentage point while those in the initiative saw no overall increase. Results for those Yots who joined the project a year later were no more convincing, as they recorded an overall increase of one-third that of non-participating Yots (0.4 percentage point compared with 1.2 percentage points) (YJB 2005f: 23; 24; 25). However, the limited data available to the researchers may have hidden some significant local changes, as during this period individual Yots recorded both large increases and decreases in the numbers of young people engaged in education, training or employment.

A promising approach? – the Bridge Course

This project has several unusual features: it has been replicated extensively in England and Wales with an apparently high degree of programme integrity, and has relatively comprehensive quantitative information on the antecedents of young people, their attendance, qualifications gained, changes in literacy and numeracy levels, and subsequent destinations. It was evaluated recently as part of the YJB's review of the education training and employment projects that it funded, and the data have been further analysed in a recent article (YJB 2003a; Hurry *et al.* in press).

There were nearly 500 young people in this evaluation with an average age of 17 from 16 projects in a variety of locations. Most were completely detached from education and training; just over one-fifth were or had been looked after by the local authority. Over two-thirds had literacy and numeracy levels assessed at below Level 1 (that of the average 11-year-old) on referral. The great majority of them (83 per cent) were referred by the Yot. Nine out of 10 were repeat offenders (88 per cent) with an average of 12 previous convictions and an average gravity score of 5.3.

There appears to have been a relatively low rate of attrition with a correspondingly high dosage of received hours of education. On average, young people were on the project for 17 out of the potential 24 weeks and undertook 22 hours per week of education with an average total of 370 hours received for each young person.

In terms of educational outcomes, those who remained for more than 15 weeks recorded modest but highly significant gains in both literacy and numeracy. About 50 per cent gained qualifications while a significant proportion were continuing to work towards them. If those who were removed to custody (9.5 per cent) or moved out of the area (2.2 per cent) are discounted, then 72 per cent of young people on the project had initial destinations of education, training or employment.

With regard to offending, there was a 67 per cent reconviction rate in the year after entry to the project, but this was accompanied by statistically significant reductions in offending in terms of both the number of offences and the gravity of offence. The average offences per young person dropped by 25 per cent from 5.1 to 3.8 comparing the year before and the year after being on the project.

In order to examine the potential effect of the programme on reoffending, the three educational outcomes of positive destination, qualifications gained, and literacy and numeracy improvements were assessed. Each of these outcomes was significantly related to reductions in offending. While there was a 72 per cent reconviction rate for those who did not have a positive destination, this fell to 57 per cent for those who did. There was a similar reduction for those who gained qualifications compared with those who did not. Reductions in the average number of offences per head were even greater, with a fall of a half for those who gained qualifications compared with a tenth for those who did not.

A further study analysed the data by regression analysis to explore predictors of reoffending. Controlling for previous offending and background factors (gender, school-leaving age, living situation, number of sessions attended and drug use), it was found that literacy and numeracy gains were significantly associated with lower rates of reoffending. The study concluded: 'It would appear that improving participants' literacy and numeracy skills may be an effective way of reducing their offending behaviour' (Hurry *et al.* in press).

The quantity and quality of data garnered by this evaluation mean that there can be much closer scrutiny of the costs incurred of this programme. Instead of simply giving a per capita cost of a place – the normal method – costs can be calculated per contact hour. This yields interesting results. The per capita cost of the Bridge Course model appeared to be more than double that of similar projects funded by the YJB, but on a cost per contact hour basis, it was up to half the cost of other projects. Again, better recording practices bring benefits in that headline costs can be deceptive if the structure, intensity and duration of intervention are not sufficiently intensive to gain high rates of attendance and retention. If we adopt a more rigorous approach to recording what is actually received by a young person in tandem with pre- and post-intervention assessment, then much more effective cost-benefit analysis will be possible in future.

The reasons for the apparent relative success of this project model for young people who often do not get access to or participate extensively in segregated provision may be as follows:

- the use of mainstream environments (principally FE colleges) to dilute delinquent peer group effects and promote behaviour modification;

- intensive supervision (one to ten caseload over and above teaching staff);

- multi-modal – the multidisciplinary project manager worked across social care, health, criminal justice issues;

- high degree of programme intensity (Stephenson 1996; DfEE 1995).

Incentives for participation

Staying on in education has been considered to be potentially protective against delinquency. The introduction of the Education Maintenance Allowance (EMA) in selected areas enabled a recent quasi-experimental study to examine the impact on juvenile crime (Feinstein and Sabates 2005). The study found that there was a statistically significant decrease in convictions for burglary by 16–18-year-old boys (but not for theft or violent offences) in the EMA areas, compared with non-EMA areas and compared with older groups in their area. Given that areas of high deprivation tend to attract multiple initiatives from government departments, which could either individually or in concert affect the results, the study looked at the Reducing Burglary Initiative (RBI). The main effect seemed to occur when both programmes were operated together rather than individually, giving rise to the main finding that there are 'clear grounds that introduction of the EMA together with the RBI programme had significant and substantive effects on conviction rates for burglary offences by 16 to 18 year olds' (Feinstein and Sabates 2005: 4). A further gain over time of staying on in education could potentially be lower unemployment, which is associated with decreases in offending.

What does not work

It is instructive to examine some examples of educational type projects or approaches that are still supported despite evidence to the contrary. One very well-known American project highlights this problem - Drug Abuse Resistance Education (DARE). Strong empirical evidence, including studies using a random assignment design, have demonstrated that DARE is not effective (Howell 2003). Yet, it remains a very large programme employing more than 50,000 police officers lecturing in nearly half of America's elementary schools. One explanation for its continuing popularity despite being apparently a failed intervention is that it is founded on a mistaken belief in the effectiveness of deterrence. It appears that fundamental beliefs in the efficacy of repressive deterrence are irresistible, particularly when combined with an apparently common-sense approach. The zero tolerance approach applied to schools has also been found to be ineffective, but this has not restricted its popularity in the USA and its potential spread to the UK (Howell 2003; Smith 2005).

More benign motives can lie behind projects where the evidence does not suggest that they are effective. Flexible provision linked to schools with the ostensible aim of reintegrating young people can often, counter-intuitively, lead to greater detachment. The youth-inclusion programme developed by the YJB is a structured youth work programme combining elements of education and personal development targeted on the 50 most at-risk young people in a neighbourhood. Referral criteria include poor attendance or exclusion from school. Its targets include reducing recorded crime by 30 per cent and reducing non-attendance and school exclusion each by 30 per cent. The outcomes have, however, included a 6 per cent increase in offending and a significant deterioration in attendance. While this approach might have made sense from a youth justice perspective, from an educational perspective it ran the risk of providing young people with an easy option educationally, and it enabled schools to divert young people who may have been challenging in school settings towards more 'appropriate' education provision without resort to exclusion (YJB 2003b).

There is a history of such alleged reintegration – or now renamed 'inclusion' – projects, whose name, in fact, is a misnomer, as they can legitimise the detachment of young people from mainstream schooling. Ironically, this programme has been expanded despite its failure to meet several of its own success criteria. The fact that permanent exclusions may have declined is probably simply a reflection of the increased non-attendance and the diversion of particular young people away from school sites.

There is a pervasive belief in the notion that 'the Devil makes work for idle hands' and that involving young people in positive extra-curricular activities can reduce delinquency. This common-sense idea is behind initiatives such as Positive Actions for Young People (PAYP), which operates in the summer, and the development of extended schools that open early and offer a range of activities after school. More generally, it underpins much youth work. However, the research evidence underpinning such approaches is equivocal.

An evaluation of several Summer Splash schemes found that youth crime did not increase dramatically during the summer holidays, and that a decline in offending was noted only where there had been little existing summer provision and where a relatively high rate of incidents was reported to the police (Loxley *et al.* 2002).

The outcomes for those activities with a clear link to more conventional interests, such as hours spent on homework, may well be associated with less delinquency, in contrast to involvement in more adult activities such as motor projects, which are associated with increases in delinquency (Harper and Chitty 2005).

For the whole range of other activities, including youth groups, volunteering, sports and individual hobbies, little effect on delinquency has been observed in the American research literature (Gottfredson 2001). One study using UK data found that increased leisure activity between ages 8 and 10 was a predictor of both lower levels of self-control between 12 and 14 years of age and of offending between the ages of 14 and 16. It is speculated that supervision exercised in the activity settings was not as effective as that of parents, which possibly reduced self-control.

Arts interventions

The power of the arts to transform the lives of people who offend has often been proclaimed. A recent review found that out of 700 projects catering for both young people and adults who had offended, 400 had used arts-based activities (Hughes 2005). A wide range of benefits is claimed, including:

- development of self-confidence and self-esteem;
- increased creativity and thinking skills;
- improved skills in planning and organising activities;
- improved communication of ideas and information;
- raised or enhanced educational attainment;
- increased appreciation of the arts;
- enhanced mental and physical health and well-being;
- increased employability of individuals;
- broadened outlook;
- reduced offending behaviour (Jermyn 2004).

The quality of the research underpinning this impressive list of claims tends not to be high. Common limitations include evaluations with small sample sizes, a lack of baseline information, lack of control groups, few appropriate measures, over-reliance on anecdotal evidence, difficulties accessing information relating to offending, and unsupported assumptions about the links between intervention and outcome (Hughes 2005). Much of the evidence relates to behavioural changes, usually of adults, within custody such as a reduction in adjudications following an arts intervention. The plethora of indirect and testimonial evidence often adduced to support the effectiveness of the arts in the criminal justice system does not come close to the rigorous methodologies required by the Home Office.

Research sponsored by the YJB and Arts Council England is currently being undertaken through the PLUS strategy, focusing on the links between engagement in the arts, educational participation, and progression and offending.

Conclusions

While evidence-based practice represents a new cultural approach for youth justice services to adopt, most approaches to preventing offending in the UK must, strictly speaking, be deemed 'unknown' or at best 'promising' rather than truly effective.

Even when the evidence base is firm, it must be emphasised that there is no magic solution when it comes to preventing offending. Using the techniques of meta-analysis provides average measures of changes in recidivism. Use of averages, of course, disguises a performance range both above and below the central score. The inference that practitioners can draw therefore is that even when they apply interventions that are rated the most 'effective', the outcomes could range from a complete cessation of offending to a significant increase.

Although there is a lack of a shared approach towards 'what works?' between educators and those in youth justice, both promising and effective approaches can be identified. In overall terms, the evidence such as it is supports those approaches that enable young people ultimately to gain and sustain employment as one of the best ways of preventing offending. The prerequisites for achieving this outcome are ensuring that attainment is high, particularly with respect to literacy and numeracy, and that young people form a strong attachment to mainstream education. Schools and colleges may have a significant positive effect, but custodial and care experiences can have equally negative consequences.

Interventions that are not strongly linked to these two key objectives of increasing attainment and preventing detachment have relatively little chance of success. For example, interventions where increasing self-esteem is the primary objective or where learning occurs in a segregated or abnormal environment are likely to be ineffective.

There are additional salutary messages. It is much clearer on what to do rather than how to do it in detail; reattaching young people to education and training is far harder than preventing detachment in the first place; the transfer of learning between different environments, such as custody, to the community is extremely limited.

Summary

❑ 'What works?' is a deceptively simple and apparently apolitical concept, but it is not value-free, and its applicability to education and to youth justice has been contested. Very few interventions have been subject to the most rigorous of evaluations, and the evidence is better suited to indicating promising approaches rather than definitive prescriptions about exactly what works.

❑ Interventions which have been evaluated to a relatively high standard and that demonstrated effectiveness in preventing detachment are the same as for tackling low attainment; they include pre-school education, family literacy, intensive reading schemes, reasoning and social skills education, and organisational change in schools.

❑ There is some evidence of a relationship between attendance, attainment (particularly in literacy and numeracy) and lower offending rates.

❑ Most studies that try to measure the effectiveness of custodial educational intervention or resettlement programmes have been compromised by weak research design, but do provide some evidence of a link between educational intervention and reduction in recidivism, although this tends to be for adults.

Chapter 10

Social policy – education, youth justice and social inclusion

Which is best, to pay for the policeman or the schoolmaster – the prison or the school?

The Times (1867)

One challenge above all stands out – tackling the scourge and waste of social exclusion.

Peter Mandelson (1997: 6)

Education and crime have been headline priorities for New Labour since its election in 1997. Social exclusion was adopted as the government's primary discourse for social policy developments, and this was underlined by the establishment of the SEU. There has been a focus on detachment processes with a concomitant emphasis on social inclusion. The recognition of the interrelated aspects of deprivation led Blair to exhort government departments and agencies that 'joined-up problems need joined-up solutions' in order to reduce social exclusion.

This chapter attempts to establish how far the discourse of social inclusion has influenced the formation of social policy across education and youth justice, and to identify any inherent tensions. It then examines just how far services have been joined up, particularly through the creation of Yots and the Connexions Service. Finally, an assessment is made of the impact of policy on the educational risk factors for offending, principally through reviewing progress against targets for detachment, attainment, custody and school improvements.

Education

Lifelong learning in its broadest sense occupies centre stage in New Labour's economic strategy, political philosophy and social policy. This high ranking in social policy objectives derives from the need to be able to compete within an increasingly globalised economy and the new and rapidly changing technologies with their fundamental impact on labour markets. Sir Michael Bichard's (the ex-permanent secretary for the DfEE in New Labour's first administration) views exemplify this:

> The new centrality of education in our society – the widespread acceptance that education is the key to our future economic success as well as the key to a better quality of life for every individual citizen (2001).

Within the political strategy of ensuring the ideological attachment of Middle England while pursuing social inclusion and reducing social security costs, four themes have come to dominate social policy in both compulsory and post-compulsory education: promoting standards; reducing long-term unemployment (and welfare costs) through the New Deal; widening participation in FE, higher education and training; and improving levels of literacy and numeracy.

In turning these policy themes into strategies that can be implemented, three main strands have emerged which contain inherent tensions and contradictions (Hodgson and Spours 1999).

1 A 'traditionalist interventionist' approach to raising achievement in schools. The Standards and Effectiveness Unit in tandem with Ofsted have centrally driven this. It has been characterised by heavy emphasis on the acquisition of literacy and numeracy skills, the rejection of so-called progressive learning methods and an overt attempt to secure middle-class support by introducing programmes for the 'gifted and talented', and promoting streaming within a diversification of types of schools available to increase choice.

2 A 'voluntarist framework/partnership' approach to lifelong learning.

3 An 'exclusion reduction' approach designed to provide funding and support for those who are detached or at risk of detaching from mainstream secondary education. This has developed increasingly in harness with attempts to widen participation in FE and latterly higher education.

Reconciling the first and last of these strands requires typical New Labour 'not only ... but also' political dexterity (Fairclough 2000). Having discovered social exclusion, New Labour has been confronted with doing something about it or standing accused of straddling a widening gap between the reality and rhetoric.

Youth justice

The Crime and Disorder Act 1998 placed a duty on statutory agencies, including education, to prevent offending. The Yots have a role to pull together all the relevant agencies in delivery of community-based provision with young offenders. LEAs are required to participate in the steering groups that oversee the multiagency work of Yots. LEAs also have to make a contribution to the staffing complement of Yots. The Detention and Training Order (DTO) introduced under the Act not only makes the objectives of the sentence explicit in its title but also spans custody and community, thus pushing education and training to the fore.

The YJB has given considerable impetus to youth justice work with education through issuing national standards, setting explicit education targets and introducing a systematic assessment that includes education and training ASSET. Additionally, as the commissioner of all secure placements, the YJB has placed education centre stage for custodial work with young people. It has also funded a series of education, training and employment initiatives. How far has all this shifted Yot work on education and training with regard to both extent and effectiveness?

Social inclusion

Social exclusion has become a common term in social policy discourses in the UK only since the creation of the SEU in 1998. But what does social *inclusion* mean in relation to both education and youth justice? How can social policy give concrete expression to inclusion?

The term is ubiquitous in both social policy and practitioner circles to the extent that it has been described as both an '"international buzzword" and "a cliché"' (Thomas and Loxley 2001: vii). No mission statement and certainly no funding applications where children and young people are concerned are free from the word. However, inclusion has been much less studied than exclusion, certainly in terms of examining what it means in practice. There are some early signs of devaluation of the term 'inclusion' already, which is coming to mean only the process of 'what we do to the excluded'. Ironically, the term has been emasculated by this appropriation and has almost become a justification of exclusion.

There is no agreed definition internationally, within UK social policy and between different disciplines. This provides so much elasticity that the term can even be stretched to justify existing segregated practices, which either contribute to social exclusion or condone the maintenance of the status quo with those who are excluded.

Several factors contribute to this. Inclusion as a concept is not yet grounded in practical experience: there is no recognised body of inclusion knowledge and practice. There are implicit policy tensions in the concept, for example, between raising standards in school and widening participation. There is always a tendency at policy level to set up dichotomies, for example, between the included and the excluded. Finally, existing service structures have become adept at 'rebranding' to accommodate new terminology rather than fundamentally changing practice and systems. Already the situation exists in some schools where, paradoxically, increasing numbers of children and young people are removed from mainstream lessons to attend so-called 'inclusion units'. If those young people who are held in custodial institutions can be described as the most socially excluded in our society, it is doubly ironic that those held in segregation for a variety of reasons in what is virtually solitary confinement should find these rebranded as 'inclusion units' as has happened in at least one YOI.

Part of the reason for the lack of a generally agreed definition lies in the mixed origin of the concept. For educators, the term 'inclusion' is very much bound up with notions of special educational need. Succeeding the use of the term 'integration', 'inclusion' in an educational context has often been used as a description of how children and young people with learning difficulties, physical disabilities or sensory impairments are assimilated within mainstream schools. Used in this rather restricted way, it tends to place boundaries around certain kinds of putative learning difficulties and disabilities.

However, the term has other roots that lie within labour market analysis. In France, for instance, the concept of inclusion is closely related to 'social insertion policies' designed to reduce unemployment and increase social cohesion and solidarity (Barry and Hallett 1998). European social policy initially focused on those aspects of social inclusion directly connected with the right to work and the desire for paid employment. Subsequently, this has been extended beyond economic rights to civil, political and social rights.

It would seem, then, that when applied to children and young people, social inclusion would be fundamentally concerned with the participation of all young people in mainstream education and training, not just with special educational needs, and would also anticipate their rights and duties as adult citizens. If social inclusion is constructed out of these different strands, it also needs to be a universal concept. Defining social inclusion, for example, as 'the attempt to reintegrate, or to increase the participation of, marginalised groups within mainstream society' (Barry and Hallett 1998: 5) is still insufficient. Given the knowledge of just how difficult this is to accomplish, that it starts from an assumption of separate 'groups' and that this represents simply the reduction of existing social exclusion, then, arguably, something more comprehensive is required.

Although not presenting a specific definition of social inclusion, the UK national action plan for social inclusion lists the following policy goals:

- preventing exclusion from happening;
- reintegrating those who become excluded;
- getting the basics right–providing the minimum standards for all (Department for Work and Pensions 2001).

Thomas and Loxley (2001: 119) constructed their definition of inclusion within the educational context out of ideas about social justice and human rights: '[inclusion] is about providing a framework within which all children–regardless of ability, gender, language, ethnic or cultural origin–can be valued equally, treated with respect and provided with real opportunities at school.' The approach to inclusion that they propose represents the evolution of comprehensive education with an emphasis on the school as a collective moral activist institution that rejects segregated education.

This emphasis on both the collective and moral activist dimensions combats two of the main criticisms of the concept of inclusion. There is a real risk that notions of inclusion are simply the latest labels to attach to the work with individuals who do not fit in. Politically, the concept is attractive in that it can be used to divert attention from the potential need for radical change and simply encourages compliance with the status quo (Barry and Hallett 1998). If inclusion is constructed around a moral activist approach that emphasises the promotion of values such as acceptance of, and respect for, difference and equality of opportunity, then it counters these arguments. Central though the 15,000 hours of schooling should be to the lives of all children and young people, social inclusion, if the concept is to mean anything, has to be manifested across communities and adopted by the relevant agencies. This involves the agencies in both accepting the centrality of mainstream schooling and interpreting inclusion so that it is given practical expression within the context of their work.

While there have been attempts to do this in social services and social work, for example, discussion of inclusion is conspicuously absent in youth justice discourses and certainly at the policymaking level. The reason for this, it has been argued, is that New Labour's policy on youth justice is the antithesis of inclusion; rather, it represents a 'nostalgic attempt to recover an imagined past in which there were only good and bad children and common-sensical ways of making the bad ones behave themselves' (Pitts 2000: 12). Other commentators consider government policy on social inclusion to be simply rhetoric that is undermined by the intense concentration on modifying the behaviour of individuals who indulge in antisocial or criminal behaviour (Smith 2003).

In fact, the whole concept of social inclusion can be reframed into the extension of social surveillance and control into the community. The schools taking on more extended community roles, neighbourhoods becoming locations for surveillance and supervision, and the implementation of targeted measures, such as youth-inclusion programmes and summer schemes, have all been seen as 'representing a Foucaultesque strategy for classifying and controlling the problematic behaviour of the young' (Smith 2003: 159).

Alternatively, with respect to New Labour's pick-and-mix approach to the different strands of criminology in formulating its youth justice policy, it 'can be argued that the emphasis on inclusionary crime prevention marks a significant departure from punitive justice, yet it retains a commitment to an ethos of individual responsibility and penal custody that seems to actively promote exclusion. Significantly, the principles of inclusion are frequently backed by coercive powers' (Muncie 2000: 31). It is difficult to detect within any of the many planning documents of the YJB signs that it sees itself as part of a wider progressive strategy that aims to overcome social inequality and division through the promotion of inclusion.

However, while the overt articulation of the principles of inclusion does appear to be absent and the YJB's stance has some inherent tensions, the underlying and potentially inclusive nature of its policies may sometimes be underestimated. In its devotion to a hard-headed, 'what works?' approach, wider theoretical arguments have often been ignored. Yet, the potential for inclusion is implicit in the Crime and Disorder Act 1998 with the statutory duty on all agencies to prevent offending. The strategic aim of increasing public confidence in the youth justice system is partly to be achieved by much greater public involvement and reconnecting the perpetrator and the victim of offences. Initiatives such as restorative justice and referral order panels have the potential to engage the community in the important matters of school attainment and detachment. Equally, they also have the potential for net widening and focusing on the behaviour of the young person rather than the structural deficiencies of the education system. Similarly, it has been argued in Chapter 9 that, in one of the few instances of the use of the word 'inclusion', youth inclusion programmes may actually act to increase detachment from school.

Nevertheless, the YJB has consistently championed the importance of mainstream education and training to young people and exhorted the other agencies to give it equal importance. The then chair of the YJB, Norman Warner, asserted: 'We don't want to create education and training ghettoes for young offenders, which would be a confession of failure' (Warner 2003). Ironically, those agencies charged with a more mainstream set of policy priorities have been less enthusiastic. The Connexions Service National Unit (CSNU), for example, did not fully adopt the YJB's education target and the LSC's first national plan omitted any reference to the educational and training needs of young people who offend (DfES/YJB 2001).

Joined-up solutions?

Figure 10.1 illustrates just how central the issue of young people out of mainstream education is in relation to the work of the central government departments and local government agencies concerned with criminal justice, health, culture and social care.

With such 'joined-up problems' what have been the 'joined-up solutions'? Not surprisingly, despite the rhetoric of joining up, most initiatives have emanated from the existing central government departments, and, while there is a new recognition that matters relating to learning and skills are not solely the prerogative of DfES centrally and LEAs locally, the approaches tend to be dominated by constraints imposed by organisational culture. The youth justice reforms, led by the YJB, and the initiatives to improve experience of public care through the Quality Protects programme under the auspices of the Department of Health, showed a new emphasis on the importance of mainstream learning and skills acquisition for young people in both the care and criminal justice systems. But both reform programmes were constrained by the traditional departmental machinery centrally and locally, the belief that these 'categories' of young people need to be educated in a completely different way from their peers, and a lack of understanding and authority to influence the basic delivery systems for education and training.

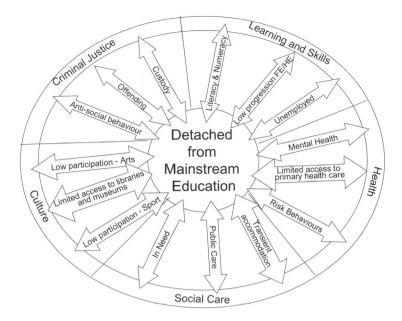

Figure 10.1 Social exclusion and government departments.

The youth justice reforms are often acclaimed by New Labour as a flagship of modernising government, but how effective are they in the crucial relationship with education? The 'processual cogs' may 'positively mesh', as Rod Morgan has observed of the new youth justice infrastructure, but are they turning where education is concerned? (Bateman and Pitts 2005: vi).

Yots are subject to a blended governance whereby they are part of local government but are also accountable to each governing body and to the courts. In recognition of the fact that the prevention of offending requires working with young people who offend across several agencies, they are the central device to ensure that youth justice work has an appropriate status expressed through the ability of managers and practitioners to gain access to appropriate services.

However, the presence of the chief education officer or other senior education manager on the steering group apparently does not often ensure adequate access to mainstream education services for many Yots (Audit Commission 2004; YJB 2006). The steering groups appear to be an uneasy alliance between agencies who may have conflicting priorities with those of the Yot. The Audit Commission surveyed Yot managers to assess the degree of congruence between Yot and governing body objectives. Only a very small proportion of education (schools and LEAs) performance indicators coincided well with those of the Yot, and nearly 60 per cent had some or considerable conflict (Audit Commission 2004).

Such tensions can lead Yots staff deliberately or inadvertently to withhold information that could cause conflict within the steering group. One study found, for example, that over 80 per cent of Yot supervising officers surveyed did not notify the steering group regarding young people of compulsory school age who did not have a full-time educational programme on release to the community part of a DTO, although this is required by national standards (YJB 2000a; ECOTEC 2001).

In the absence of direct control over access to education and training, the YJB and Yots have had to rely on exhortation and local agreements. The YJB has attempted to formalise the relationships between Yots and key educational agencies by providing the use of protocols to define access to appropriate educational provision. Under their national standards, effective protocols are required between Yots and LEAs and also with local LSCs. There appears to be considerable variation in the perceived effectiveness of these protocols. To the extent that these protocols are indicative of the health of the working relationship between Yots and LEAs, there is cause for concern. Nearly one in three (30 per cent) Yots reported that they did not even have a protocol with their LEA. A further one in five Yots felt that their protocol was ineffective (YJB 2006).

Post-16 education and training links appear to be even more attenuated between Yots and local LSCs, only just over one in three (35 per cent) reportedly having a protocol in place. Even where there was a protocol, over two-thirds (69 per cent) responded that the protocol was ineffective (YJB 2006).

Yot education staff

LEAs are required to nominate a representative to Yots. This contribution to resourcing varies very considerably between Yots across England and Wales and averaged 5 per cent nationally in 2003/4 (Audit Commission 2004). Regionally, this varied between 9.3 per cent in the Eastern region to just 2.77 per cent in Wales (YJB 2004c). Similar variations are recorded more locally, as within the London region, contributions from LEAs ranged from over 10 per cent to less than 1 per cent of the Yots' total budget.

There were also variations in the working arrangements, as while some educators were directly employed by the Yots, 43 per cent appeared to be in temporary positions. There appears to be a lack of clarity or consistency over the role of these staff, some undertaking core Yot work and others operating mainly as more specialist advisers. Staff involved in core work and holding case responsibility carry out associated mainstream tasks such as completing ASSET. The varied uses to which the staff are put are also reflected in how other Yots use them. Apparently, only one in four of the education representatives in Yots believe it likely that they would see all young people under supervision who had an educational problem (YJB 2004c). Whether absorbed into mainstream Yot activities or acting as a specialist, the great majority (75 per cent) were providing interventions themselves largely through one-to-one contact. This could include teaching when no other provision is available (Audit Commission 2004). The fact that nearly all of these staff were based wholly in the Yot means they could be at risk of losing touch with their employer, the LEA.

The simple presence of educational representatives within Yots does not guarantee the resolution of educational difficulties; indeed, there may have been unintended consequences, as LEAs and schools may 'use seconded staff to relieve themselves of responsibility for providing services to young offenders and their families' (Audit Commission 2004: 63). There appear to be three main problems with the education role within Yots:

1 Authority – if timely access to suitable education or training provision is the number one priority, as many managers and practitioners believe, any education representative needs to have either the professional credibility of a senior management background within schools or colleges, or equivalent status within a LEA.

2 Absorption – the pressure of mainstream Yot work draws the focus of the education worker inwardly towards the young person and the youth justice system away from the crucial external relationships.

3 Absolution – the very existence of Yots containing an educational representative can tend to allow both LEAs and schools to transfer responsibility. This is manifested by some Yots attempting to establish their own educational provision and in some instances register them as schools.

Ironically, given that many of the staff were either on secondment or had previously been employed by the LEA, one of the most commonly noted difficulties in the role was liaison with the LEA:

Pushing the boundary of expectation of provision for school-aged young offenders: it is unconsciously accepted that there are holes in the education safety net. Yot and educational establishment perspectives on this often conflict, and this interface has to be managed. It is easy to harbour feelings of failure on both sides ... The Yot serves as a 'disclosing agent' for the number of young people drifting or plummeting out of the state education system (YJB 2004c: 71).

Connexions Service

The development and implementation of the Connexions Service was potentially one of the most exciting social policy developments of the last 20 years. When launched, the key aim of the Connexions Service was 'to enable all young people to participate effectively in appropriate learning ... [and] to play a central role in helping to deal with problems experienced by young people, removing any wider barriers to effective engagement in learning that young people are suffering' (DfEE 2000: 32). For the first time, there was an attempt to unite a range of disciplines and professionals including non-educators within an educational/learning framework, with effective participation and progression in mainstream learning for all young people as its goal. While attempting to build on effective partnership and multiagency working, it went further by introducing the new role of personal adviser. This role had the potential to fill the gap of 'one accountable professional' who spans health, social care and criminal justice issues, where these form the barriers to a young person's inclusion in and progression in mainstream education.

There were some considerable threats to its success in achieving its aim. It had some in-built barriers that prevented it being as successful as it might have been. Arguably, the construction and implementation and relative failure of the Connexions Service represents a microcosm of the extent to which new inclusive strategies within the overall theme of reforming public services have had their effectiveness diluted.

While any change programme needs to accept compromises, the vested interests largely determined the shape of the Connexions Service, with the inevitable perpetuation of existing cultures in meeting the needs of socially excluded young people.

In practical terms, the service was largely the product of a 'shotgun wedding' between careers companies and the youth service. At the time, careers companies emphasised the potential threat Connexions presented to guidance services for less disadvantaged young people;

and some elements of the youth service did not feel that they and the young people with whom they work shared the values and approaches of all elements of mainstream education.

A central policy dilemma was created in that Connexions was intended to be 'a universal but targeted service'. It was argued with some justification that a Connexions Service that catered only for the socially excluded would face difficulties. It may itself have become a marginalised service, devalued in the eyes of young people, its practitioners perceived as having lower professional status by mainstream professionals. The concern was that it would not have the impact it ought to in shifting the culture of schools and colleges, and would be vulnerable to significant reductions when the economy experienced a downturn. On the other hand, this may have been a justification for using career company revenues rather than a properly funded youth support service.

The service had to balance the needs of the majority and the socially excluded minority, bring about major cultural change within careers companies and the youth service, and embed the personal adviser role in institutions whose infrastructure was already close to overload. The risk was that the needs of the socially excluded received less attention than the SEU's Bridging the Gap report – the genesis of the service – had intended. In the event, that arguably proved to be correct, but, on the contrary, it was claimed that the needs of young people in school became relatively neglected (DfES 2005a).

Crucially, the CSNU was not established on the lines of the YJB: it remained within the departmental structures of DfES and was largely staffed by civil servants. As a result, its independent voice was much more limited. Given the concerns voiced by Sir Michael Bichard regarding the lack of experience of senior civil servants in operational delivery (*Financial Times*, 3 July 2001), these were serious weaknesses for an initiative intended to transform existing services. Not surprisingly, the central unit was absorbed within the new Children's Service structure in the DfES and lost its identity and authority.

Initially, the role of the personal adviser was to be that of a new professional (DfEE 2000). In the face of opposition from the vested interests in youth work and careers guidance, this was diluted to a new 'professionalism'. In effect, many existing professionals were simply rebadged so that at particular times they could act as 'personal adviser', thereby missing the point entirely.

The Connexions Service, then, was caught on the New Labour 'not only … but also' hook (universal but targeted), lacked the authority of a cross-departmental agency with a degree of autonomy from the civil service, and ended up as an amalgam of careers and youth services with no identifiable new professionals at its core as promised but rather using the rhetoric of a 'new professionalism'. Without a succinct definition of what was so different about the service, it failed to gather significant political support both centrally and locally. Despite the committed efforts of many chief executives and practitioners, all that is likely to remain of the Connexion Service, like the Cheshire cat's smile, is its brand name. Hopefully, in some areas, a much more effective configuration of the youth support service combining perhaps the Connexions Service, the Yot and the youth service will emerge.

Assessment

Working in partnership between agencies and their professionals is increasingly coming to be defined as the exchange of data. Assessment, planning and review processes are the main medium for the collation and distribution of data. Paradoxically, although each new initiative proclaims its commitment to working in partnership, the creation of additional assessment systems reduces further the effectiveness of data exchange, which is already operating at a relatively low level.

One of the findings repeated with monotonous regularity by a succession of both academic studies and government audits and inspections is that the information gathered on young people experiencing major difficulties in education tends to be both limited and tardy. This is greatly compounded when a young person enters the care or the criminal justice systems. This failure on an individual level is replicated at a macrolevel and stymies coherent and effective policymaking.

The main source for information on individuals is through professional assessment. The apparently straightforward task of acquiring and aggregating such information faces two major barriers. Firstly, there is a proliferation of assessment systems which a young person with multiple adversities can almost simultaneously become subject to. Secondly, the nature and purpose of assessment varies significantly among professions.

Given that these young people frequently cross the agency boundaries of health, social care, criminal justice and education, they can be subject to a barrage of multiple, uncoordinated assessments. Unsurprisingly, the result is considerable duplication of effort, and substantial gaps in the professional knowledge of the learning and other important needs of young people who are socially excluded.

Each new initiative tends to bring with it a new assessment, planning and review system for practitioners and young people and their parents/carers to participate in. Although the Connexions Service initially promised that it would 'seek to develop a common assessment tool' (DfEE 2000: 43), it ended up developing its own assessment, planning and review system (APIR), so that practitioners and young people had yet another such bureaucratic system to contend with.

Reflecting on the continued failure to gather timely and accurate information in the youth justice system, particularly that relating to education through assessment, the Audit Commission (2004: 98) recommended that the government, 'in developing one overall assessment tool for children at risk ... should consider having a common core of questions that follow a child, supplemented by specialist sections for different agencies'. This was intended to influence the implementation of the consultation paper *Every Child Matters*, (DfES 2003) which recommended the development of a common assessment instrument for all agencies dealing with children and young people at risk. The Audit Commission report recognised that it will prove extremely difficult, if not impossible, to agree on a common format for all relevant agencies and professionals and to discard all existing procedures.

In fact, the problems of assessment are far more fundamental than simply improved document design, administrative process and managerial will. Assessment processes lie at the very heart of each profession's practice. Consequently, each assessment process is jealously guarded, as to abandon it will be to breach the distinctiveness of each professional grouping and be seen as a serious threat to identity and status. What is more, despite the rhetoric about needs, assessment is usually the means by which a particular agency rations access to its resources, and such authority cannot or will not be readily transferred to others outside.

Given the professional cultural value of each assessment process, it is entirely predictable that a common approach that relies heavily on exhortation and goodwill will not be successful. An approach that is too discretionary will be sidelined or, worse, will become yet another layer of information gathering and create further transmission problems. For a common approach to be successful, it must be built into the initial training of all relevant professions and be part of a major continuing professional development programme. It would also have to replace significant elements of existing assessment processes along the lines recommended by the Audit Commission. Although this would require a high level of design skills, it will require a much higher level of political authority to ensure compliance across social work, youth justice and education staff. In fact short of a major professional realignment or even reconstruction the common assessment framework championed by *Every Child Matters* will probably have only a superficial impact.

Children's services and education reforms

Children's services are currently in the early stages of major reorganisation, and education faces potentially far reaching reforms. The infrastructure of children's services, both centrally and locally, is being integrated following the inquiry report into the death of Victoria Climbié, which catalogued poor communication between the agencies, a lack of coordinated services and a confusion of accountabilities. The Children Act 2004 and the Green Papers *Every Child Matters* and *Youth Matters* (DfES 2005d) established the main themes for integrating children's services, revolving around five key outcomes and providing a framework for all planning, commissioning, providing and inspection of services.

The recent schools White Paper, *Higher Standards, Better Schools* (DfES 2005c) put forward further reforms in relation to admissions, status, leadership and governance of schools within a wider context of giving greater autonomy to schools for better parental choice.

Yet, there are major tensions between these two reform programmes, and the position of young people in the youth justice system is unclear. The YJB remains within the remit of the Home Office, and the relationship of Yots with the new configuration of services is not defined in detail.

Despite the compelling logic that schools are a universal service as the main justification for the transfer of responsibility to the DfES from the Department of Health, schools may be able to choose the level of their involvement. The extension of the quasi-market in education may cause school intakes to become more socially unbalanced.

There is a striking contrast between the language of children's services focusing on 'integration' and 'partnership' with that applied to the prospective status of schools and their greater 'autonomy'. While a new duty to cooperate has been laid on many services, schools are not classified as 'statutory partners', but rather there is an expectation that local authorities and children's trusts will engage with schools. The Children Act 2004 imposed a statutory duty upon local authorities to 'promote the educational achievement of looked after children' (a potential precedent for young people in the youth justice system). Again, this requirement has not been attached to schools. The overarching Children and Young People's Plan is also permissive rather than prescriptive as regards young people in youth justice system.

Social policy outcomes

The success of social policy initiatives in relation to detachment, attainment, school improvement and care, and custodial reforms can increasingly be measured against an array of targets. But as Vulliamy and Webb (2001: 368) warned in a Home Office publication, 'in taking official quantified data for granted – whether at the level of school, LEA or the DfEE – recorded change in such data may reveal more about institutional responses to government target setting than about the impact of a specific educational innovation'. It is unlikely that this institutional response is confined to education. As far as youth justice is concerned, YJB reports on engagement in education, and successive reviews of custodial education have indicated that official returns from Yots and YOIs may considerably overstate how many young people are in education, training or employment and how much education they are in receipt of (YJB 2003c, 2004b, 2006).

Detachment

Exclusion from school may appear to be of relatively little significance compared with some of the major socio-political issues; yet, it has emblematic importance. It encapsulates some of the fundamental social policy dilemmas that confront New Labour, and it represents a challenge in microcosm to the 'third way'. If it is demonstrated that a formal process of exclusion from mainstream education has deleterious consequences for the individual, imposes high costs on communities, and is itself a significant cause of social exclusion, its existence cannot be reconciled with the current government's social policy thrust.

At the heart of the problem is the widening gap between power and responsibility: schools have an increasing amount of individual authority, including the right to exclude their pupils, while LEAs, with a shrinking resource base, are accountable for the education of those excluded pupils.

Exclusion from school – both the concept and its practical outcomes – poses several paradoxes that have a broader socio-political application. At the level of an individual school, it may be perceived as the solution to a problem, but from the perspective of other agencies or the community, it represents the creation of further problems and demands. There is an interesting contrast in attitudes, in that some young people are to be excluded from school as punishment, while those who do not attend are to be returned to school as a punishment ('playing truant' after all implies some degree of enjoyment).

When policy focuses on exclusion from school, it is forced to confront a range of fundamental issues: for example, the discriminatory attitudes and processes within schools and the wider education system, which are having a negative impact on a significant number of young people, including young people from certain ethnic minority groups, young people at risk of offending, and those who are in the care of the local authority. Are the needs of young people who have multiple disadvantages compatible with the disproportionate exercise of individual choice by better-off parents? How is the quasi-market in education to be managed so that the needs of diverse and often disadvantaged groups of children and young people are met?

The initially high-profile exclusion target was achieved relatively rapidly with numbers falling from over 12,000 to 8,000; however, political pressures saw ministers abandon a reduction target for exclusions, and they have now started to rise again, reaching nearly 10,000 in 2004 although falling slightly in 2005.

The trend for total absences from all schools is downwards from 1997 to 2005, but this is mainly due to a reduction in authorised absence. Unauthorised absence has increased particularly at maintained secondary schools, where it is about 18 per cent higher in 2005 than 1997 (DfES 2005b). Given the particular blunt method (percentage of half-days missed) used for measuring non-attendance, these figures may mask significant variations up or down in terms of those young people who are largely or completely detached from primary and secondary school and most at risk of offending.

Reducing the numbers of those not in education, training or employment (NEET) was the highest priority for the Connexions Service. As has been seen in earlier chapters, this is a critical age group for youth justice supplying the great majority of those in custody. According to the CSNU, significant reductions were achieved, although these figures appear to be contradicted by their own colleagues in DfES. The provisional Connexions figures for 2005 are 129,000 young people, in contrast to 220,000 according to the statistical release by DfES. What is more, the trend is rising, probably driven by an overall weakening of demand for labour but also possibly influenced by the curtailment of LSC-funded programmes.

Care needs to be taken in interpreting these figures, as the baseline data have always had a degree of imprecision, the counting rules include young people on only minimal part-time provision and there are many young people whose whereabouts are unknown (see Figure 4.3, Chapter 4).

In fact, the NEET population has remained very stable being either 9 or 10 per cent of 16–18-year-olds for 13 out of the last 15 years.

Since the introduction of the Connexions Service, the proportion out of education, training and employment has, if anything, increased from 9 per cent in 2000 to 11 per cent in 2005 (DfES 2006a).

Developments in the 16–19 education and training system, which is particularly relevant to young people involved in more persistent and serious offending, have not been promising. The authoritative Nuffield Review concluded that the system was characterised by 'only modest rates of participation and attainment compared with our European neighbours, is not comprehensive and has suffered massive academic drift'. (Hayward *et al.* 2005: 127). Increases in participation have been overwhelmingly a middle-class phenomenon, and this polarisation has left other young people behind.

The widely promoted guarantee is that all 16-year-olds are guaranteed an offer of learning or training, but, in practice, eligibility is confined to those of Level 2 attainment, whereas the majority of those at risk in the youth justice system and probably beyond are below this level. Similarly, the initial rapid expansion of Entry to Employment (E2E) programmes was halted, as its outcomes were refocused to Level 2 qualifications thereby excluding many of those at risk.

This disjuncture between the LSC as the funder of the key training programmes for young people referred by Connexions and Yots has been a major fault line in ensuring access.

The YJB's target of 90 per cent of Yots-supervised young people being in suitable full-time education training or employment has not been reached; the national reported average is 75 per cent. This figure has to be treated circumspectly for a number of reasons. Understandably, Yots do not have detailed registration systems, and while arrangements may have been made for full-time education, training or employment, the quality assurance on attendance is often unsatisfactory. The counting rules appear to have a number of loopholes in that despite the fact that the target was originally framed 'at the beginning during and end of sentence', the counting rules in many areas include information at the point of case closure and may well often simply represent arranged destinations rather than the receipt of education or training. In addition, the interpretation of 'suitable' is rather flexible and the inclusion of attendance at leisure facilities, for example, may be more distantly related to reducing educational risk factors than, say, attendance at literacy and numeracy classes. Consequently, the recording by some Yots of over 90 per cent of young people in suitable, full-time education, training or employment may need to be treated with considerable scepticism, particularly when compared with Yots, who claim to apply a more rigorous approach and return figures closer to 30–40 per cent.

While it was not a specific target, the government required that local educational authorities provide all excluded children and young people with suitable full-time education by the autumn of 2002. This is not routinely monitored by the DfES, but the evidence suggests that provision commonly falls far short of this and that there are significant delays in getting access even to part-time provision for those who are excluded.

Despite a significant expansion in both on- and off-site segregated provision, there still appears to be a significant shortfall (see Chapter 3). On balance, the major educational risk factor for offending of being detached from mainstream education and training appears to have been little ameliorated during this period. While significant new resources have been pumped into segregated provision both on and off school sites, this may have had the perverse effect of stimulating demand still further.

Attainment

The two major strategies designed to lift attainment levels are the literacy and numeracy strategy aimed at primary schools and the basic skills strategy, Skills for Life, which is the adult equivalent. These have been overlaid with a range of programmes such as Excellence in Cities. Progress in literacy and numeracy (measured against government targets) has stalled, and although it was apparently higher in 2004, nearly a quarter of children still do not achieve the expected standard at age 11. Some analysts have even argued that the significant increase that occurred between 1995 and 2000 was largely illusory (Frater 2005).

GCSE grades at A–C have seen consistent incremental increases. This headline figure disguises the fact that proportionately more boys are not achieving this standard and a growth in the proportion who failed altogether.

The basic skills strategy was claimed to have achieved the target of 750,000 new qualifications in literacy and numeracy, but its performance has been roundly criticised by the Chief Inspector of the Adult Learning Inspectorate (ALI): 'in provision for adult literacy and numeracy there has been a depressing lack of improvement and a failure to tackle weaknesses of the past four years' (ALI 2005: 18). Part of the reason for this, he argued, was the adoption of too high a threshold in the working definition of literacy and numeracy by Skills for Life, thus missing those most disadvantaged, such as the majority of young people in youth justice population.

The education targets for young people in the care system differ markedly in their construction in that they are 'convergence' targets. This is a potentially useful approach. It takes account of the fact that peers in the general population may well be improving and emphasises that these young people are part of the mainstream and that the aspiration is for them to rejoin it with regard to attainment and progression. It possibly guards against the well-attested low educational expectations that can become self-fulfilling for young people beset with multiple adversities. Of course, it does throw into stark relief just how poor the education outcomes are for young people in the care system.

Since 2002 and the impact of the Quality Protects initiative, there has been some convergence; that is, many young people in the care system have been improving at a faster rate than their peers in the general population. However, it is very likely that none of the attainment targets will be met.

Custody

The SEU's Bridging the Gap report (1999) set out an action plan (endorsed by the prime minister and Parliament), which included requirements of Yots for baseline assessment of a young person's educational needs at the start of a sentence with an exit assessment to measure progress. Targets were to have been set for the education/ training value which Yots would add, while those under 16 in custody were supposed to receive at least 30 hours of education and personal development per week, with similar requirements for 16- and 17-year-olds. In the event, the reforms attempted by the YJB appear to have fallen well short of this. Chapter 7 described the statistical alchemy practised upon the figures for access, participation and progression in education in YOIs.

School organisation

The number of low-performing schools has fallen. There are some signs that targeting primary schools in deprived areas can result in greater than average increases. Education Action Zones were in effect replaced by the Excellence in Cities programme, which covered 2400 schools in 58 deprived areas. In these schools, the proportion of 16-year-olds getting five or more GCSE grades A–C increased at twice the rate of other schools.

Managerialism and management information

Critics of New Labour's youth justice reforms emphasise the introduction of 'a technocratic managerialism with no principles or independent rationale' (Smith 2003: 3). Others argue that 'managerialism stresses the need to develop a connected, coherent, efficient and above all *cost-effective* series of policies and practices' (Muncie and Hughes 2002: 5). Yet, paradoxically, very little is known about the access to and participation and progression in education, training and employment of young people who offend. Managerialism cannot flourish without management information, but this is often lacking in both youth justice and educational settings. Ofsted, for example, was withering in its criticisms in relation to young people detached from mainstream school: 'Most significantly, schools and LEAs are not tracking pupils and do not have a comprehensive view of their whereabouts, achievements or destinations. There is insufficient monitoring of the quality and range of alternative provision' (Ofsted 2004: 5). These weaknesses directly affect those young people of most concern to Yots, 'indicating a high potential for pupils to be lost to the system, to be accessing minimal education and training opportunities, and to be out of school for a large proportion of the school week without the knowledge of the LEA' (Ofsted 2004: 25).

Within custodial education, the paucity of management information, particularly with regard to outcomes, may even be preventing recognition of some progress. A recent YJB review of the implementation of its education reforms in YOIs concluded that 'despite the increased inputs particularly through new posts and increased expenditure on resources the fundamental weaknesses in monitoring and reporting systems effectively prevent this review from establishing equivalent improvements in either outputs (e.g. number of educational hours received by individual young people) or outcomes such as learning gains' (YJB 2005c: 7). Central government may espouse modernisation through managerialism, but this is often blocked by the fear of exposing underresourcing or underachievement locally coupled with the low priority given to many of these young people by mainstream services.

Conclusions

The period 1997 to 2006 has seen an almost unprecedented surge in the amount of legislation on education and crime. Despite the recognition of joined-up problems, the creation of joined-up solutions has often been elusive, and the great range of initiatives has often had centrifugal effects, as people concentrate on devising and implementing rather than making linkages. While the concept of social exclusion has gained some currency in that there is greater appreciation by policymakers of processes that combine to detach people from mainstream life, social inclusion remains underdeveloped conceptually and appears to be largely an exercise in rebranding in its implementation. This is because there is no accepted definition across education and youth justice, and it faces serious opposition from many practitioners, and possibly the public, and can be seen as conceptually at odds with the thrust of social policy on youth justice.

The plethora of targets means that there are somewhat crude measures to judge the impact of social policy on the key educational risk and protective factors in relation to offending. There has been considerable emphasis on improving attainment with some success for the general population, although the rate of increase is flattening. Many young people most at risk, however, fall outside the range of the targets. There is early and limited evidence that attainment increases at a faster rate in schools in deprived areas where there is a concentration of initiatives on them.

Despite some initial success in the reduction of permanent exclusion from school and a shrinkage in the number of young people recorded as not in education training or employment, both appear to have been reversed, and there remains a very significant problem regarding the access and participation in mainstream education and training for young people most at risk.

The Quality Protects programme has clearly enhanced the educational experiences for some young people in the care system, and there is much greater clarity over just how poor their educational outcomes are compared with their peers in the general population. The reforms of education in custody appear to have been less successful, as they are hampered by the size of the juvenile custodial population, the consistently weak articulation between work in custody and community, and the lack of recognition for the need of a programme comparable with Quality Protects. The most promising initiative in relation to the education of young people who offend was the Connexions strategy, which is perceived at best to have had only limited success.

The contradiction between the rhetoric of social inclusion and the reality of segregationist education policies and exclusionary youth justice policies is a fault line running through New Labour's social policy. A benign judgement would see this fault line opening up only under the intense pressure of general election campaigns but generally being gradually closed by stealth through approaches to both education and youth justice that encourage progressive personal and social development within the mainstream. A bleaker perspective is that eventually the fundamental incompatibilities between social inclusion and the exclusionary dynamics within education and youth justice will pull apart. As public expenditure on education and youth justice begins to ebb, the failure of social inclusion will be seen on the high water-mark of renovated or newly built PRUs. The politics of behaviour will supersede the niceties of social inclusion and custodial, and out-of-school and training populations will increase further.

Central to the whole New Labour project is the drive to ensure that Middle England does not desert state education or the National Health Service, with the obvious negative consequences for those with multiple disadvantages, who would be left with the residual, significantly inferior services. This has meant that in the short term more emphasis has been placed on helping raise the achievement of the majority, and that reassuring gestures have been made repeatedly to illustrate that government policy is tough on those who are perceived as threatening to the well being of the majority through their behaviour in school and in the community. If, over the medium term, the politics of reassurance do not evolve into the positive promotion of inclusion that will bring benefits for the majority as well as the minority, then this approach will be ultimately self-defeating, as the socially excluded will be left further behind. The cost to the economy and to the well-being of society as a whole will continue to rise.

Summary

❑ Education and youth justice have been two dominating social policy themes that are increasingly converging in the politics of behaviour where zero tolerance is promoted on the streets and in the classroom.

❑ While the social exclusion discourse has provided a framework for policy analysis, social inclusion lacks consistent definition and is largely absent from youth justice initiatives. The notion of inclusion appears to be increasingly confined to describing interventions with those who are excluded.

❑ A much more focused approach has been taken towards the education of young people in public care with a raft of support measures, convergence targets and management information, and the Children Act 2004 imposes a statutory duty to ensure their education.

- ❑ The emphasis on discipline in schools and the abandonment of the exclusion and non-attendance targets is likely to lead to increased detachment of young people at risk.
- ❑ There have been some significant social policy setbacks, such as the relative failure of the Connexions Service and the continuing high level of the juvenile custodial population.
- ❑ While there has been an increased recognition of the existence of significant numbers of young people receiving a limited or non-existent education outside mainstream school, this has led to the formation of a significant segregated education sector that is of variable quality and will prove difficult to maintain in more constrained economic circumstances.
- ❑ In preventing offending, the YJB has placed great emphasis on the importance of young people participating and progressing in education. It has had only limited success with its two main challenges: influencing mainstream education to fulfil its duties and bringing about a progressive change in the quality of custodial education.

Chapter 11

Conclusions

At this point in our history we must enter once again into the debate that preceded mass schooling over a century ago: namely, what sort of society do we want to create, and how can the education system help us to reach such a society?

David Hargreaves, *New Statesman* (29 November 1999)

We should rightfully have the power to arrest all these little beggars, loafers, and vagabonds that infest our city, take them from the streets and place them in schools where they are compelled to receive education and moral principles.

Chicago Board of Education (1898)

Relationship of education and youth justice

In the public mind, education performs a variety of functions, but the socialisation of young people into conforming to norms of behaviour is a high priority. Failing to comply with internal rules or not attending school are transgressions that are perceived as a threat first to society rather than a loss for the individual in terms of foregone learning. The boundaries between transgression and delinquent behaviour are becoming increasingly blurred. This is reflected in various sentencing process biases. Engagement with mainstream education is perceived as a significant mitigating factor. But there is a deep ambivalence too. Despite the importance accorded to schools in preventing crime, committing an offence can result in double jeopardy whereby a young person can receive a custodial sentence and be removed from a school roll. A violent act within the school can result in both a prosecution and an exclusion.

Education has long been perceived as having a powerful corrective role for those young people who have committed offences. This has two aspects. There is the rational chain: learn to read and write, gain qualifications, become employed, stop offending and pay taxes. But this is accompanied by the more visceral notion of schooling as instilling discipline. To many, education is a rather punitive rite of passage.

These impulses led to the creation of the reformatories and industrial schools. The corrective power of schooling was widely recognised, as was the overt moral reclamation through Christian values and social control through monotonous labour. For much of the nineteenth century, the history of schooling was the history of youth justice. The withering away of the reformatories perhaps owes more to their financial and management costs than any waning in the public belief in their efficacy. While the residential component may be untenable, it is still an attractive proposition, and it may be rediscovered. Certainly, the attachment to day schools that would be little different in ethos from a late nineteenth-century industrial school is still strong. The Conservative Party manifesto drafted by its current leader for the 2005 General Election contained a pledge to create 24,000 places in 'Turnaround Schools'. As city academies and specialist schools proliferate, how long will it be before the twenty-first century version of the reformatory emerges?

Both education and youth justice systems have expansionary tendencies. Children start education earlier and stay longer - schools themselves are open longer. In youth justice, sentencing powers have increased, the age of responsibility has decreased, and the remit extends to those who have not yet committed crimes. The two separate expanding systems increasingly overlap: restorative justice and police officers in schools; youth-inclusion programmes and the prosecution of parents whose children do not attend school. But both systems contain powerful exclusionary dynamics that appear to be strengthening.

The positive and negative effects of schools on the likelihood of a young person's offending remain controversial. There are significant gaps in our knowledge regarding the causal and temporal order of educational underachievement and detachment in relation to the onset, persistence and desistance from delinquency. On balance, it seems harder to sustain the belief that schools simply process a given intake than to accept institutional influences on the propensity to offend. This is not to deny the importance of compositional effects either directly or indirectly on delinquency. Relationships with teachers and peers may well be influential on delinquent behaviour, but we do not know exactly how and in what circumstances. Attachment to school appears to be an important social bond and an integral part of development. Again, how this is achieved for a given individual or groups of young people appears to be speculative and to reside in the nebulous concept of school ethos.

The two principal educational risk factors for offending appear to be low attainment and weak engagement in school, culminating in complete detachment. The majority of those in the youth justice system appear to have very low levels of attainment, and many are barely functionally literate or numerate. Detachment from mainstream school or post-16 education, training or employment is the most striking educational characteristic of these young people. While both detachment and low attainment are predictive of offending, and the evidence, at least as far as exclusions are concerned, is increasing of a causal relationship, the transmission of risk is much less clear. Detachment may develop through greater involvement in delinquent peer groups and engaging in other risk behaviours, such as substance misuse, and an increase in unsupervised time. This could be reinforced through a bias in processing towards higher disposals, particularly custodial sentences, ultimately lowering the chances of employment. Attainment may well have a reciprocal relationship with detachment, although there is little evidence to show that it acts directly. Indirect effects could be transmitted, for example, through an expression of low self-esteem as a learner or through aggressive behaviour leading to exclusion. Low attainment at school-leaving age is associated with subsequent non-participation at ages 16–18, which strongly predicts later unemployment (which appears to have an independent effect on offending).

Current scale and nature of the problem

It has been argued that, to all intents and purposes, there is an ill-defined group of young people beset by multiple disadvantages who usually have difficulties gaining access to, participating in and progressing within mainstream education. It may therefore make much more sense for social policy to focus on reducing the size of the population that is outside mainstream education, training and employment rather than to subdivide it into categories defined largely according to professional roles or agency responsibilities. If the risk transmission mechanisms discussed above are accurate, the route taken out of the mainstream may be irrelevant, it is the simple fact of being detached for prolonged periods that increases the current and future risks. The taxonomy of the detached – 'permanent exclusions', 'fixed-term exclusions', 'informal exclusions', 'self-exclusions' and 'truancy' of various kinds – is unconvincing and has little practical meaning for those working in the youth justice system. The confusion of accountabilities compounds the issue, meaning that a series of subpopulations are counted often in very different ways. While it is in the interests of some agencies to highlight the scale of the problem, for most there are vested interests in minimising it in order to achieve government targets or ration access by other agencies to scarce resources.

Despite the promotion of an annual census in each local authority area by both the YJB and the Audit Commission, there seems to be considerable reluctance to do this census. This is odd, since the one simple measure and target population would provide a focal point for a range of agencies to join up their approaches. An annual census would enable trends to be identified. Of course, the strong suspicion is that for many local authorities such an exercise would simply highlight deficiencies in resources, agency performance and monitoring systems.

From what figures are available, it is estimated that well over one-third of a million children and young people up to the age of 18 are outside mainstream school, FE, training or employment. Young people in the youth justice system figure prominently, constituting perhaps as much as one-third of this wider population.

The disaffection discourse tends to be dominant in the social policy sphere and common among practitioners. For a concept that is so widely accepted, it is remarkably unsupported by any robust evidence. Its utility is derived from its lack of definition and location of problems within the young person. Its use can absolve mainstream education from its shortcomings and comes close at times to justifying the supposed uneducable status of some young people. Disaffected is probably a simplistic description of the complex and contradictory attitudes that many young people have to different educational institutions.

The main conclusion is that there is a deep-rooted cultural mismatch between the youth justice and education systems. The very different professional backgrounds, environments and objectives lead to collective behaviours that often tend to detach young people who offend from mainstream education and constitute barriers to their reintegration. This cultural mismatch has some salient characteristics.

Despite working with the same young people albeit at different points in their educational careers, there is virtually no professional cross-pollination between staff in youth justice and education. Not only are there conflicting objectives and targets but there is also a lack of knowledge of the priorities and specific targets placed on each other. For instance, awareness of the YJB's education targets within schools and FE colleges is likely to be almost non-existent. There is an ever-present tension between the focus of the youth justice system on the single young person and management of the group that characterises educational institutions. There are few practical professional links between the two systems; for example, there is little synchronisation between sentence length and, for example, examination and course commencement. The everyday workings of the youth justice system often disrupt a young person's participation in education through for example court appearances, remands to custody or case reviews.

There is often confusion over the accountability for the education of young people involved in offending. Responsibility for the education or training of these young people appears to be a baton that is regularly passed and frequently dropped between schools, LEAs, custodial institutions and LSCs, with Yots and Connexions partnerships being rather inconsistent intermediaries.

Evidence-based practice

Ostensibly, the commitment to evidence-based practice is one of the main ways of joining up government and ensuring that multiagency working is more effective. Could the 'What works?' movement provide a bridge across the cultural divide between youth justice and education? The prospects seem limited. Even within youth justice, the enthusiastic adoption of this approach has been criticised as simplistic, and within education many have doubted its applicability to the complexities of the learning process. Perhaps the principal barrier to its adoption, though, is that it is really a highly political approach, in that only certain types of interventions have public approval irrespective of demonstrable effectiveness or lack of it. For instance, if community sentences that were perceived as too lenient by the public were found through rigorous evaluation to be much more effective in reducing reoffending than custody, there would still be little chance in the current climate of their introduction at the expense of custody. Conversely, there are examples of programmes that continue to have both public and professional support yet are demonstrably ineffective.

There is a major deficit in relevant information both on the educational needs and behaviours of the young people and on the outcomes of intervention. While it may be unfair to accuse the different agencies of deliberately arranging this situation in order to prevent rigorous scrutiny of their costs and outcomes, it is certainly both cause and effect of the deep divisions that lie between them.

On a broader level both in central and local government, there is little evidence of an evaluation ethos, let alone a research and development approach. Much of the evidence tends to come from North America. The justifications include the opportunity costs, most managers lack of awareness of the cost of rigorous research designs, and implementation timescales that need to produce early results. Underlying this is perhaps the failure for professions to be sufficiently self-critical and consider that their interventions may be even ineffective or harmful. Nearly a decade of significant increases in public expenditure on education and youth justice and wave upon wave of reforms and initiatives have not seen a commensurate increase in knowledge of what works, as research and evaluation have often been neglected.

Effectiveness of New Labour's education and youth justice reforms

Education and youth justice are not only highly topical politically but also have always been politicised. While 'law and order' has become increasingly significant as a party political issue over the last 25 years, this has been joined by educational standards and behaviour. These two dominating political themes have converged in a politics of behaviour where 'zero tolerance' policies are to be pursued on the streets and in the schools. In relation to education, the New Labour strategy has been to try to ensure the middle-class attachment to state education particularly in large urban areas. Rather than attacking private education directly, it has sought to persuade the middle class to participate in a quasi-market within state education with the extension of choice, increased diversity of schools, programmes for the gifted and talented, and a drive on standards. While one justification of this strategy is that it ultimately will increase social inclusion, the short-term trade-off may be increased numbers of young people who become detached from mainstream classes, enter on-school units, and end up in some kind of out-of-school provision, sometimes one largely notional. Ironically, this education strategy may, at least in the short term, be exacerbating the risk factors for offending for some young people.

Conceptually and practically, social inclusion is at best weakly developed; and at worst, it actually confirms the socially excluded status of many young people. The SEU has failed to deliver on its initial promise, partly because it has been unable to articulate any concept of social inclusion, confining itself instead to describing interventions with those who are excluded, and partly because its influence over departmental policy has declined considerably since its inception. Its initial critical reports have been superseded by cheerleading for government policies.

The youth justice reforms have received fierce criticism and are accused of continuing a carceral bonanza, criminalising social policy and drawing many more children and young people into the criminal justice system. Less polemical assessments emphasise the creation of a coherent local multiagency infrastructure linked to a relatively independent and authoritative national body. While the social inclusion discourse appears to have barely influenced the policies and programmes promoted by the YJB, it has at least emphasised the crucial role of mainstream education and has attempted to reform custodial education, albeit with limited success.

One of the main barriers to the access and participation of many young people in the youth justice system is the attitude of many professionals. While there is evidence that many teachers feel that mainstream school is not appropriate for young people who have offended, more ostensibly benign attitudes pose at least as much of a block. The social work ethos often puts a priority on meeting the emotional and relationship needs of a young person first, so that education is a second-order problem. The argument is often used that young people with multiple challenges in their lives cannot cope with full-time education. Their 'disaffection' with traditional schooling is raised repeatedly as a justification for a ragbag of part-time learning programmes, usually with a significant leisure activity component.

Containment education based upon a 'pool and ping-pong' curriculum is readily justified in these circumstances. Some Yots interpret the YJB's requirement for full-time education (defined as 25 hours per week) for those on ISSPs as 15 hours' education supplemented by a range of casework. Clearly, Yots are facing major structural challenges in gaining access to suitable full-time placements, but to hide behind flimsy notions of disaffection or to focus on other issues as a priority at the expense of education is unacceptable. After all, the track record of social work in resolving the emotional needs of young people is much weaker than that of education in providing a route to employment and independence.

The vested interests of some voluntary organisations lead them to use similar arguments. Much of their provision occurs outside mainstream education, so great emphasis is placed on preparing the young people for mainstream programmes rather than actually introducing them relatively immediately to full-time education or training.

Such attitudes in consequence deflect interest from measuring hard outcomes, such as improvements in literacy and numeracy or qualifications gained, and maintaining standard school practices, such as detailed monitoring of attendance. The void in our knowledge about the educational experiences and outcomes for young people in the youth justice system becomes self-perpetuating. Those responsible for mainstream services can ignore this hidden population, and assessing more or less effective approaches to the engagement and progression of these young people becomes almost impossible.

Everything points to the conclusion not only that becoming detached from mainstream education is a significant risk factor for offending but also that entry into the youth justice system tends further to detach young people, and lower their attainment and their chances of a successful transition to FE and employment, compared with those of similar backgrounds. Until this is widely recognised by policymakers, managers and practitioners within both education and youth justice, the educational failure of significant numbers of young people will continue with potential knock-on effects on their offending.

At a time when the numbers in custody, placed in segregated education, or not engaged in education, training or employment are all at a historically high level what are the prospects for improving this situation? The realistic answer is that they are pretty limited. An increasingly anxious and threatened public (despite most objective risks having fallen or stayed the same), a growing political punitive consensus on crime by young people, the expansion of market forces in education, a more constrained outlook for growth in public expenditure, and a point in the political cycle where radical professional reform is untenable are formidable obstacles.

Segregated education has been used to control or to rescue the children of the poor for over 200 years, and its rebranding under the social inclusion banner has only strengthened its position. Clearly, mainstream education as currently constructed needs its safety valve, and where schools have increased power and a greater share of education resources, but no enduring responsibility for placement, the movement out of school is unlikely to be reversed.

The most likely response by policymakers is to continue to conceptualise the problem as the inherent difficulties of the young person and to conceive of offenders as a discrete category of learners. This has already begun with the creation of the Offenders' Learning and Skills Service. This ineluctably draws policy and provision further down the cul-de-sac of segregated provision and the creation of an offending learning identity. The YJB's National Specification for Learning and Skills (for young people on a DTO in prison service accommodation) has seen its scope extended to adults and more emphasis placed on resettlement to earn its new title, of the 'Offenders' Learning Journey'. Consequently, the basic policy and practice question becomes 'how do we engage these young people in education?' rather than 'how do we engage the education and training system in meeting the needs of young people at risk of offending or reoffending?'

A possible way forward?

There is perhaps no greater management challenge than that of transforming the culture of organisations. Therefore, radically changing the cultures within schools and the support and specialist agencies, given current public opinion, is not a realistic short-term option. Any programme for change has to be designed along the grain of current social policy development.

Following a 25-year campaign initially sparked by academics and promoted vigorously by some voluntary organisations, policymakers accepted that the experiences of young people in the care system increased their already high risks of education failure. Modest but significant progress has been made in reducing some of these risks, and a higher priority is given to education within social work. However, it must be borne in mind that public and professional opinion does not have an innate sympathy when a young person is perceived as an offender as opposed to a victim of neglect or abuse.

It is interesting that in the USA the Department of Justice and the Department of Education developed a joint initiative, Youth Out of Education Mainstream (YOEM). This initiative was founded on a recognition that although different approaches would be necessary, the primary issue was simply the number of young people outside mainstream education whatever the reason. The YOEM initiative had three goals: to reduce the number of young people in danger of leaving or who had already left mainstream education; to concentrate on those at risk of delinquency; and to raise awareness of this growing problem (Ingersoll and LeBoeuf 1997).

Given this model and the experience of the measures taken to improve educational outcomes for young people in the care system, the design and introduction of an educational framework akin to the Quality Protects initiative for those in the youth justice system could provide a way forward.

The starting point would be a detailed national assessment of those detached from both compulsory education and post-16 education, training and employment, using a simple single measure for all up to the age of 19. This would be supplemented by an annual local census led by local authorities. These exercises would need to be sufficiently rigorous to distinguish between what is ostensibly arranged and what is actually received by young people and to flush out part-time provision and dubious practices such as extended study leave. This would enable the identification of priority young people in the youth justice system, such as those without any provision. Other ideas to be borrowed from the findings of social care research would include a focus on placement stability. To this end, schools should retain responsibility for the education of young people remanded or sentenced to custody. Currently, many young people aged 16-18 are experiencing multiple training or employment placements and spending significant periods completely detached, but this is not always picked up by the current tracking system of Connexions.

Convergence targets on both detachment and attainment could be introduced, as has been done for young people in the care system. Their value lies in the fact that while they highlight the extent of their educational failure compared with their peers it also links them to mainstream expectations. If the attainment levels of those in the care system can be monitored there is no reason that this cannot be done for those in the youth justice system.

There needs to be a transfer of commissioning authority for placements to either Yots or whatever configuration of youth support services evolve from Connexions. Currently there is a substantial deficit in the supply of appropriate placements. It may be that the role of education in Yots could be upgraded to provide greater leverage for those of compulsory school age and possibly an LSC representative for those aged 16–18.

As far as custodial education is concerned, the sheer scale of the underfunding in both capital and revenue precludes significant improvement with the current level of the custodial population. More significantly, though, it is difficult to escape the conclusion that a large-scale investment could be counter-productive. Not only might the image of secure colleges encourage more custodial sentences, given the concerns of magistrates with education, but also the exclusionary nature of custody would serve to detach young people further from education and training.

The only chances of significant improvement lie in a very significant reduction in the custodial population and a complete reconfiguration of the juvenile secure estate. Reduction of demand in the absence of changes in public opinion could probably be achieved only through measures such as transferring cash-limited funds to court areas so that they commission custodial placements with the potential for redeployment of resources. Security-focused regimes, except for those convicted of grave crimes, need to be replaced by education-focused institutions, such as FE colleges, with the prison service not having any input.

Public opinion has some interesting strands tangled around notions of education and punishment as indicated by the Unlocking Learning project, that could be woven into more community-based education and training interventions rather than custodial ones. Equally, according to other surveys, substantial numbers of the public would volunteer to work with young people in the youth justice system to help with literacy and numeracy. There is, however, a very real risk of simply replacing YOIs with reformatories, and the motley array of out-of-school provision with a twenty-first-century version of industrial schools.

Arguably, these are palliatives in the absence of a truly inclusive and appropriately resourced education system. Even if that was to come about, it would be unrealistic to expect such a system to overcome all the fundamental social and economic inequalities that underlie poor educational outcomes and much involvement in offending.

As this book illustrates, very little is known about some of the young people who concern us the most. Research is necessary in three main areas:

- to establish the basic educational demographics of the youth justice system;
- to chart the educational exclusion careers of young people in the context of their involvement in the care and criminal justice system;
- to determine points of intervention, understand better the processes of detachment, and develop robust evaluations of what works in ensuring better access, participation and progression in education.

The very significant costs of segregated education will bring its expansion to an end, but this is unlikely to mean more inclusionary policies; rather, there will be even more obfuscation of the numbers detached from mainstream education. The reality will be, in effect, a three-tier system comprising mainstream schooling, segregated education in its various forms, and those receiving nothing at all. The history of mass education is shorter than that of penal education, and it has never attempted to cater for all children and young people. It is not that inclusion has been tried and failed – it has never been attempted. As Ron Edwards, one of the leading researchers in the effective schools movement in America observed, 'We can, whenever and wherever we choose, successfully teach all children *whose schooling is of interest to us.* We already know more than we need to in order to do that. Whether or not we do it must finally depend upon how we feel about the fact that we haven't so far' (Coffey and Gemignani 1994: 4).

References

Abrams, F. (2005) 'Better behaved', *Prospect Magazine*, 117: 12–17.

Adey, P., Fairbrother, R. and William, D. (1999) *A Review of Research on Learning Strategies and Learning Styles*. King's College, London School of Education.

Adult Learning Inspectorate (ALI) (2005) *Annual Report of the Chief Inspector 2004–05*. Coventry: Adult Learning Inspectorate.

Alexander, K., Entwisle, D. and Dauber, S. (1993) *On the Success of Failure – A Reassessment of the Effects of Retention in the Primary Grades*. Cambridge: Cambridge University Press.

Alexander, K., Entwisle, D. and Horsey, C. (1997) 'From the first grade forward: early foundations of high school drop out', *Sociology of Education*, 70: 87–107.

Altschuler, M. and Armstrong, T. (1999) *Reintegration, Supervised Release and Intensive Aftercare*. Washington, DC: Office of Juvenile Justice and Delinquency Prevention.

Armstrong, D., Hine, J., Hacking, S., Armaos, R., Jones, R., Klessinger, N., and France, A. (2005) *Children, Risk and Crime: The On Track Youth Lifestyles Survey*. London: Home Office Research Study No. 278, Research Development and Statistics Directorate.

Arts Council England (ACE) (2005) *Access, Participation and Progression in the Arts for Young People on Detention and Training Orders*. London: Arts Council England.

Audit Commission (1996) *Misspent Youth: Young People and Crime*. London: Audit Commission.

Audit Commission (1999) *Missing Out: LEA Management of School Attendance and Exclusion*. London: Audit Commission.

Audit Commission (2004) *Youth Justice 2004: A Review of the Reformed Youth Justice System*. London: Audit Commission.

Aynsley-Green, A. (2003) *Do Ye Hear the Children Weeping, O My Brothers, Ere the Sorrow Comes with Years?* Great Ormond Street Hospital for Children. Nottingham: Russell Press.

Bailey, V. (1987) *Delinquency and Citizenship: Reclaiming the Young Offender, 1914–1948.* Oxford: Clarendon Press.

Baker, K., Jones, S., Roberts, C. and Merrington, S. (2002) *The Evaluation of the Validity and Reliability of the Youth Justice Board's Assessment for Young Offenders: Findings from the First Two Years of the Use of ASSET.* Oxford: Centre for Criminological Research, University of Oxford.

Baldwin, D., Coles, B. and Mitchell, W. (1999) 'The formation of an underclass or disparate processes of social exclusion? Evidence from two groupings of "vulnerable youth"', in R. MacDonald (ed) *Youth, the 'Underclass' and Social Exclusion.* London: Routledge.

Ball, C. and Connolly, J. (2000) 'Educationally disaffected young offenders: youth court and agency responses to truancy and school exclusions', *British Journal of Criminology*, 40: 594–616.

Ballas, D., Rossiter, D., Thomas, B., Clarke, G. and Dorling, D. (2005) *Geography Matters: Simulating the Local Impacts of National Social Policies.* York: Joseph Rowntree Foundation.

Barber, M. (1997) *The Learning Game: Arguments for an Education Revolution.* London: Indigo.

Barry, M. (1998) 'Social exclusion and social work: an introduction', in M. Barry and C. Hallett (eds) *Social Exclusion and Social Work: Issues of Theory, Policy and Practice.* Dorset: Russell House Publishing.

Barry, M. and Hallett, C. (eds) (1998) *Social Exclusion and Social Work, Issues of Theory, Policy and Practice.* Dorset: Russell House Publishing.

Bateman, T. and Pitts, J. (eds) (2005) *The RHP Companion to Youth Justice.* Dorset: Russell House Publishing.

Battistich, V., Solomon, D., Watson, M. and Schaps, E. (1997) 'Caring school communities', *Educational Psychologist*, 32: 137–51.

Berg, I. and Nursten, J. (1996) *Unwillingly to School.* London: Gaskell.

Bernstein, B. (1975) *Class, Codes and Control.* London: Routledge and Kegan Paul.

Berridge, D., Brodie, I., Pitts, J., Porteous, D. and Tarling, R. (2001) *The Independent Effects of Permanent Exclusion from School on the Offending Careers of Young People.* RDS Occasional Paper No. 71, Crown Copyright.

Bichard, M. (2001) *Financial Times,* 3 July.

Biehal, N., Clayden, J., Stein, M. and Wade, J. (1992) *Prepared for Living? A Survey of Young People Leaving the Care of Three Local Authorities.* London: National Children's Bureau.

Blyth, E. and Milner, J. (1996) 'Black boys excluded from school: race or masculinity issues?', in E. Blyth and J. Milner (eds) *Exclusion from School: Inter-professional Issues for Policy and Practice.* London: Routledge.

Bonta, J. (1996) 'Risk-needs assessment and treatment', in A. Harland (ed) *Choosing Correctional Options That Work.* Thousand Oaks, CA: Sage.

Bowles, R., Pradiptyo, R. and Garcia Reyes, M. (2006) *Estimating the Impact of the Safer School Partnerships Programme.* York: University of York.

Bradshaw, J., Kemp, P., Baldwin, S. and Rowe, A. (2004) *The Drivers of Social Exclusion: A Review of the Literature for the Social Exclusion Unit in the Breaking the Cycle Series.* London: Office of the Deputy Prime Minister.

Bridges, A. (1998) *Increasing the Employability of Offenders: An Inquiry into Probation Service Effectiveness.* Oxford: Probation Studies Unit Report No. 5.

Brodie, I. (2000) 'Children's homes and school exclusion: redefining the problem', *Support for Learning,* 15(1): 25–9.

Burney, E. (2005) *Making People Behave: Anti-Social Behaviour, Politics and Policy.* Cullompton: Willan Publishing.

Burrell, J. (1992) *The Times,* 7 December.

Bynner J. (2002) *Young People's Changing Routes to Independence.* York: Joseph Rowntree Foundation.

Bynner, J., McIntosh, S., Vignoles, A., Dearden, L., Reed, H. and Van Reenen, J. (2001) *Improving Adult Basic Skills – Benefits to the Individual and to Society.* Sheffield: DfES, Research Brief 251.

Byrne, D. (2005) *Social Exclusion.* Maidenhead: Open University Press.

Carlebach, J. (1970) *Caring for Children in Trouble.* London: Routledge and Kegan Paul.

Carlen, P., Gleeson, D. and Wardhaugh, J. (1992) *Truancy: the Politics of Compulsory Schooling.* Buckingham: Open University Press.

Carpenter, M. (1968) *Reformatory Schools for the Children of the Perishing and Dangerous Classes, and for Juvenile Offenders.* London: Woburn Press.

Centre for Longitudinal Studies (1970) *British Cohort Study (BCS70).* London: Institute of Education.

Centre for Longitudinal Studies (1970) *National Child Development Study.* London: Institute of Education.

Clarke, J. (2002) 'The three Rs – repression, rescue and rehabilitation: ideologies of control for working-class youth', in J. Muncie, G. Hughes and E. McLaughlin (eds) *Youth Justice: Critical Readings.* London: Sage.

Coffey, D. and Gemignani, M. (1994) *Effective Practices in Juvenile Correctional Education: A Study of the Literature and Research 1980-1992.* Washington, DC: Office of Juvenile Justice and Delinquency Prevention.

Coffield, F., Mosely, D., Hall, E. and Ecclestone, K. (2004) *Learning Styles and Pedagogy in Post-16 Learning: A Systematic and Critical Review.* London: Learning & Skills Research Centre.

Cole, T. (1989) *Apart or A Part? Integration and the Growth of British Special Education.* Milton Keynes: Open University Press.

Cole, T. (1996) *Special Educational Needs: Historical Perspectives – A Course Reader.* Birmingham: University of Birmingham.

Coles, B. (2000) *Joined-up Youth Research, Policy and Practice: A New Agenda for Change?* Leicester: Youth Work Press.

Collishaw, S., Maughan, B., Goodman, B. and Pickles, A. (2004) 'Time trends in adolescent mental health', *Journal of Child Psychology and Psychiatry,* 45 (8): 1350–1362.

Cooke, R. (2000) 'Exclusion from school', *Curriculum,* 21 (3): 152–155.

Copeland, I. (1999) *The Making of the Backward Pupil in Education in England 1870-1914.* London: Woburn Press.

Cromwell, P. and del Carmen, R. (1999) *Community-Based Corrections.* Belmont, CA: Wadsworth.

Croll, P. and Moses, D. (2003) *Young People's Attitudes to School and Their Trajectories into Post-Compulsory Education: A Preliminary Analysis of Data from the British Household Panel Survey.* University of Reading: Institute of Education.

Croninger, R. and Lee, V. (2001) 'Social capital and dropping out of school: benefits to at-risk students of teachers' support and guidance', *Teachers College Record,* 103: 548–81.

Cullingford, C. (1999) *The Causes of Exclusion: Home, School and the Development of Young Criminals.* London: Kogan Page.

Cullingford, C. (2002) *The Best Years of Their Lives? Pupils' Experiences of School.* London: Kogan Page.

Daniels, H., Cole, T., Sellman, E., Sutton, J., Visser, J. and Bedward, J. (2003) *Study of Young People Permanently Excluded from School.* School of Education, University of Birmingham: Queens Printer.

Department of Education and Science (1978) *Special Educational Needs* (The Warnock Report). London: HMSO.

DfE (1994) *Pupils with Problems.* London: Department for Education.

DfEE (1994) *The Education of Pupils with Emotional and Behavioural Difficulties.* Circular 9/94. London: DfEE.

DfEE (1995) *More Willingly to School?: An Independent Evaluation of the DfEE's Truancy and Disaffected Pupils (TDP) GEST Programme.* London: DfEE.

DfEE (1997) *Excellence for All Children: Meeting Special Educational Needs.* London: The Stationery Office.

DfEE (1999) *Permanent Exclusions from Schools in England 1997/98 and Exclusion Appeals Lodged by Parents in England 1997/98.* Statistical Press Release SFR 11/1999, 16.

DfEE (1999) *Social Inclusion: Pupil Support.* Circular 10/99. London: DfES.

DfEE (2000) *Connexions: The Best Start in Life for Every Young Person.* Nottingham: DfEE Publications.

DfES (2003) *Every Child Matters.* Green Paper. Norwich: DfES.

DfES (2005a) *GCSE and Equivalent Results for Young People in England* 2004/05 (Provisional). London: DfES.

DfES (2005b) *Pupil Absence in Schools in England: 2004/05 (Revised).* SFR56/2005. London: DfES.

DfES (2005c) *Higher Standards, Better Schools for All – More Choice for Parents and Pupils,* White Paper, London: TSO.

DfES (2005d) *Youth Matters,* Green Paper, London: DfES.

DfES (2006a) *Participation in Education, Training and Employment by 16–18-Year-Olds in England: 2004 and 2005.* SFR 21/2006. London: DfES.

DfES (2006b) *Permanent and Fixed Period Exclusions from Schools and Exclusion Appeals in England, 2004/05.* SFR 24/2006. London: DfES.

DfES/YJB (2001) *Working Together: Connexions and Youth Justice Services.* Nottingham: DfES.

DoH (1991) *Patterns and Outcomes in Child Placement: Messages from Current Research and Their Implications.* London: HMSO.

DWP (2001) *United Kingdom National Action Plan on Social Inclusion 2001–2003.* London: Department for Work and Pensions.

Desforges, C. and Abouchaar, A. (2003) *The Impact of Parental Involvement, Parental Support and Family Education on Pupil Achievement and Adjustment: A Literature Review.* DfES Research Report No. 433. London: Queens Printer.

Dishion, T., Patterson, G., Stoolmiller, M. and Skinner, M. (1991) 'Family, school, and behavioral antecedents to early adolescent involvement with antisocial peers', *Developmental Psychology*, 27(1): 172–80.

Ditchfield, J. and Catan, L. (1992) *Juveniles Sentenced for Serious Offences: A Comparison of Regimes in Youth Offender Institutions and Local Authority Community Homes.* London: Home Office.

Doble, J. (2002) 'Attitudes to punishment in the US – punitive and liberal opinions', in J. Roberts and M. Hough (eds) *Changing Attitudes to Punishment.* Cullompton: Willan Publishing.

Donnison, D. (1998) *Politics for a Just Society.* London: Macmillan.

Downes, D. and Morgan, R. (2002) 'The skeletons in the cupboard: the politics of law and order at the turn of the millennium', in M. Maguire, R. Morgan and R. Reiner (eds) *The Oxford Handbook of Criminology.* Oxford: Oxford University Press.

Durkheim, E. (1956) *Education and Sociology.* New York: The Free Press.

Dustmann, C., Rajah, N. and Smith, S. (1997) *Teenage Truancy, Part-Time Working and Wages.* London: Institute for Fiscal Studies.

ECOTEC (2001) *An Audit of Education and Training Provision Within the Youth Justice System.* London: Youth Justice Board.

Eslea, M. and Smith, P. (1998) 'The long-term effectiveness of anti-bullying work in primary schools', *Educational Research*, 40: 203–18.

Fairclough, N. (2000) *New Labour, New Language?* London: Routledge.

Farrell, K. and Tsakalidou, K. (1999) *Recent Trends in the Re-integration of Pupils with Emotional and Behavioural Difficulties in the United Kingdom.* University of Manchester: Research Report.

Farrington, D. (1993) 'Understanding and preventing bullying', in M. Tonry (ed) *Crime and Justice: An Annual Review of Research*, (Vol. 17, pp. 381–458). Chicago: University of Chicago Press.

Farrington, D. (2002) 'Developmental criminology and risk-focused prevention', in M. Maguire, R. Morgan and R. Reiner (eds) *The Oxford Handbook of Criminology.* Oxford: Oxford University Press.

Farrington, D. (2003) 'Key results from the first forty years of the Cambridge Study in Delinquent Development', in T. Thornberry and M. Krohn (eds) *Taking Stock of Delinquency: An Overview of Findings from Contemporary Longitudinal Studies.* New York: Kluwer Academic/Plenum Publishers.

Farrington, D., Gallagher, B., Morley, L., St. Ledger, R. and West, D. (1986) 'Unemployment, school leaving and crime', *British Journal of Criminology*, 26: 335–56.

Feinstein, L. and Sabates, R. (2005) *Education and Youth Crime: Effects of Introducing the Education Maintenance Allowance Programme.* DfES Research Brief No. RCB01-05. Nottingham: DfES.

Fergusson, D., Lynskey, M. and Horwood, J. (1997) 'The effects of unemployment on juvenile offending', *Criminal Behaviour and Mental Health*, 7: 49–68.

Firth, H. and Horrocks, C. (1996) 'No home, no school, no future: exclusions and children who are "looked after"', in E. Blyth and J. Milner (eds) *Exclusion from School*. London: Routledge.

Flood-Page, C., Campbell, S., Harrington, V. and Miller, J. (2000) *Youth Crime: Findings from the 1998/99 Youth Lifestyles Survey*. London: Home Office Research Study No. 209, Research Development and Statistics Directorate.

Frater, G. (2005) *Death of Dyslexia?* http://www.basic-skills.co.uk/site/print.php?p=1624.

Fredericks, J., Blumenfeld, P. and Paris, A. (2004) 'School engagement: potential of the concept, state of the evidence', *Review of Educational Research*, 74 (1): 59–109.

Frost, N. and Stein, M. (1989) *The Politics of Child Welfare: Inequality, Power and Change*. Hemel Hempstead: Simon and Schuster International Group.

Furlong, V. (1985) *The Deviant Pupil: Sociological Perspectives*. Milton Keynes: Open University Press.

Galloway, D. (1985) *Schools and Persistent Absentees*. Oxford: Pergamon.

Gillborn, D. (2002) *Education and Institutional Racism*. Inaugural lecture, London: Institute of Education, University of London.

Goldson, B. (ed.) (2000) *The New Youth Justice*. Dorset: Russell House Publishing.

Goldson, B. (2002) 'New punitiveness: the politics of child incarceration', in J. Muncie, G. Hughes and E. McLaughlin (eds) *Youth Justice: Critical Readings*. London: Sage.

Goodall, E. (2005) *School's Out? Truancy and Exclusion*. London: New Philanthropy Capital.

Gottfredson, D. (2001) *Schools and Delinquency*. Cambridge: Cambridge University Press.

Gottfredson, M. and Hirschi, T. (1990) *A General Theory of Crime*. Stanford, CA: Stanford University Press.

Gould, S. (1996) *The Mismeasure of Man*. London: Penguin.

Graham, J. (1988) *Schools, Disruptive Behaviour and Delinquency*. London: Home Office Research Study No. 96, HMSO.

Graham, J. and Bowling, B. (1995) *Young People and Crime*. London: Home Office.

Gray, J., McPherson, A. and Raffe, D. (1983) *Reconstructions of Secondary Education*. London: Routledge and Kegan Paul.

Gregg, P. (2000) *The Impact of Youth Unemployment on Adult Unemployment in the NCDS*. Bristol: University of Bristol, Department of Economics.

Griffin, P. (1999) 'Juvenile probation in the schools', *NCJJ in Focus*, 1(1): 1–10.

Grigg, R. (2002) 'Educating criminal and destitute children: reformatory and industrial schools in Wales, 1858-1914', *Welsh History Review*, 21 (2): 292–327.

Grimshaw, R. and Berridge, D. (1994) *Educating Disruptive Children: Placement and Progress in Residential Special Schools for Pupils with Emotional and Behavioural Difficulties*. London: National Children's Bureau.

Hagell, A. and Shaw, C. (1996) *Opportunity and Disadvantage at Age 16*. London: Policy Studies Institute.

Hansard Written Answers (2005a) House of Commons www.parliament.the-stationery-office.co.uk/pa/cm200405/cmhansrd/cm050221/text/50221w75. htm [21 February 2005].

Hansard Written Answers for 4 July 2005 (pt 39) (2005b) House of Commons www.publications.parliament.uk/pa/cm200506/cmhansard/cm050704/text/50704w39.htm.

Hargreaves, A. (1989) 'The crisis of motivation and assessment', in A. Hargreaves and D. Reynolds (eds) *Education Policies: Controversies and Critiques*. London: Falmer Press.

Hargreaves, D. (1996) *Teaching as a Research-Based Profession: Possibilities and Prospects*. Teacher Training Agency Annual Lecture.

Hargreaves, D. (1997) 'Education', in G. Mulgan (ed.) *Life After Politics: New Thinking for the Twenty-First Century*. London: Fontana Press.

Harper, G. and Chitty, C. (2005) *The Impact of Corrections on Re-offending: A Review of 'What Works'*. Home Office Research Study 291. London: Home Office Research, Development and Statistics Directorate.

Hawkins, J., Smith, B., Hill, K. *et al.* (2003) 'Understanding and preventing crime and violence: findings from the Seattle Social Development Project', in T. Thornberry and M. Krohn (eds) *Taking Stock of Delinquency: An Overview of Findings from Contemporary Longitudinal Studies*. New York: Kluwer Academic/Plenum Publishers.

Hayward, G., Stephenson, M. and Blyth, M. (2004) 'Exploring effective educational interventions for young people who offend', in R. Burnett and C. Roberts (eds) *What Works in Probation and Youth Justice: Developing Evidence-Based Practice*. Cullompton: Willan Publishing.

Hayward, G., Hodgson, A., Johnson, J., Oancea, A., Pring, R., Spours, K., Wilde, S. and Wright, S. (2005) *The Nuffield Review of 14-19 Education and Training Annual Report 2004-05*. Oxford: University of Oxford Department of Educational Studies.

Hayward, R. and Sharp, C. (2005) *Young People, Crime and Antisocial Behaviour: Findings from the 2003 Crime and Justice Survey*. London: Home Office Findings 245.

Hazel, N., Hagell, A., Liddle, M., Archer, D., Grimshaw, R. and King, J. (2002) *Assessment of the DTO and Its Impact on the Secure Estate Across England and Wales*. London: Policy Research Bureau.

Heal, K. (1978) 'Misbehaviour among schoolchildren: the role of the school in strategies for prevention', *Policy and Politics*, 6: 321–32.

Hendrick, H. (2002) 'Constructions and reconstructions of British childhood: an interpretative survey, 1800 to the present', in J. Muncie, G. Hughes and E. McLaughlin (eds) *Youth Justice: Critical Readings*. London: Sage.

Her Majesty's Chief Inspector of Prisons (1997) *Young Prisoners: A Thematic Review by HM Chief Inspector of Prisons for England and Wales*. London: Home Office.

HM Inspectorate of Prisons (2006) *Annual Report of HM Chief Inspector of Prisons for England and Wales 2004–2005*. London: The Stationery Office.

Herrenkohl, T., Hawkins, D., Chung, I., Hill, K. and Battin-Pearson, S. (2001) 'School and community risk factors and interventions', in R. Loeber and D. Farrington (eds) *Child Delinquents: Development, Intervention, and Service Needs*. London: Sage.

Hibbett, A., Fogelman, K. and Manor, O. (1990) 'Occupational outcomes of truancy', *British Journal of Educational Psychology*, 60: 23–36.

Hobcraft, J. (2002) 'Social exclusion and the generations', in J. Hills, J. Le Grand and D. Piachaud (eds) *Understanding Social Exclusion*. Oxford: Oxford University Press.

Hobbs and Hook Consulting (2001) *Research into Effective Practice with Young People in Secure Facilities*. London: Youth Justice Board.

Hodges, H. (1982) 'Madison Prep – alternatives through learning styles', in J. Keefe (ed.) *Student Learning Styles and Brain Behaviour Progress, Instrumentation, Research*. Reston VA: National Association of Secondary School Principals.

Hodgson, A. and Spours, K. (1999) *New Labour's Educational Agenda: Issues and Policies for Education and Training from 14+*. London: Kogan Page.

Home Office (2001) *Making Punishments Work: Report of a Review of the Sentencing Framework for England and Wales* (Halliday Review). London: Home Office Communication Directorate.

Home Office (2004) *The Role of Education in Enhancing Life Chances and Preventing Offending*. London: Home Office Development and Practice Report 19.

Hough, M. and Park, A. (2002) 'How malleable are attitudes to crime and punishment? Findings from a British deliberative poll', in J. Roberts and M. Hough (eds) *Changing Attitudes to Punishment*. Cullompton: Willan Publishing.

Hough, M. and Roberts, J. (2004) *Youth Crime and Youth Justice*. Bristol: Policy Press.

Howard League (2001) *Missing the Grade: Education for Children in Prison*. London: Howard League for Penal Reform.

Howell, J. (2003) *Preventing and Reducing Juvenile Delinquency: A Comprehensive Framework*. London: Sage.

Hughes, J. (2005) *Doing the Arts Justice: A Review of Research Literature, Practice and Theory*. Canterbury: Unit for the Arts and Offenders, Centre for Applied Theatre Research.

Huizinga, D., Weiher, A., Espiritu, R. *et al.* (2003) 'Delinquency and crime: some highlights from the Denver Youth Survey', in T. Thornberry and M. Krohn (eds) *Taking Stock of Delinquency: An Overview of Findings from Contemporary Longitudinal Studies*. New York: Kluwer Academic/Plenum Publishers.

Humphries, S. (1981) *Hooligans or Rebels? An Oral History of Working-Class Childhood and Youth 1889–1939*. Oxford: Basil Blackwell.

Hurry, J., Brazier, L. and Moriarty, V. (2006) 'Improving the literacy and numeracy skills of young people who offend: can it be done and what are the consequences?', *Literacy and Numeracy Studies*, 14 (2): 61–74.

Hurry, J., Brazier, L., Snapes, K. and Wilson, A. (2005) *Improving the Literacy and Numeracy of Disaffected Young People in Custody and in the Community: Summary Interim Report of the First Eighteen Months of Study.* London: National Research and Development Centre.

Hurt, J. (1984) *Education and the Working Classes from the Eighteenth Century to the Twentieth Century.* Lancaster: History of Education Society, 1985.

Hustler, D., Callaghan, J., Cockett, M. and McNeill, J. (1998) *Choices for Life: An Evaluation of Rathbone CI's Work with Disaffected and Excluded School Pupils.* Manchester Metropolitan University: Didsbury Educational Research Centre.

Inner London Education Authority Research and Statistics Division (1986) *The Junior School Project.* London: ILEA.

INCLUDE (2000) *Approaches to Effective Practice for Yots: Engaging Young Offenders in Education, Training and Employment.* London: Youth Justice Board.

Indermaur, D. and Hough, M. (2002) 'Strategies for changing public attitudes to punishment', in J. Roberts and M. Hough (eds) *Changing Attitudes to Punishment.* Cullompton: Willan Publishing.

Ingersoll, S. and LeBoeuf, D. (1997) *Reaching Out to Youth Out of the Education Mainstream.* Washington, DC: Office of Juvenile Justice and Delinquency Prevention.

Jackson, S. (1987) *The Education of Children in Care.* Bristol: School of Applied Social Studies, University of Bristol.

Jackson, S. and Martin, P. (1998) 'Surviving the care system: education and resilience', *Journal of Adolescence*, 21: 569–83.

Jermyn, H. (2004) *The art of inclusion. Research Report 35.* London: Arts Council.

John, P. (1996) 'Damaged goods? An interpretation of excluded pupils' perceptions of schooling', in E. Blyth and J. Milner (eds) *Exclusion from School: Inter-Professional Issues for Policy and Practice.* London: Routledge.

Josi, D. and Sechrest, D. (1999) 'A pragmatic approach to parole aftercare: evaluation of a community reintegration program for high-risk youthful offenders', *Justice Quarterly*, 16: 51–80.

Kaplan, H. (2003) 'Testing an integrative theory of deviant behavior: theory-syntonic findings from a long-term multi-generation study', in T. Thornberry and M. Krohn (eds) *Taking Stock of Delinquency: An Overview of Findings from Contemporary Longitudinal Studies.* New York: Kluwer Academic/Plenum Publishers.

Kauffman, J. (2001) *Characteristics of Emotional and Behavioural Disorders of Children and Youth.* Upper Saddle River, NJ: Merrill Prentice-Hall.

Kendall, S., Kinder, K., Halsey, K., Fletcher-Morgan, C., White, R. and Brown, C. (2002) *An Evaluation of Alternative Education Initiatives.* London: DfES.

Kinder, K., Wakefield, A. and Wilkin, A. (1996) *Talking Back: Pupil Views on Disaffection.* Slough: NFER.

Kinder, K., Halsey, K., Kendall, S., Atkinson, M., Moor, H., Wilkin, A., White, R. and Rigby, B. (2000) *Working Out Well, Effective Provision for Excluded Pupils.* Slough: NFER.

Levitas, R. (2005) *The Inclusive Society?: Social Exclusion and New Labour*. Basingstoke: Palgrave Macmillan.

Lipsey, M. (1995) 'What do we learn from 400 research studies on the effectiveness of treatment with juvenile delinquents?', in J. McGuire (ed) *What Works: Reducing Reoffending*. Chichester: Wiley.

Lipsey, M. (1999) 'Can rehabilitative programs reduce the recidivism of juvenile offenders?', *Virginia Journal of Social Policy and the Law*, 6: 611–41.

Lipsey, M., Wilson, D. and Cothern, L. (2000) *Effective Intervention for Serious Juvenile Offenders*. Washington, DC: Office of Juvenile Justice and Delinquency Prevention.

Lloyd, G. and Padfield, P. (1996) 'Reintegration into mainstream. "Gi'e us peace!"', *British Journal of Special Education*, 23 (4): 180–6.

LoBuglio, S. (2001) 'Time to reframe politics and practices in correctional education', in J. Comings, B. Garner and C. Smith (eds) *Annual Review of Adult Learning and Literacy*. Vol. .2 San Francisco, CA: Jossey-Bass.

Loeber, R.. and Farrington, D. (eds) (2001) *Child Delinquents: Development, Intervention, and Service Needs*. London: Sage.

Loeber, R., Farrington D., Stouthamer-Loeber, M. *et al.* (2003) 'The development of male offending: key findings from fourteen years of the Pittsburgh Youth Study', in T. Thornberry and M. Krohn (eds) *Taking Stock of Delinquency: An Overview of Findings from Contemporary Longitudinal Studies*. New York: Kluwer Academic/Plenum Publishers.

Lombroso, C. (1911) *Crime: Its Causes and Remedies*. Boston: Little, Brown.

Loxley, C., Curtin, L. and Brown, R. (2002) *Summer Splash Schemes 2000: Findings from Six Case Studies*. London: Home Office, Research, Development and Statistics Directorate.

MacDonald, R. (ed) (1997) *Youth, the 'Underclass' and Social Exclusion*. London: Routledge.

Magarey, S. (2002) 'The invention of juvenile delinquency in early nineteenth-century England', in J. Muncie, G. Hughes and E. McLaughlin (eds) *Youth Justice: Critical Readings*. London: Sage.

Maguin, E. and Loeber, R. (1996) 'Academic Performance and Delinquency', in M. Tonry (ed) *Crime and Justice: A Review of the Research*, Vol. 20. Chicago: University of Chicago Press.

Mair, C. and May, G. (1997) *Offenders on Probation*. London: Home Office.

Malcolm, H. Wilson, V., Davidson, J. and Kirk, S. (2003) *Absence from School: A Study of Its Cause and Effect in Seven LEAs*. Research Report 424. London: Department for Education and Skills.

Mandelson, P. (1997) *Labour's Next Steps: Tackling Social Exclusion*. Pamphlet 581. London: Fabian Society.

Mansell, W. (2005) *Times Educational Supplement*, 2 September.

Marland, M. (1993) *The Craft of the Classroom*. Oxford: Heinemann Educational.

Martinson, R. (1974) 'What works? Questions and answers about prison reform', *The Public Interest*, 10: 22–54.

Maughan, B., Mortimore, P., Ouston, J. and Rutter, M. (1980) 'Fifteen thousand hours: a reply to Heath and Clifford', *Oxford Review of Education*, 6 (3): 289–303.

Maughan, B., Pickles, A., Hagell, A., Rutter, M. and Yule, W. (1996) 'Reading problems and antisocial behaviour: developmental trends in comorbidity', *Journal of Child Psychology and Psychiatry*, 37: 405–18.

May, C. (1999) *Explaining Reconviction Following a Community Sentence: The Role of Social Factors.* HORS 192. London: Home Office.

May, M. (2002) 'Innocence and experience: the evolution of the concept of juvenile delinquency in the mid-nineteenth century', in J. Muncie, G. Hughes and E. McLaughlin (eds) *Youth Justice: Critical Readings.* London: Sage.

Mayhew, P. and Van Kesteren, J. (2002) 'Cross-national attitudes to punishment', in J. Roberts and M. Hough (eds) *Changing Attitudes to Punishment.* Cullompton: Willan Publishing.

McGuire, J. (1995) *What Works: Reducing Re-offending: Guidelines from Research and Practice.* Chichester: Wiley.

McIntosh, S. (2003) *The Early Post-School Experiences of the Unqualified/Low Qualified: Using the Labour Force Survey to Map the 14–16 Year Old Low-Achievers.* London: Centre for Economic Performance.

McMahon, G., Hall, A., Hayward, G., Hudson, C., Roberts, C., Fernandez, R. and Burnett, R. (2004) *Basic Skills Programmes in the Probation Service: Evaluation of the Basic Skills Pathfinder.* London: Home Office.

McRobbie, A. and Thornton, S. (2002) 'Rethinking moral panic for multi-mediated social worlds', in J. Muncie, G. Hughes and E. McLaughlin (eds) *Youth Justice: Critical Readings.* London: Sage.

Midwinter, E. (1970) *Nineteenth Century Education.* London: Longman Group Limited.

Mihalic, S., Irwin, K., Elliott, D., Fagan, A. and Hansen, D. (2001) *Blueprints for Violence Prevention.* Washington, DC: Office of Juvenile Justice and Delinquency Prevention.

Mitchell, L. (1996) 'The effects of waiting time on excluded children', in E. Blyth and J. Milner (eds.) *Exclusion from School: Inter-Professional Issues for Policy and Practice.* London: Routledge.

Moffitt, T. (1993) 'Adolescence-limited and life-course persistent antisocial behavior: A developmental taxonomy', *Psychological Review*, 100: 674–701.

Moore, R., Gray, E. Roberts, C., Merrington, S., Waters, I., Fernandez, R., Hayward, G. and Rogers, R. (2004) *ISSP, The Initial Report.* London: Youth Justice Board.

Moore, S. (2002) 'Child Incarceration and the New Youth Justice', in B. Goldson (ed) *The New Youth Justice.* Lyme Regis: Russell House Publishing.

Morgan, R. (2002) 'Imprisonment: a brief history, the contemporary scene, and likely prospects', in M. Maguire, R. Morgan and R. Reiner (eds) *The Oxford Handbook of Criminology.* Oxford: Oxford University Press.

Morris, M. and Rutt, S. (2004) *Analysis of Pupil Attendance Data in Excellence in cities (EiC) Areas: An Interim Report.* London: HMSO.

Mortimore, J. (1991) *The Unqualified School Leaver: A Literature Review.* Post-16 Education Centre Report No. 9, University of London, Institute of Education.

Mortimore P. (1995) 'The positive effects of schooling', in M. Rutter (ed.) *Psychosocial Disturbances in Young People: Challenges for Prevention*. Cambridge: Cambridge University Press.

Mortimore, P., Davies, J., Varlaam, A. and West, A. (1983) *Behaviour Problems in Schools: An Evaluation of Support Centres*. London: Croom Helm.

Mortimore, P., Sammons, P., Stoll, L., Lewis, D. and Ecob, R. (1988) *School Matters: The Junior Years*. Wells: Open Books.

Muncie, J. (2000) 'Pragmatic realism? Searching for criminology in the new youth justice', in B. Goldson (ed) *The New Youth Justice*. Dorset: Russell House Publishing.

Muncie, J. and Hughes, G. (2002) 'Modes of youth governance', in J. Muncie, G. Hughes and E. McLaughlin (eds) *Youth Justice: Critical Readings*. London: Sage.

Muncie, J., Hughes, G. and McLaughlin, E. (eds) (2002) *Youth Justice: Critical Readings*. London: Sage.

Munn, P., Lloyd, G. and Cullen, M. (2000) *Alternatives to Exclusion from School*. London: Paul Chapman.

MVA Consultancy (1991) *Links Between Truancy and Delinquency*. Scottish Office: Education Department.

NACRO (1988) *School Reports: A Second Look*. London: NACRO.

NACRO (2003) *Missing Out: Key Findings from Nacro's Research on Children Missing School*. London: NACRO.

National Audit Office Report (2005) *Improving School Attendance*. London: The Stationery Office.

National Commission on Education (1993) *Learning to Succeed*. London: Heinemann.

Newburn, T. (2002) 'The contemporary politics of youth crime prevention', in J. Muncie, G. Hughes and E. McLaughlin (eds) *Youth Justice: Critical Readings*. London: Sage.

Newburn, T. and Shiner, M. (eds) (2005) *Dealing with Disaffection: Young People, Mentoring and Social Inclusion* Cullompton: Willan Publishing.

Office for National Statistics (ONS) (2000) *The Mental Health of Children and Adolescents in Great Britain*. London: ONS.

Office for National Statistics (2000a) *Psychiatric Morbidity Among Young Offenders in England and Wales*. London: ONS.

Office for National Statistics (2005) *Permanent and Fixed Period Exclusions from Schools and Exclusion Appeals in England, 2003/2004*. London: DfES.

Ofsted (1995) *Pupil Referral Units: The First Twelve Inspections*. London: The Stationery Office.

Ofsted (1996) *Exclusions from Secondary Schools 1995/96*. London: The Stationery Office.

Ofsted (2003) *Annual Report of Her Majesty's Chief Inspector of Schools: Standards and Quality in Education 2001/2002*. London: The Stationery Office.

Ofsted (2004) *Out of School*. London: The Stationery Office.

Ofsted (2005) *The Annual Report of Her Majesty's Chief Inspector of Schools 2003/04*. London: The Stationery Office.

O'Keeffe, D. (1994) *Truancy in English Secondary Schools: A Report Prepared for the DfEE.* London: HMSO.

Olweus, D. (1983) 'Low school achievement and aggressive behavior in adolescent boys', in D. Magnusson and V. Allen (eds) *Human Development: An Interactional Perspective.* New York: Academic Press.

Olweus, D. (1993) *Bullying at School: What We Know and What We Can Do.* Oxford: Blackwell.

Osler, A. (1997) *The Education and Careers of Black Teachers: Changing Identities, Changing Lives.* Buckingham: Open University Press.

Osler, A., Watling, R., Busher, H., Cole, T. and White, A. (2001) *Reasons for Exclusions from School.* Research Report No. 244. London: Department for Education and Skills.

Parker, R. (1990) *Away from Home: A History of Child Care.* Ilford: Barnardo's.

Parsons, C. (1996) 'Measuring the real cost of excluding children from school', paper presented at The National Children's Bureau Conference, Exclusion or Inclusion and the School System - Retaining or Rejecting the Disaffected Child, London, 9 July.

Parsons, C. (1999) *Education, Exclusion and Citizenship.* London: Routledge.

Parsons, C. and Howlett, K. (2000) *Investigating the Reintegration of Permanently Excluded Young People in England.* Ely: INCLUDE.

Parsons, S. and Bynner, J. (1998) *Influences on Adult Basic Skills: Factors Affecting the Development of Literacy and Numeracy from Birth to 37.* London: Basic Skills Agency.

Pawson, R. (2000) 'The evaluator's tale', in D. Wilson and A. Reuss (eds) *Prison(er) Education: Stories of Change and Transformation.* Winchester: Waterside Press.

Payne, J. (2002) *Attitudes to Education, and Choices at Age 16: A Brief Research Review.* Policy Studies Institute: Report to the DfES Advisory Panel on Research Issues for the 14–19 Age Group.

Pearce, N. and Hillman, J. (1998) *Wasted Youth: Raising Attainment and Tackling Social Exclusion.* London: Institute for Public Policy Research.

Pearson, G. (1983) *Hooligan: A History of Respectable Fears.* Basingstoke: Macmillan.

Pearson, G. (1994) 'Youth, crime and society', in M. Maguire, R. Morgan and R. Reiner (eds) *The Oxford Handbook of Criminology.* Oxford: Oxford University Press.

Pearson, G. (2002) 'Youth crime and moral decline: permissiveness and tradition', in J. Muncie, G. Hughes and E. McLaughlin (eds) *Youth Justice: Critical Readings.* London: Sage.

Pitts, J. (2000) 'The new youth justice and the politics of electoral anxiety' in B. Goldson (ed.) *The New Youth Justice.* Dorset: Russell House Publishing.

Pitts, J. (2005) 'The recent history of youth justice in England and Wales', in T. Bateman and J. Pitts (eds) *The RHP Companion to Youth Justice.* Dorset: Russell House Publishing.

Platt, A. (1969) *The Child Savers: The Invention of Delinquency.* Chicago: University of Chicago Press.

Platt, A. (2002) 'The triumph of benevolence: the origins of the juvenile justice system in the United States', in J. Muncie, G. Hughes and E. McLaughlin (eds) *Youth Justice: Critical Readings*. London: Sage.

Pond, C. and Searle, A. (1991) *The Hidden Army, Children at Work in the 1990's*. Birmingham City Council: Education Department, Low Pay Unit.

Porporino, D. and Robinson, F. (1992) *Can Educating Adult Offenders Counteract Recidivism?* Ottowa: Research and Statistics Branch of the Correctional Service of Canada.

Pring, R. (2004) 'Conclusion: evidence-based policy and practice', in G. Thomas and R. Pring (eds) *Evidence-Based Practice in Education*. Maidenhead: Open University Press.

Pruden, D., Young, S., Thomas, K., Boden, H. and Singleton, C. (2005) *Practical Solutions to Identifying Dyslexia in Juvenile Offenders: Report of a Joint Project of the British Dyslexia Association and HM Young Offender Institution Wetherby 2004–2005*. Reading: British Dyslexia Association.

Putnam, R. (2000) *Bowling Alone: The Collapse and Revival of American Community*. New York: Simon and Schuster.

Raynor, P. (2004) 'Opportunity, motivation and change: some findings from research on resettlement', in R. Burnett and C. Roberts (eds) *What Works in Probation and Youth Justice: Developing Evidence-Based Practice*. Cullompton: Willan Publishing.

Reid, K. (1999) *Truancy and Schools*. London: Routledge.

Reuss, A. (1999) 'Prison(er) education', *The Howard Journal*, 38 (2): 113–127.

Rice, M. and Brooks, G. (2004) *Developmental dyslexia in Adults: A Research Review*. London: NRDC.

Roberts, J. (2002) 'Public opinion and the nature of community penalties: international findings', in J. Roberts and M. Hough (eds) *Changing Attitudes to Punishment*. Cullompton: Willan Publishing.

Roberts, J. and Hough, M. (eds) (2002) *Changing Attitudes to Punishment*. Cullompton: Willan Publishing.

Roberts, J. and Stalans, L. (1997) *Public Opinion, Crime, and Criminal Justice*. Boulder, CO: Westview Press.

Rowe, J., Hundleby, M. and Garnett, L. (1988) *Child Care Placements: Patterns and Outcomes*. London: DHSS.

Rutter, M. (1983) 'School effects on pupil progress: findings and policy implications', *Child Development*, 54 (1): 1–29.

Rutter, M., Maughan, B., Mortimore, P. and Ouston, J. (1979) *Fifteen Thousand Hours: Secondary Schools and Their Effects on Children*. London: Open Books.

Rutter, M., Giller, H. and Hagell, A. (1998) *Antisocial Behaviour by Young People*. Cambridge: Cambridge University Press.

Rutter, M., Tizzard, J. and Whitmore, K. (eds) (1970) *Education, Health and Behaviour*. London: Longman.

Ryan, A. and Patrick, H. (2001) 'The classroom social environment and changes in adolescents' motivation and engagement during middle school', *American Educational Research Journal*, 28: 437–60.

Ryrie, A. (1981) *Routes and Results: A Study of the Later Years of Schooling.* Dunton Green: Hodder and Stoughton for the Scottish Council for Research in Education.

Sarno, C., Hearnden, I., Hedderman, C. and Hough, M. (2000) *Working Their Way Out of Offending: An Evaluation of Two Probation Employment Schemes* (HORS 218). London: Home Office.

Sayer, K. (1993) 'Language matters: the changing vocabularies of special needs', in G. Thomas and A. Loxley (2001) *Deconstructing Special Education and Constructing Inclusion.* Buckingham: Open University Press.

Saylor, W. and Gaes, G. (1997) 'PREP: training inmates through industrial work participation and vocational and apprenticeship instruction', *Corrections Management Quarterly*, 1 (2): 32–43.

Schoon, I. (2003) *How to Motivate Demotivated 14–16 Year Old Learners, with Particular Reference to Work Related Education and Learning.* London: Centre for Economic Performance.

Schorr, L. (1988) *Within Our Reach: Breaking the Cycle of Disadvantage.* New York: Doubleday.

Shah, M. (2001) *Working with Parents.* Oxford: Heinemann Educational Publishers.

Sheehy, E. (2004) 'Advancing social inclusion: the implications for criminal law and policy', *Canadian Journal of Criminology and Criminal Justice*, 46 (1): 73–95.

Shore, H. (2002) 'Reforming the juvenile: gender, justice and the child criminal in nineteenth-century England', in J. Muncie, G. Hughes and E. McLaughlin (eds) *Youth Justice: Critical Readings.* London: Sage.

Shore, H. (2003) '"Inventing" the juvenile delinquent in nineteenth-century Europe', in B. Godfrey, C. Emsley and G. Dunstall (eds) *Comparative Histories of Crime.* Cullompton: Willan Publishing.

Slavin, R. (2002) 'Evidence-based education policies: transforming educational practice and research', in G. Thomas and R. Pring (eds) (2004) *Evidence-Based Practice in Education.* Maidenhead: Open University Press.

Smith, D. (1998) 'Social work with offenders: the practice of exclusion and the potential for inclusion', in M. Barry and C. Hallett (eds) *Social Exclusion and Social Work.* Lyme Regis: Russell House Publishing.

Smith, D. (2006) 'Youth crime and justice: research, evaluation and "Evidence"', in B. Goldson and J. Muncie (eds) *Youth Crime and Justice.* London: Sage.

Smith, D. and Tomlinson, S. (1989) *The School Effect.* London: Policy Studies Institute.

Smith, J. (2005) *The Guardian*, 24 June.

Smith, R. (2003) *Youth Justice: Ideas, Policy, Practice.* Cullompton: Willan Publishing.

Social Exclusion Unit (SEU) (1998) *Truancy and School Exclusion.* London: Cabinet Office.

Social Exclusion Unit (1999) *Bridging the Gap: New Opportunities for 16–18 Year Olds Not in Education, Employment or Training.* London: Cabinet Office.

Social Exclusion Unit (2002) *Reducing Re-offending by Ex-prisoners*. London: Cabinet Office.

Social Exclusion Unit (2003) *A Better Education for Children in Care*. London: Office of the Deputy Prime Minister.

Sparkes, J. and Glennerster, H. (2002) 'Preventing social exclusion: education's contribution', in J. Hills, J. Le Grand and D. Piachaud (eds) *Understanding Social Exclusion*. Oxford: Oxford University Press.

Squires, P. and Stephen, D. (2005) *Rougher Justice: Anti-social Behaviour and Young People*. Cullompton: Willan Publishing.

Stalans, L. (2002) 'Measuring attitudes to sentencing', in J. Roberts and M. Hough (eds.) *Changing Attitudes to Punishment*. Cullompton: Willan Publishing.

Steedman, H. and Stoney, S. (2004) *Disengagement 14–16: Context and Evidence*. Centre for Economic Performance. Discussion Paper No. 654.

Stein, M. and Carey, K. (1986) *Leaving Care*. Oxford: Basil Blackwell.

Stephenson, M. (1996) 'Cities in schools: a new approach for excluded children and young people', in E. Blyth and J. Milner (eds) *Exclusion from School*. London: Routledge.

Stephenson, M. (2004) *Unlocking Learning*. London: Esmee Fairbairn, Rethinking Crime and Punishment.

Steurer, S., Smith, L. and Tracy, R. (2001) *Three State Recidivism Study*. Lanham, MD: Correctional Education Association.

Stott, D. and Wilson, D. (1977) 'The adult criminal as a juvenile', *British Journal of Criminology*, 17 (1): 47–57.

Stratta, E. (1970) *The Education of Borstal Boys*. London: Routledge and Kegan Paul.

Sutton, P. (1992) *Basic Education in Prisons: Interim Report*. Hamburg: UNESCO Institute for Education.

Teague, P. and Wilson, R. (eds) (1995) *Social Exclusion, Social Inclusion*. Belfast: Democratic Dialogue.

Thomas, G. and Loxley, A. (2001) *Deconstructing Special Education and Constructing Inclusion*. Buckingham: Open University Press.

Thomas, G. and Pring, R. (eds) (2004) *Evidence-Based Practice in Education*. Maidenhead: Open University Press.

Thornberry, T. and Krohn, M. (eds) (2003) *Taking Stock of Delinquency: An Overview of Findings from Contemporary Longitudinal Studies*. New York: Kluwer Academic/Plenum Publishers.

Times Educational Supplement (TES) (1989) 3 November.

Times Educational Supplement (2005) 2 September.

Tolbert, M. (2002) *State Correctional Education Programs: State Policy Update*. Washington, DC: National Institute for Literacy.

Tomlinson, S. (1982) *A Sociology of Special Education*. London: Routledge and Kegan Paul.

Topping, K. (1983) *Educational Systems for Disruptive Adolescents*. Beckenham: Croom Helm.

Torgerson, C., Brooks, G., Porthouse, J., Burton, M., Robinson, A., Wright, K. and Watt, I. (2004) *Adult Literacy and Numeracy Interventions and Outcomes: A Review of Controlled Trials*. London: National Research and Development Centre.

Tremblay, R., Vitaro, F., Nagin, D. *et al.* (2003) 'The Montreal Longitudinal and Experimental Study: rediscovering the power of descriptions', in T. Thornberry and M. Krohn (eds) *Taking Stock of Delinquency: An Overview of Findings from Contemporary Longitudinal Studies.* New York: Kluwer Academic/Plenum Publishers.

Trinder, L. (2000) 'Introduction: the context of evidence-based practice', in L. Trinder with S. Reynolds (eds) *Evidence-Based Practice: A Critical Appraisal.* Oxford: Blackwell Science.

Utting, D. (1999) *A Guide to Promising Approaches.* London: Communities That Care.

Utting, D. and Vennard, J. (2000) *What Works with Young Offenders in the Community?* Ilford: Barnado's.

Vernon, J. and Sinclair, R. (1998) *Maintaining Children in School: The Contribution of Social Service Departments.* National Children's Bureau and Joseph Rowntree Foundation.

Visser, J. (2003) *A Study of Children and Young People Who Present Challenging Behaviour.* University of Birmingham.

Vulliamy, G. and Webb, W. (2001) 'The social construction of school exclusion rates: implications for evaluation methodology', *Educational Studies,* 27 (3): 358.

Warner, N. (2003) Speech at the Youth Justice Board Conference 'Reducing Youth Offending – The Role of Learning and Skills' held at Church House, London on 30 January 2003.

Webb, R. and Vulliamy, G. (2004) *A Multi-agency Approach to Reducing Disaffection and Exclusions from School.* London: DfES.

Weissberg, R. and Caplan, M. (1998) *Promoting Social Competence and Preventing Antisocial Behavior in Young Urban Adolescents.* Philadelphia: Temple University, Center for Research in Human Development and Education, Laboratory for Student Success.

West, A. and Pennell, H. (2003) *Underachievement in Schools.* London: RoutledgeFalmer.

West, D. and Farrington, D. (1973) *Who Becomes Delinquent?* London: Heinemann.

West, D. and Farrington, D. (1977) *The Delinquent Way of Life* London: Heinemann.

Wilkin, A., Hall, M. and Kinder, K. (2003) *Learning Support Unit Strand Study.* Slough: NFER.

Wilkinson, C. (1995) *The Drop Out Society: Young People on the Margin.* Leicester: Youth Work Press.

Williamson, H. and Middlemiss, R. (1999) 'The emperor has no clothes: cycles of delusion in community interventions with "disaffected" young men', *Youth and Policy,* 63: 13–25.

Willms, J. (2003) *Student Engagement at School: A Sense of Belonging and Participation. Results from PISA 2000.* Paris: Organisation for Economic Co-operation and Development.

Wilson, D. and Reuss, A. (eds) (2000) *Prison(er) Education: Stories of Change and Transformation.* Winchester: Waterside Press.

Young, J. (2002) 'Crime and social exclusion', in M. Maguire, R. Morgan and R. Reiner (eds) *The Oxford Handbook of Criminology*. Oxford: Oxford University Press.

Youth Justice Board (2000a) *National Standards for Youth Justice*. London: Youth Justice Board.

Youth Justice Board (2000b) *Youth Survey*. London: Youth Justice Board.

Youth Justice Board (2001) *Risk and Protective Factors Associated with Youth Crime and Effective Interventions to Prevent It*. London: Youth Justice Board.

Youth Justice Board (2002a) *The National Specification for Learning and Skills for Young People on a Detention and Training Order in Prison Service Accommodation*. London: Youth Justice Board.

Youth Justice Board (2002b) *Key Elements of Effective Practice – Education, Training and Employment*. London: Youth Justice Board.

Youth Justice Board (2002c) *Evaluation of the PLUS Programme*. London: Youth Justice Board.

Youth Justice Board (2002d) *Unlocking Basic Skills for Yots: Assessing the Level of Need Basic Skills Toolkit for Yots*. London: Youth Justice Board.

Youth Justice Board (2003a) *Youth Justice Board Intervention Programme: Education, Training and Employment*. Central Evaluators' Final Report. London: Youth Justice Board.

Youth Justice Board (2003b) *Evaluation of the Youth Inclusion Programme*. London: Youth Justice Board.

Youth Justice Board (2003c) *Progress Report on the Implementation of the National Specification for Learning and Skills for Young People on the Custodial Phase of a Detention and Training Order*. London: Youth Justice Board.

Youth Justice Board (2004a) *Corporate and Business Plan 2004/5 to 2006/7*. London: Youth Justice Board.

Youth Justice Board (2004b) *Progress Report on the Implementation of the Youth Justice Board's National Specification for Learning and Skills in the Juvenile Prison Estate 2003-04*. London: Youth Justice Board.

Youth Justice Board (2004c) *Health, Education and Substance Misuse Workers in Youth Offending Teams and the Health/Education Needs of Young People supervised by Youth Offending Teams*. London: Youth Justice Board.

Youth Justice Board (2005a) *Youth Justice Annual Statistics 2003/04*. London: Youth Justice Board.

Youth Justice Board (unpublished) (2005b) *Diversity in Learning: Establishing the Cognitive Styles and Learning Strategies of Young People in the Youth Justice System*. London: Youth Justice Board.

Youth Justice Board (2005c) *Progress Review on the Implementation of the Youth Justice Board's National Specification for Learning and Skills 2004-2005*. London: Youth Justice Board.

Youth Justice Board (2005d) *Volunteering in Youth Justice*. London: Youth Justice Board.

Youth Justice Board (2005e) *Monitoring and Evaluating the Safer School Partnerships Programme*. London: Youth Justice Board.

Youth Justice Board (2005f) *Keeping Young People Engaged Year 2: Final Report September 2004–August 2005*. London: Youth Justice Board.

Youth Justice Board (2006) *Barriers to Engagement in Education, Training and Employment for Young People in the Youth Justice System.* London: Youth Justice Board.

Youth Justice Trust (2004) *On the Case: A Survey of Over 1,000 Children and Young People Under Supervision by Youth Offending Teams in Greater Manchester and West Yorkshire.* Manchester: Youth Justice Trust.

Youth Justice Trust (2004b) *The Learning Alliance National E2E Offender Pilot*: Final Evaluation Report August 2004. Manchester: Youth Justice Trust.

Zhang, M. (2003) 'Links between school absenteeism and child poverty', *Pastoral Care*, March: 10–17.

Index